May the Lord in his mercy be kind to Belfast

Tony Parker

Henry Holt and Company
New York

For **Gill Coleridge**
best of agents, best of friends
with much love

Henry Holt and Company
Publishers since 1866
115 West 18th Street
New York, New York 10011

Henry Holt® is a registered trademark
of Henry Holt and Company, Inc.

First published in the United States in 1994 by
Henry Holt and Company, Inc.
Originally published in the United Kingdom in 1993 by Jonathan Cape.

Library of Congress Cataloging-in-Publication Data
Parker, Tony.
    May the Lord in his mercy be kind to Belfast / Tony Parker.—1st
American ed.
        p.   cm.
    Originally published: J. Cape, 1993.
    Includes bibliographical references.
    1. Belfast (Northern Ireland)—Politics and government.   2. Belfast
(Northern Ireland)—social conditions.   3. Violence—Northern Ireland—
Belfast.   I. Title.
DA995.B5P37   1994
941.6'7—dc20   93-40754
                                                                          CIP

ISBN 0-8050-3053-0

First American Edition—1994

Printed in the United States of America
All first editions are printed on acid-free paper.∞
    3   5   7   9   10   8   6   4   2

Excerpt from "Little Gidding" in *The Complete Poems and
Plays of T. S. Eliot* is reproduced by kind permission of
Faber & Faber Ltd. "Ballad to a Traditional Refrain" by
Maurice James Craig is reproduced by kind permission of
Jonathan Williams.

Contents

May the Lord in his mercy be kind to Belfast

Red brick in the suburbs, white horse on the wall,
Eyetalian marble in the City Hall:
O stranger from England, why stand so aghast?
May the Lord in His mercy be kind to Belfast.

This jewel that houses our hopes and our fears
Was knocked up from the swamp in the last hundred years
But the last shall be first and the first shall be last:
May the Lord in His mercy be kind to Belfast.

We swore by King William there'd never be seen
An All-Irish Parliament at College Green,
So at Stormont we're nailing the flag to the mast:
May the Lord in His mercy be kind to Belfast.

O the bricks they will bleed and the rain it will weep,
And the damp Lagan fog lull the city to sleep;
It's to hell with the future and live on the past:
May the Lord in His mercy be kind to Belfast.

'Ballad to a Traditional Refrain'
Maurice James Craig

1 *To arrive where we started*

The Head of the Northern Ireland Probation Service is Breidge Gadd. As she was someone I already knew, she was the first person I went to see.

'I'm thinking of coming to stay for a while in Belfast,' I said. 'To do a book of interviews with people whose lives have been affected in some way by the Troubles – perhaps a lot, or only just a little.'

'That shouldn't be much of a problem,' she said. 'Just talk to everyone.'

She offered contacts, put forward suggestions, struck sparks and as usual threw out provocative thoughts and contentious ideas. We had lunch. 'Oh yes and by the way,' she said as I was leaving, 'don't always refer to "the Troubles" until you know something about who you're talking with.'

'No?' I said. 'Really? Why not?'

She smiled. 'I'm sure it won't be long before you find out,' she said. 'That and a few other things. Put your toes in the water first.'

Two months, thirty-odd letters and twenty-seven phone calls later, after some reading and thinking and more talking to other people, I went back again to Belfast to meet five women who'd been suggested by different individuals and organisations as being possibly suitable as an assistant for me.

Of one, the first thing I'd been told was 'she'd be ideal, because her name's Teresa Green. So with a Catholic Christian name and a good sound Protestant surname, she could use either – which'd be a terrific advantage.' Someone recommending someone else said: 'She'd be most suitable: her name's Barbara you see, which is completely non-informative. In fact she's a Protestant but she's married to a Catholic – though she only says so when it's necessary. Another thing is they live in Stranmillis, which nowadays everybody knows of as a mixed Bohemian area, so that'd be a plus too.' Part of the description of a third person was: 'Her only drawback is she spent some of her childhood in Cheltenham, so she sometimes comes out with an English accent now and again without realising it.' Until I enquired myself, no mention had up till then been made about whether the person concerned could maintain confidentiality, was reliable and persistent, approachable and easy-mannered, unafraid of being in strange places, not worried about being confused, could drive a car, had a quiet speaking voice, or possessed any of another twelve qualities which, in my innocence, I'd thought might be helpful for the work.

Yet these introductory remarks about Christian and surnames, where people lived and what sort of accent they had, were all offering me an important glimpse, if only I'd been able to see it, of the totally different world I was to inhabit and become immersed in when, not long afterwards, I went to stay in Belfast for a while 'to do a book of interviews'.

Breidge had been right: everyone had been affected, was all the time affected, and each day in their lives was becoming increasingly affected, by what was happening in this wretched and unhappy part of the United Kingdom. And however irrelevant and unimportant it seemed to me, a middle-class English agnostic pacifist, I soon and quickly started to learn what first and most mattered in Northern Ireland today – which is that no relationship can proceed unless certain basics are clarified to begin with. The first thing you need to know about someone as soon as you meet them – and they equally need to know about you – is whether each or both of you is Protestant or Catholic. To be 'neither' is not sufficient. You can be 'neither' now but in that case what matters is 'where did you begin?' Or in other words, what were your parents, what were your grandparents or failing that your great grandparents? What is your *origin*? This must be, and almost always unfailingly is, established within the first minute, or at the most, two. Once on a social occasion my wife happened to tell someone she'd never met before that her ancestors had been in the siege of what was known as Londonderry in 1689. It was true: but jokingly though she'd intended it, immediately came the only half-humorous response: 'Where were they? Inside the city or besieging it?'

The need for knowledge of someone's present faith or antecedents isn't for the purpose of expressing empathy or antagonism, but purely so that any following conversation can continue with greater ease. Once you know whether you share common background, or you do not, thereafter you can avoid saying the wrong thing, or wrong word, to unwittingly cause offence.

Anyone born and brought up in Northern Ireland can do this effortlessly, practised since birth: almost by extra-sensory perception, it seems at times. More than one person told me casually and in passing, making nothing of it because it seemed quite normal, that they could usually tell at first glance merely by looking at someone what they were. I found this incredible – until, before long, I became aware I was trying to do it myself: and, when I sometimes got it right, was coming to regard it as a skill. Then, even more incredibly, came the discovery after a while, that I was beginning to *want* to know, and bothering to try and find out. I started to ask myself why I cared. Curiosity of course, was the answer, no more than that. But what happened then to its all being 'irrelevant and un-important'? No really it was just curiosity, that's all. Honestly, no more than that. But tell yourself whatever you like: you do wonder, you do listen, you do notice, and you want to find out. Insidiously it pervades, it corrodes you. It really does.

Because of such things as these. If you are Protestant and 'British', you'll always call the second biggest city in Northern Ireland 'Londonderry': if you're Catholic and/or Nationalist, you'll only refer to it as 'Derry'. Nationalists and Catholics speak of 'the North', 'Ireland' or, intentionally aggressive, 'the Six Counties'. 'Northern Ireland' and 'Ulster' are Protestant terminology: and to speak of 'the Province' in front of a Nationalist is provocative, even if it wasn't intended. This was the point of Breidge's admonition: Catholics, and particularly Republicans, never talk about 'the Troubles' – they use the blunter 'the war' or 'the struggle'. Even in the *minutiae* of pronunciation there are giveaways: the Department of Health and Social Security's initials are pronounced 'DHSS' by Protestants, but by Catholics 'D Haitch SS'. So too with the IRA: more correctly 'The Provisional IRA', its members are only called 'Provos' by

Protestants: to Republicans, Nationalists and Catholics they're 'the Provies', the slightly-changed sound with its more moderating softness perhaps revealing something else as well. These are only some of the more obvious pointers. But in every conversation there'll come the faintest of suppressed grimaces, or the slightest flicker in an eye, if a 'wrong' word is used revealing you to be one of the 'others'.

Nearly everything that was said to me within the first two or three days of my arriving contained a myriad of clues. At the time though I was oblivious to it all.

*

1 *Taxi-driver from the airport*
– And how are you then today sir? It's a fine afternoon now to be sure isn't it? It's been like this all day here from first thing this morning, so it has. Over from the mainland are you sir? Did you have a good flight? On business or pleasure are you? And is this your first visit to us now, or have you been in the Province before? How long'll you be staying with us then? Well sure that'll be long enough for you to get a good idea of the place so it will. A very nice hotel you're staying at, everyone who stays there says it's very nice. Will you have the time to look around the city while you're here? If the weather stays like this you'll see it at its best you will. A fine wee place you know, Belfast, not like you're having on the television or in the newspapers all the time. A lot of those people, you know, they come over here for two days, then they go back with all sorts of stories, you wonder where they get them so you do. Now what's the hold up ahead of us, an accident is it? Oh no, just the routine police check that's all, he's waving everyone through, no problem.

So where's your own home town sir, where do you come from? Well now is that so? I had an auntie lived in Crumpsall, that's not so far from Manchester now is it? I was there once myself when I was a schoolboy, I went for a holiday with my brother. I remember Manchester was a very fine city it was. Carlisle, do you know that? A lot of my father's family came from up that way, my wife and I're always saying we'll go there one day for a holiday, a caravan you know, something like that. Very nice people up in the north of

England from what I remember of them. They're almost as nice as Belfast people so they are, and I can't say better than that.

2 *Hotel receptionist*

– Hello, can I help you? Oh yes sir, that's right, we have your reservation. Welcome to Belfast. Three nights isn't it? Would you like a smoking or a non-smoking room sir? That'll be Room 339 then, would you mind filling in this wee registration card for me please? Would you like a call in the morning? And what paper would you like? Thank you, I'll put that down for you. Would you like this evening's paper with our compliments? It's a pleasure. I'll ring for the porter to show you to your room. Did you have a pleasant flight over, comfortable was it, on time? Will you be taking dinner with us this evening, should I reserve a table in the restaurant for you? Have you been to Belfast before, are you familiar with the city? Let me give you this wee map then to help you find your way around. We're here, then the city square is along here, these streets are where the best shops are; and the cinemas are on this corner here, and the Opera House theatre is here. Oh and there's a very nice wee park just here if you feel like an evening stroll later and a breath of fresh air. And there's a night-club two streets along this way, if you fancy something like that. Now they close the barriers at the end of the square here at night, so you can only get back to the hotel this way. Ah Patrick there you are, will you take this gentleman up to Room 339 please. Enjoy your stay sir.

3 *Man in park*

– Here Campbell! I hope he's not bothering you. Oh you'll be from England now won't you, where'd you live? Really now? Well I know East Anglia right enough I do, my wife comes from Peterborough. We go there every year we do. Sit down now Campbell, there's a good man. So are you living here yourself then, or just over for a visit? So how long will you be in Belfast then? Sure and it's a great place, you'll like it I'm sure. Will you be at the University now? Well that's a very nice part around there, so it is. Football, are you interested in that by any chance? Well there's a good match at Windsor Park next Tuesday evening. If you get the opportunity you should go and watch Linfield, they're playing very

well just now so they are. Oh yes they're my team all right, I've
supported them ever since I was a wee boy. Linfield and Glasgow
Rangers, those are my teams they are, aye. Stay still will you now
Campbell, behave yourself for this gentleman from England. He's
only a wee puppy yet you know, six months that's all. Well he's a
Jack Russell I suppose you'd say, or most of him is. Good night to
you now, my name is Donald McDowell by the way, it's been nice
to meet you. Enjoy your stay. Bradbury Place, Shaftesbury Square,
anywhere round these parts if you're walking on, it's all a good area
this way, you'll be perfectly safe. Come along now Campbell.
Goodnight.

4 *Estate agent*
– What area were you looking for rented accommodation in sir?
Have you any preference for any particular part of the city? Would
you want to be central, or on the outskirts perhaps? The Malone
Road of course, that's a good area, handy for the south of the city.
Or the north, or the east perhaps, would you fancy something in that
direction, say towards Holywood which is a nice area? Can you give
me an idea what sort of price you had in mind? Well I'm sure we
could find you something suitable at around that figure. I'd imagine
something on the east side of the Lough – maybe even towards
Bangor if you don't mind a fifteen or twenty minute journey in.
What about facilities nearby, would you want it to be handy for a
golf club say, or a particular church? No? Well then I'm sure we can
offer you several places to choose from. Definitely let's say on the
east and to the north, that's where most of our properties tend to be
anyway.

5 *Woman at a coffee-bar table*
– Oh how interesting, what form will it take? Interviews with what
sort of people? What a fascinating idea, I'm sure you won't have the
slightest difficulty in getting people to talk. I'm afraid we've all got
rather the gift of the gab as they say, a little too much at times
sometimes I think. Have you done that sort of thing before? America
and Russia, really, how interesting! And now it's the turn of Belfast:
well good, we do rather feel at times no one's very interested in us
much. What'll its theme be, historical? Present day, oh what a good

idea! I do hope you'll stress the positive side of things here, please do do that won't you? So many people who come here give a completely false picture, it makes one so angry you know. They write only about the negative things as I call them. Heaven knows there're enough dreadful things to write about all over the world without picking on Belfast. You really must stress the absolute ordinariness of everyday life here you know, how we all live perfectly normal lives apart from just an odd bomb scare or something now and again. Oh look – here's my daughter coming to join us. She'll tell you what life's like from a schoolgirl's point of view, why don't you ask her?

6 *Fifteen-year-old schoolgirl*
– I think it's brilliant is Belfast, it's a real top place to live. I wouldn't like to live anywhere else, honestly I wouldn't, not ever. People from outside you know, they're really surprised when they come here and find out what it's like, they really are. They think it's all bombs going off all the time, everybody shooting one another and all stuff like that. They can't believe it, the smart shops, all the things in them, the clubs, the discos, all the young people enjoying themselves. The newspapers and the television, all they ever show's bombs and buildings and fires and shootings and all stuff like that. They don't show you what a great place Belfast is. I mean look at me, I've never been shot at, I've never even heard shooting except once in a while somewhere in the distance. People should come and see for themselves. Belfast's no different from anywhere else: it's great, it is, it's really really great.

7 *University professor*
– I do think one should acknowledge how remarkable the city and its inhabitants are. Despite all the difficulties of the past fifty years or more – the troubles, the decline of the local economy, the running down of the shipyards, the collapse of manufacturing industry and so on, there's still a great deal here that is good. We have a university of worldwide renown, and a lively and thriving artistic and intellectual community centred on it. The spirit and cheerfulness of the people under extremely trying circumstances is quite remarkable. There is a certain amount of poverty, one must admit, and some I suppose one

might call them unsavoury areas such as the Falls or the Shankill Road, but by and large there are no more than in other major cities. And quite large parts of Belfast are in spirit just as good or even better than any other capital city in Europe.

8 *Housewife, Dundonald*

– It makes me laugh you know sometimes, it really does. My husband's mother lives in Yorkshire: and if I've asked her once I've asked her twenty times, why doesn't she come over and have a holiday with us and see what it's like for herself? But will she? No she will not. 'You'll never get me over there,' she says. 'Never in all my life. I'd be absolutely on tenterhooks all the time I would.' I honestly think she imagines when I go down the garden to hang out the washing I have to crawl along the path on all fours. What can you say to someone who thinks it's all like that? I hope you'll help straighten some people's ideas out with your book.

9 *Car-hire firm manager*

– Here now have this wee map, we give it free to all our customers. Where you're staying, now that's very handy for Crawfordsburn Country Park you know – any day you want, you'll be able to go there, a beautiful place beautifully kept up, and that's the truth so it is. You must take yourself a drive around there every day. Then on a Sunday if you were to come this way look, along the Ards peninsula – go right to the bottom here and across the Strangford ferry, then back home again this way up this side. Beautiful. Then another day you should go this way north to Larne, then take the coast road. Very spectacular it is, really spectacular, all through Ballycastle here, right up to Port Rush. You won't find grander scenery anywhere else in the world. You've heard of the Giant's Causeway? Of course you have, well as you see it's clearly marked here. And so it should be, it's the most famous spot in the whole of Ireland. And don't miss a chance to go south this way too: the Mountains of Mourne, that's the loveliest area of all, you can't even begin to imagine the beauty of it. I do you know, I really envy you, coming to Northern Ireland for the first time – as beautiful a land as God ever made they say it is, and that's exactly true.

10 *Chemist's shop assistant*

– Just the one fillum you want to have developed and printed is it sir? With pleasure, no problem, it'll be back here for you tomorrow. We don't process them here on the premises ourselves, we send them away. They go either to Johnson and Hunter or Collins and Sullivan, which would you prefer? Well it's just as you please sir: they both take exactly the same length of time, they'll be back here by ten o'clock. No they're the same price, there's no difference. Johnson and Hunter give you a free fillum with them – but then of course so do Collins and Sullivan too. Well it's for you to say which one you'd like sir. Really no preference? Then we'll send them to Johnson and Hunter shall we, OK?

11 *Newspaper letter*

Dear Sir, I'm sure many other people beside myself will have been angered by the so-called 'documentary' shown on BBC television last night, which purported to give a picture of present-day Belfast. What a biased, inaccurate and one-sided travesty it was – and absolutely typical of the presentation of our city in the mainland media, press and television alike. According to my dictionary, a 'documentary' is supposed to be 'a factual filmed report' – but last night's effort fell very short of that, in fact the impression it gave of what's going on here was so exaggerated it could almost be described as 'complete fiction'. What sort of an impression are the people who make these programmes trying to give – that we all live in daily fear for our lives? What rubbish! Yours sincerely, 'Belfast citizen and proud of it.'

2 *Some not always accurate nor appropriate clues*

A 'clue' was originally a ball of thread (from the old English word '*cleowen*'), because the only way to find the way out of the mythological Cretan Labyrinth was by following a path marked with a hanging thread. 'I haven't a clue' is a current colloquial usage meaning 'I haven't an inkling' or 'I haven't the vaguest idea' (what you are talking about, or referring to, etc.)

(Brewer's *Dictionary of Phrase and Fable*, Cassell 1981.)

The title of Chapter 1 is taken from 'Little Gidding', one of T. S. Eliot's *Four Quartets*. Its setting in the lines immediately before and after it (of which the last is perhaps the most appropriate) is:-

> We shall not cease from exploration
> And the end of all our exploring
> Will be to arrive where we started
> And know the place for the first time.

1   All the private-car taxi-drivers at Belfast International Airport are likely to be Protestants. There is a security checkpoint, manned by the armed Royal Ulster Constabulary, on the access road: any driver recognised as a Catholic, or not recognised and producing for identification a driving licence showing a Catholic surname or Catholic-area home address, is likely to be held up for questioning. He won't be though if he's already known as a Protestant.

There is an immediate presumption that any arriving Englishman will be Protestant too. (Much later a 20-year-old Catholic university student told me that until her first visit there two years previously, she'd never known there were any Catholics in England.) So the affably garrulous and inquisitive taximan was taking it for granted one Protestant was talking to another: and, kindly, was using such expressions as 'the mainland' and 'the Province' because he knew they would be acceptable, and perhaps faintly flattering too in the hint of awareness of social and ethnic standing.

Which hotel you're staying at conveys, in conjunction with other pointers, whether you might be Catholic: there are two or three Belfast hotels which only Catholics stay at.

Quickness to stress Belfast's virtues, and anxiety for you not to believe impressions given by the media, is characteristic and constant, and the driver was only the first of many wanting to pre-empt any already-formed ideas. Mentioning family connections with places in England is also a regularly-occurring conversational theme.

2 Belfast hotels are renowned for the friendliness and solicitude with which they greet and treat their guests, and their hard work to ensure they have a comfortable stay and want to return. It's not something which needs much effort on their part: Northern Irish people have great natural warmth and charm. Offering a choice of smoking or non-smoking bedrooms is a grace far too few hotels in the rest of the United Kingdom have yet adopted. Again there was the immediate desire to lay emphasis on the city's attractions and facilities: which can seem at times almost to border on nervousness.

3 Someone who's given his dog a Scottish name is bound to be a Protestant: even before he tells you his own name to confirm it you'll know that – and that he's not exactly reticent about other people knowing it. Outspoken allegiance to Linfield F.C., and particularly Glasgow Rangers – without even waiting to be asked – is also a clear signal of Puritan fundamentalism. Again there was the immediate identification with a part of England. (Even though to someone living in Suffolk, claiming Peterborough as 'East Anglia' is trying to give it a cachet it doesn't have.) The casual mention of some areas of the city as 'safe' and including them in 'these parts' indicates without

question Protestantism: no part at all of Belfast would be described as
that by any Catholic to anyone.

4   Obviously the estate agent was Protestant and presumed I would
be too, coming from England and coming to him. Hence there was
no mention of property in west Belfast, which is almost entirely
Catholic. There was still a slight doubt in his mind at the beginning
though.

   The Malone Road is, it's true, 'a good area', and a popular one for
mainly professional middle-class people. It used to be almost entirely
Protestant, but now has Catholic residents as well: by the time
you're high enough up the social ladder to want property there, your
financial standing counts for more than your religious affiliation. If I
had been Catholic I would have known that, and expressed at least an
initial interest, just as an aware Protestant would know of Holywood
as 'a nice area'. The large Catholic church there was burned down in
somewhat mysterious circumstances a year or two ago.

   Bangor is middle-class respectability personified, or likes to think
of itself as such. It has a yachting marina built with financial help
from the EEC. 'Facilities . . . a golf club or a particular church' was a
final baiting of a hook to try and learn a little more.

5   Someone pressing you to convey the 'positive' side of life in
Northern Ireland is in all probability Protestant middle-class. The
stressing of 'the absolute ordinariness of everyday life', and of
everyone living perfectly normal lives apart from the odd bomb
scare or something, is of course an expression of hope that it might,
in reality, be just that. There's also often an underlying suggestion
that it would be bad taste to look at things in any other way. A
similar kind of attitude's common among supporters of the Tory
Party, who take for granted the idea that their political outlook is the
'natural' one and anything else is not indulged in in polite society any
more than one would ever dream, for example, of eating one's peas
off a knife.

6   Being a well brought-up girl (and in the presence of her mother)
Cheryl, as I later learned her name was, naturally put on her best
manners and brightest front for someone she'd been introduced to as

a writer from England on a visit. When we met again some weeks later, though, and were able to talk on our own and for longer, her attitude and opinions were not so effervescent.

7   It was reputedly Sainte-Beuve (1804-69) who first used the phrase 'une tour d'ivoire', describing the garret in which Alfred de Vigny secluded himself – thus bringing into parlance the (often correct) cliché describing where academics live rent free and with security of tenure. It's a very different surrounding to the one inhabited by working-class Catholics in the Falls Road, or Protestants in the Shankill area – two of the best known districts of Belfast for their respective religious affinities.

There are many others too, also with ready-made assumptions about their orientation. Gradually, through reading and hearing their repetition, you come to know the names, and the almost automatic conclusion about the religion of people who live there. Some writers even draw sketch maps to preface books they've written, to help their readers identify:-

as predominantly Catholic areas: Falls, Andersonstown, Divis, Ardoyne, Turf Lodge, Ballymurphy, Clonard, Twinbrook, Poleglass, Cliftonville, the enclave in Short Strand, Milltown where the cemetery has an IRA burial plot, Suffolk, Flax Street, Whiterock, New Lodge, Oldpark, Leanadoon, the Glen, Beechmount, Springfield, New Barnsley, Moynard;

and as predominantly Protestant: Shankill, Rathcoole, Finaghy, Glencairn, Sandy Row, Ballybeen, Woodvale, Ballymacarrett, Seymour Hill, The Village, Annadale Flats, Sydenham, Castlereagh, Windsor, Knocknagoney, Ballynafeigh, Donegall Road, Woodstock Road, Tiger Bay.

There are many others where, if you live there, assumptions about your religious background will be usually, but not always accurately, made.

Some names and initials of groups of people, too, constantly occur and re-occur. Briefly, inadequately, and certainly none too accurately, these are only initial guidelines. Most of them are taken from some of the books listed in the Bibliography in an Appendix.

'Members of the Security Forces' sometimes means the police, sometimes soldiers, and sometimes both together, as they often are. It is also sometimes a veiled reference to the SAS.

'The police' are the Royal Ulster Constabulary (RUC). After the Metropolitan Police, they are the second largest force in the United Kingdom. They wear heavy protective body armour, carry revolvers and automatic rifles, and have large numbers of armoured vehicles and helicopters. Protestants like them, but not many Catholics do.

The Ulster Defence Regiment (UDR) was until recently a locally recruited Army regiment of full and part-time soldiers. It served only in Northern Ireland, and was almost entirely Protestant.

'The Army' sometimes refers to them, and sometimes to soldiers of British regiments, who serve tours of duty of either six months in barracks unaccompanied, or of two years in Army quarters with their wives and families.

In general terms, 'Loyalists' are Northern Irish Protestants who want to remain British citizens (about two-thirds of the population). Unionists and Democratic Unionists are separate but similar Protestant political parties who adhere firmly to this principle.

The Ulster Defence Association (UDA) is the largest Protestant (and allegedly paramilitary) organisation: at one time it claimed to have 40,000 members. It is now illegal. Two small extremist paramilitary groups have separated from it: they are the Ulster Freedom Fighters (UFF), and the Ulster Volunteer Force (UVF) which is sometimes called 'the secret army'.

Nationalists, who are usually but not always Catholic, do not want Northern Ireland to remain part of the United Kingdom; and Republicans want it to be part of a united socialist Ireland. The political party of the latter is Sinn Fein.

The Irish Republican Army (IRA) is sometimes called 'the terrorist wing' of Sinn Fein: at other times Sinn Fein is accused of being 'the political wing' of the IRA.

In 1970 the IRA split into two sections – the 'Official' and the 'Provisional'. A number of small extremist paramilitary groups subsequently broke away from the former: the best known are the Irish National Liberation Army (INLA) and the Irish People's Liberation Organisation (IPLO) who in turn split from the INLA. In 1976 the Official IRA was formally disbanded when its militants renounced violence as a solution and dedicated themselves to left-wing parliamentary politics. General references to the IRA usually mean, strictly speaking, the Provisional IRA.

8   Dundonald is a Protestant area on the eastern outskirts of Belfast. It has had, and continues to have, its fair share of what are sometimes referred to as 'incidents'. It's rare for bullets actually to be flying across back gardens, and it's not necessary to move around the whole time on all fours. Nevertheless life there isn't precisely the same as it is in, say, Wetherby.

Bravado may be an admirable attitude, but when it's expressed one may reflect that it is presumably existing for some reason.

9   It might be almost the apotheosis of anxiety to suggest one shouldn't look at the centre, and ignore that and concentrate on the scenery instead. Supporters of apartheid in South Africa have been known to suggest a similar attitude.

Crawfordsburn is upper-middle-class Protestant: huge sums of public money and grants have been expended on the laying out and keeping up of its beautiful civic park by the shore of Lough Neagh. The Ards Peninsula, of which Strangford is at the most southerly point, returns a Unionist member to Parliament with one of the largest majorities in the Six Counties. Neither Sinn Fein nor the SDLP bother even to put up candidates at elections there, and the votes of other parties are derisory. Larne, Ballycastle and Portrush are similarly places where Protestants dominate.

The Mountains of Mourne – an area of such implacable Protestantism that it once even voted Enoch Powell in as its member of Parliament, *faute de mieux* – have scenery so beautiful that when it's not raining, which it sometimes isn't, even rigorousness approaching bigotry can almost be temporarily forgotten. For creating the whole area God should rightly be congratulated.

10   An almost perfect example, this, of an utterly clueless Englishman being baffled by an everyday situation, to the extent of not even being aware he was in it. Only several weeks later did the penny suddenly drop.

Johnson and Hunter are of course at once recognisable merely by their name as being Protestant. Just as Collins and Sullivan are Catholic, as surely all but the dimmest of the dim would be expected to recognise. So naturally, if you're Protestant you'll want your fillum developed and printed by Protestants, and by Catholics if you're Catholic. Naturally. You wouldn't want to give patronage and financial support to the other side.

When at last it became clear I didn't know this, being not only an ignoramus but probably an unbeliever as well, the young woman had to make the decision herself.

And of course, because of which she chose, apparently randomly but on reflection most certainly not, it was obvious what she was.

11 It might be argued with some justification that far from darkening the present situation in northern Ireland, the mainland media are minimising what is happening by publishing a very small proportion of the reports which appear, daily and numbingly, in Belfast's own newspapers. If readers in the rest of the United Kingdom really were aware of what happens and continues to happen, ceaselessly but apparently acceptably, day after day and night after night in one of our largest cities, they might possibly eventually begin to ask themselves what their reaction would be if it was going on in Birmingham or Manchester, and whether they would allow it to continue as it has now done for over 20 years?

Thus Lennon and McCartney sang.

3 *I read the news today Oh Boy*

(A small selection of cuttings from Belfast morning, evening and weekly newspapers over a period of eight weeks)

The AA today issued tips about what to do in traffic queues at security checks in Belfast. 'The two main dangers are damage to the clutch, and engine over-heating,' said a spokesman. Motorists are advised to apply the handbrake and put the gears in neutral, or switch the engine off if traffic is being held up for longer than two or three minutes at a time. 'It does of course depend on the condition of the car,' the spokesman said. 'Sometimes it is a bad idea to switch the engine off if there are going to be problems getting it started again.' Drivers should also make sure their radiators are kept full, as sitting in jams can result in a rise in the running-temperature of the car.

An arms haul was uncovered in a false grave during a security operation at the west Belfast City Cemetery on the Falls Road late this morning. A bolt-action rifle, a sawn-off shotgun, and three litres of nitrobenzine were found.

Shots were heard in the Glengoland area in the west of the city during the night last night, and the police say they are investigating.

A 26-year old man was recovering in hospital today from gunshot wounds to his left leg. The victim, whose condition is described as comfortable, was accosted by two masked men in Ballybean Square shortly after 8.30 pm last night.

Incendiary devices exploded at three stores in the Belfast area early today, causing minor damage. Two devices ignited at Wellworths in Shore Road, and in Glengormley two devices detonated at Stewarts in the Northcott Centre and at Crazy Prices around 2.30 pm. Two incendiary devices found at the new opened Co-Op stores at Yorkgate were defused by Army bomb experts shortly after 9.30 pm last night.

A 38-year old Dundonald man was forced to flee through an upstairs window after two armed men burst into his house at Vionville Heights at around 11.15 pm last night. The gunmen fired one shot but no injuries were caused.

A 27-year old man was injured in the back and legs last night when shots were fired at him in Newtownards Road. The gunmen used a Ford Sierra car hijacked from the Dundonald area the previous day. Anyone who can give information to help detectives investigating the shooting is being asked to telephone the police on 818080.

Army technical officers carried out a controlled explosion on a device left in an east Belfast taxi office shortly before 7.00 pm last night. The area was evacuated and the road closed whilst Security Forces dealt with the alert.

The IRA today created chaos among rush hour traffic in the greater Belfast area. Security Forces defused a 2½ lb Semtex bomb found in a waste bin on the ground floor of River House in High Street, and last night between 4.00 pm and 11.00 pm seventeen suspect vehicles and hoax calls were investigated. Railway, bus and police stations throughout Belfast were the main targets. Shoppers at Castle Court in the city centre were left stranded until 11.00 pm when the all clear was given. The M1 city-bound carriageway was also closed for a time.

Police and troops today threw a ring of steel around Belfast in a bid to thwart the IRA's renewed bombing campaign against commercial targets in the city centre. Checkpoints were set up from around 7.00 am on all main roads, and Security Forces were put on full alert. The roadblocks caused widespread disruption during the morning rush hour traffic, and the AA reported three-mile tailbacks on the M2, with traffic on the Sydenham Bypass and the Ormeau Road moving only very slowly.

An Australian tourist told today of how he was mugged in a phone kiosk within minutes of arriving in Belfast. Brian Hillier (29) from Adelaide was today recovering at a friend's house in north Belfast after being set upon by three youths in Donegall Square East in the city centre yesterday. They kicked him to the ground and snatched his rucksack as he was phoning his friend Ian Graham from the city centre kiosk at around 5.00 pm.

A Roman Catholic take-away delivery man was murdered in south Belfast yesterday, when he was shot dead at the wheel of his car a few yards from the Chinese restaurant for which he worked in Ormeau Road. Two masked men jumped out of a doorway and fired four or five shots into the car.

Tens of thousands pounds' worth of damage was caused to the four-storey Next shop in Donegall Place when fire destroyed it in a blaze which started around 2.00 am this morning. It was opened in 1988 and employed around 60 part and full-time staff.

Michael Logue (22) died from extensive injuries when a booby-trap bomb exploded under his car early on Monday morning after he had been visiting his girlfriend. In a statement the IRA admitted that Mr Logue had been killed 'by mistake', and offered 'deepest regrets' to his family.

Colm Mahon, a 39-year old Roman Catholic who worked at Frames Two Bar & Restaurant in Little Donegall Street was shot in the head in the doorway of the premises just before 1.00 am yesterday. He was rushed to the Mater Hospital but was found to be dead on arrival.

Morning rush hour traffic was severely delayed in parts of Belfast today as Security Forces mounted checkpoints to combat the recent upsurge in terrorist activity. Tailbacks on the M1 motorway stretched back for up to four miles towards Lisburn. Motorists also encountered holdups on main roads, including Ormeau Road, where cars were bumper to bumper from UTV House to the Ravenhill roundabout.

A policeman suffered serious eye injuries, and 16 other people were injured, after an IRA van exploded in Belfast city centre yesterday, causing widespread damage. Eight RUC officers, two UDR men and seven civilians were among those hurt in the explosion in Glengall Street shortly before 10.00 pm. The bomb, estimated to have contained up to 400 lbs of explosives, was packed into the back of a hijacked transit van and left near the side entrance of the Europa Hotel. A 30-minute warning had been given, but Security Forces were still evacuating hundreds of people from the hotel, the Grand Opera House, a bingo hall and nearby pubs when the device exploded.

Edward Broffey (50) was seriously ill in hospital today after a murder bid in Belfast. He was standing in a newsagent's shop in Corporation Street at around 7.45 pm last night when a lone gunman entered and fired a number of shots, hitting him in the arm, leg, face and back. The gunman then made off on foot, and the victim was rushed to hospital where he underwent emergency surgery. Mr Broffey, who comes from the Turf Lodge area, was charged with the murder of 12 people following the bombing of La Mon House in 1978. He was later acquitted, but received a 5-year gaol sentence for

being a member of the IRA, which conviction was quashed by the
Court of Appeal. He was released in 1981 after being in prison for 1
year. The attack on him was condemned by Sinn Fein, who claim it
was carried out by a Loyalist death squad.

A major clear-up operation got underway today in the wake of a
1,000 lb IRA van bomb explosion which struck at the heart of the
city's 'Golden Mile'. Extensive damage estimated at several million
pounds was caused to thirty buildings within a 200-yard radius,
including the Europa Hotel and the Grand Opera House, when the
device exploded in a hijacked van in Glengall Street last week. The
bomb blew a 9 ft wide by 6 ft deep crater in the road adjacent to the
Europa. Virtually every window in the front facade was shattered,
and a gaping hole blown in the ground-floor storage area. A
suspended ceiling collapsed in the restaurant. Up to thirty cars
parked in Glengall Street and the hotel forecourt were destroyed.

A Roman Catholic taxi driver was seriously injured today when a
lone motorcycle gunman shot him in front of scores of south Belfast
primary school children. The victim had just dropped the children at
St Michael's School, Ravenhill Road, shortly before 9.00 am when
the gunman launched the murder bid. The taxi driver, who worked
for Regal Taxis of Cromac Street, is in hospital and his condition is
described as serious: he was shot in the face and stomach. It is
believed he was targeted by Loyalist paramilitaries, in retaliation for
last night's IRA attacks which left four Protestants dead and three
injured.

A man was shot in the leg in the Shankill Road area of Belfast last
night. Two masked gunmen approached him as he walked along
Sherbrook Close, and opened fire. His condition was said to be
satisfactory in hospital.

Harry Ward was gunned down at 3.15 pm yesterday, as he tried to escape from the Diamond Jubilee Bar near the city centre. Gunmen burst in and shot him, but they were apparently looking for someone else.

Gerald Maggin of Springmartin Road was found dead in a stolen Vauxhall Cavalier last Sunday after police opened fire on the vehicle in the Poleglass area.

Last night 11 bags of fertiliser, a key ingredient for homemade explosives, were found under the floorboards of a parochial hall attached to Clonard Monastery off the Falls Road. Rector Father John O'Donnell said that no members of the Clonard community group had any knowledge of when, how or by whom the materials had been placed there. 'Just over a year ago the Community assigned Clonard Hall for use by the Clonard Youth Club,' he said. 'We deeply regret that those young people's lives were put at risk by those who placed explosive materials under the floor of the hall.'

Police are investigating reports of shots being fired in the vicinity of Oldpark RUC Station, north Belfast, last night.

Police opened fire on a car which failed to stop at a vehicle checkpoint near the city centre last night. Two shots were fired at the car in Exchange Street West, close to St Anne's Cathedral, at 10.45 pm.

Almost a hundred families were forced to flee from their north Belfast homes in freezing temperatures early today after suspected firebomb attacks on business premises. Simultaneous fires destroyed buildings housing Rite Price Carpets on York Road, along with Talbot Textiles and the neighbouring Cotton Print curtain shop in Dargan Crescent. More than sixty firemen and eight appliances were used to tackle the blazes shortly after 2.30 am.

Windsor House in Bedford Street was devastated last night by an 800 lb IRA bomb. Every window in the office block was shattered when the bomb exploded at around 9.30 pm.

Ten bomb alerts caused disruption in Belfast at different times yesterday. Police carried out searches at the International and City airports and within other parts of Belfast, and in many areas traffic was considerably delayed.

Hotel guests and students had to jump from their beds after a bomb alert in Belfast City centre early this morning. Nearly a hundred students at Brunswick House, and guests at the Plaza Hotel, were evacuated shortly after 7.00 am after a suspect van was discovered abandoned in Franklin Street between Bedford Street and Adelaide Street.

A 17-year old youth was recovering in hospital today after being shot in the legs in Friendly Street near the city centre just after midnight last night.

On Thursday last week, a Ballysillan taxi driver survived, though with horrific injuries, when he was blown up in his taxi as he turned off Sandy Row. The would-be killers later admitted that they had targeted the wrong man.

Yesterday was a day of disruption caused by bomb alerts throughout the city centre, including an explosion in a car parked in the Castle Court car park. Several other cars were damaged by the blast.

Employees at an engineering company in Dungannon were

evacuated for two hours following a hoax bomb warning at 8 o'clock this morning.

A policeman was treated for shock in hospital yesterday evening after terrorists fired shots into the RUC Station in North Queen Street. A number of cars inside the complex were damaged in the attack which occurred at 6.15 pm, but police say that no one was hit, and no fire was returned.

At the inquest yesterday on 24-year-old UDR soldier Colin McCullough, his fiancee said she was sitting beside him in his car at a beauty spot near Oxford Island, when shots were fired through the driver's side window. The soldier was struck by a total of 13 bullets. The IRA afterwards claimed responsibility for the murder.

A 21-year-old man was recovering in hospital today following an apparent 'punishment' shooting in east Belfast. He sustained a gunshot wound to his left leg when he was accosted by two masked men as he walked along a path in Knocknagoney Park at around 10.00 pm last night.

In Glanbawn Avenue shortly before 6 o'clock last night, a man in his 20s was shot in both legs in an apparent punishment-type shooting. His condition in hospital is said to be stable.

An examination of the preparation and placing of recent IRA bombs in Belfast assumes the involvement of up to two dozen people for a single device. The bombs are based on readily-available chemical fertiliser, with huge quantities needed for 500-600 lb bombs, brought into the city area from the surrounding countryside. The devices, incorporating sophisticated timing devices, detonators, and primers (usually Semtex) are constructed by experts working independently: and the separate elements, some scarce and valuable, are gathered by different individuals knowing only what they need to be told. Stock piles of the explosive must be stored at safe houses, and delivery to targets carried out by further individuals.

The Prevention of Terrorism Act has not been a success. In the 18 years in which it has been in force, 86 per cent of those who have been held under it were later released, and only 3 per cent have actually finally been charged with terrorist offences.

Statistics in the Child Care (Northern Ireland) newsletter reveal a grim picture of deprivation in the Province. A staggering 39 per cent of children live in the poverty trap – members of families earning less than £122 per week. Families here are twice as dependent on Supplementary Benefit to support their incomes as are families in the rest of the UK. Some 95,000 children have only one parent, and 70 per cent of those one-parent families live on benefits. Northern Ireland has the highest unemployment rate of any region in the UK.

A masked Loyalist gunman walked into a chemist's shop in west Belfast yesterday and shot dead a 26-year-old Catholic mother of two. She was hit five times in the body and face, and died almost instantly. The Ulster Freedom Fighters last night claimed responsibility for shooting the woman, saying her brother was a member of Sinn Fein.

A man was shot dead in east Belfast today only minutes after the all-party talks on the future of Northern Ireland resumed. The victim was one of a number of men fired on near a community centre in the Ligoniel district.

Two lorries were burned out in Dungannon early today. They had been parked in George Street, and were attacked around 1.45 am.

Letters to the Editor

Sir – The people of Ulster say take the handcuffs off the Security Forces and let them get on with the job. You can't win a war with one hand in your pocket and the other one tied behind your back.

Sir – Martial law should be introduced in Northern Ireland. The vast majority of residents here agree that the Civil Authorities – in this case the British Government – have failed to function as one would expect. They have had over 20 years to defeat the terrorists. It's time the Civil Authorities took the war to the terrorists and brought peace and prosperity to the long-suffering people of the Province. (Signed) 'No Surrender'

Sir – I would like to point out that in the New Year's Honours List there is a great omission – failure to recognise the fortitude and courage of the ordinary law-abiding people of Northern Ireland. During the Second World War the people of Malta received recognition in the form of the George Cross for their stand during the German air raids. For 22 years the people of Northern Ireland have withstood bombing and intimidation with courage second to none. Surely now it is time for this to be recognised by the award of the George Cross.

4 *Three women*

Vicky Murray

Rose Murphy

Doreen Prescott

Vicky Murray

She lived in a small modern semi-detached house at the end of a cul-de-sac off the city's outer ring road. A small thin woman with a pinched angular face, she sat on the edge of the seat of the armchair, her voice thin and tired, clasping and unclasping her hands, her fingers nervously turning her wedding ring round and round while she spoke. She was twenty-eight.

– I'm afraid. Of everything, everybody, everywhere. They make me afraid because I don't know what's going on. I don't understand any of it. Somebody said if I did I'd probably be even more afraid. I don't know, perhaps I might, perhaps I mightn't. I'm afraid for myself but even more I'm afraid for my kids. They don't understand, I don't understand: and they keep asking me to explain it to them and I can't, I don't understand it any more than they do. You see I'm not Irish, I'm not northern Irish, I'm not Belfast: I'm Lancashire, and nobody's ever been able to explain it to me. Protestants, Catholics, Ulster, the Republic, nationalism or whatever they call it – I don't, I don't understand any of it. People say to me 'What are you?' and I say to them 'What do you mean, "What are you?"' They say 'Well are you Protestant or Catholic or what?' When I say I'm not anything they always say 'Well you must be something. Even if you're not, your mother and father must have been something, what were they?' When I say I've no idea you see the look on their faces: they're saying to themselves 'She must be something, but she's not letting on.' It's a nightmare, that's the only way I can describe it.

And I don't want to say anything against my husband. Alan was a good man, he was, he was a very good man, do you know what I mean? My mother wrote and said 'He got you into all this, it was

Alan got you into it, why don't you bring the kids and come back home?' Well I can't, I don't see it like that. As I see it, things'd be no different if I went back to Blackburn, I'd be just as frightened there as I am here. And I'd want to come back here again, because you never know, if I'm here it might all get sorted out one day, you just never know. If I was there, it couldn't get sorted out because then I'd know even less about what's going on than I do now. I know it sounds daft, but I do – some days I get the feeling one day someone's going to walk in through that door and explain it all to me, to tell me what it's all about. Either that, they're going to explain it, or they're going to walk in and kill me. One or the other, I don't know which. Some days, to be honest I feel I don't really mind which it is. All I know is I just don't want to go on like this.

This isn't making much sense is it? Well how it is, that's the fact, it doesn't make sense. You mightn't think it only I'm a very shy person, I don't talk much. I don't like talking to people much really at all, I don't do it if I can avoid it. I don't mean you, I don't mind talking to you, it's different with strangers. But people who you know, if you talk to them they start saying 'Well why don't you do this?' or 'Had you thought of that?' You end up even more confused than you were. Then afterwards you start thinking over what they said, and you think 'Well yes perhaps they're right, I should've thought of that, why didn't I think of that?' Only it's all no help to you, it just makes things ten times worse.

I said I'd talk about Alan didn't I . . . yes, well that's what it's all about, it's all about Alan. If there hadn't been Alan none of it would have begun, and I wouldn't even be here. I met him in Blackpool when I was seventeen. I'd gone for a weekend with a friend, a girl I worked with, and he was there for a week on his holidays with a friend of his. Well to tell you the truth about it, what happened was I'd met him the year before when he was there on his holidays too. I was only sixteen then. It was nothing more than just a holiday romance sort of thing: we only met two days before he was going back. I thought that was the end of it, I didn't expect to see him again. We didn't write or anything, so I was very surprised when it was a year later and he rang me up. He said he was in Blackpool with his same friend as before, and why didn't me and my friend come over at the weekend to see them? He was being a bit crafty about it actually: he said his friend wanted to see my friend, he didn't say it was his idea, that it was him wanted to see me. I asked him about it a few years afterwards, you know, why he'd put it like that. He said he knew I was shy and he didn't think I'd come if I thought it was him that was after me.

I was shy, I think he was right, I think probably I wouldn't have gone. I was shy and I didn't know anything, I hadn't really been out with boys much at all, he was the first one. He was very good looking and he was a lot older than me, twenty-four or twenty-five I think he was at that time. And he had this lovely voice, this northern Irish accent, I thought it was beautiful. In fact I still do when it's someone with a quiet voice like Alan's got. I was swept off my feet as they say.

I hadn't, I hadn't ever met anybody like him, and after the weekend when he kept ringing me up every night, I mean all the way from here to Blackburn every time, it knocked me over. I mean I was, I was mad about him, but I couldn't believe he felt the same sort of thing for me. He kept saying he wanted to marry me, he wanted to marry me. After a couple of weeks when I missed I was scared of telling him because I thought he'd want no more to do with me. That's what I'd always heard about boys, that was what they did. So I didn't tell him on the phone until the next time, when I was sure. He said 'Well that's it then.' Just like that, and I did, I felt awful, I thought he meant that was the end. I said 'What do you mean?' He said 'Well that's it isn't it then, now you'll have to marry me.'

It was all very quick, I mean the wedding and everything. My mum kept saying 'You don't know anything about him, you ought to wait, lots of people nowadays don't get married straight away, you don't have to, you don't know his family or what he does or anything.' She liked him when he came to England to see her though, she said he seemed very nice and quiet and polite and everything. I came over to Belfast and I met his family, well his mother: her and his dad were divorced and he hadn't seen him for years. But she was nice his mum, her and me we got on together straight away. He didn't have any brothers or sisters, so we lived with his mum till the baby was born: Robert that is, ten years ago now. And Alan had a good job and everything, he worked for an electrical firm. I never knew properly just what he did, I don't understand these things and I didn't really ask.

At the beginning everything was absolutely fine. His mum was very nice: she said I was like a daughter for her that she'd always wanted and not had. The neighbours and everyone were very nice, they're very friendly the northern Irish people. And Alan and me . . . well, you know I've looked back on it and I've looked back on it, and I still can't see anything that was wrong. That's if there really was anything that was wrong. I don't even know that, I don't know anything for positive at all. I'd have said we were happy as far as I could tell. I know I was, I was happy: and I think he was. Only you see Alan was like me, we were both the same sort – people who didn't talk much, both of us were like that.

That's what I meant when I said earlier on that if you talk to people you know, they put ideas in your head. There was this one friend, I mean she was a friend, but she upset me more than anyone. She said to me one day, she said 'Vicky' she said, 'are you absolutely sure in your own mind Alan mightn't have got somebody else?' I said yes of course I was sure, I knew it, I was sure he hadn't. I was sure, definitely, until she said that: it'd never crossed my mind. Only it was only after she'd said it that I started thinking 'Well I don't know, perhaps she might be right', I hadn't thought.

He went out at night sometimes, but I mean all men do that don't they? They go and play darts or have an evening with their mates at the pub, there's nothing wrong with that. I wasn't going to ever be one of those wives who was always saying 'Where've you been, what've you been doing, who were you with?' and that sort of thing. I mean I knew there was the political thing, the UDA, I knew he was in that. But I never really knew anything about what it was. They've got their headquarters and everything on Gawn Street, that building with the painting on the end of the wall and the Union Jack and all the rest of it: but it's not a crime to belong to it, I thought it was just a club sort of thing. I thought it'd be something you know like the Territorial Army, to kind of defend you if you were invaded sort of idea. I know they had marches sometimes, bands, but that side of it didn't interest Alan much, he didn't go to any of those.

From what I can understand of it, it's all to do with Irish history and so on. But it's mostly political and I don't know much about it, and it didn't have nothing to do with me. I thought if Alan wants to tell me about it one day he will, but until he does I shan't ask him if he doesn't talk about it. I mean that first time, when the police came and they were asking me how long he'd been involved with UDA, how often he went out to their meetings and so on, I said I'd no idea. It was true, I hadn't. That's another thing somebody said: they said 'Well he was your husband, you know, you should've tried to take more interest.' I suppose perhaps I should. Only it never seemed to have much for women in it, so I never bothered.

The first time the police came would be two years ago, two years next month. It was eight o'clock at night, and there was this knock at the door and these two plainclothes men came in. They said they were police and showed me their identity and everything, and they asked was Alan in, they said they wanted to talk to him. I said he was away on a contract job for his firm, which he was, and they said to tell him when he came back they wanted a word with him down at Castlereagh police station. When Alan came back and I told him he just nodded, that was all. Then he went upstairs to see the kids and kiss them goodnight: he was playing about with Tina our daughter, she was six then and I remember him carrying her round on his shoulders. He didn't seem worried or anything, no different from like he usually was.

I think I asked him it'd be about a week later, had he been to the police at Castlereagh? He said yes he had. I asked him was it anything special and he said no, just something about the car that's all. And I remember him say 'You haven't mentioned it to anyone have you, me going to Castlereagh?' I said no, and he said well I shouldn't because he didn't want it getting around: he thought his firm wouldn't like it, it was their car and he hadn't told them. I thought the licence had expired or the MOT, or something like that. And we never heard no more from the police again – well I never heard, let's put it like that.

Then the next thing that happened, this'd be about a year ago now. Another night, he wasn't away but he was out, and there was this knock again on the door and this man was there. It was a man on his own. I'd never seen him before, and he said he was a friend of Alan's and was he in? I said no he wasn't, and then before I could say anything else, he pushed in past me and said he'd wait for him then. He came in just like that, and he sat down where you're sitting now. Somehow I didn't like the look of him at all. He was polite enough, nice weather we've been having and that sort of thing, but he kept kind of looking round the room all the time. Whenever there was any sort of a sound, immediately he seemed to kind of well, tense himself. And the really peculiar bit was when there was a noise upstairs, and he looked at me and I thought perhaps he was thinking it was Alan. So I said 'The kids.' And he nodded, and he said 'Oh yes, Robert and Tina isn't it?' I thought 'Well I wonder how he knew that?' Then I thought oh well, perhaps he worked with Alan or something, and Alan'd been talking about the children at work.

When it came to eleven o'clock or after and there was still no sign of Alan, I started getting really nervous. So I said to this man I thought perhaps Alan had gone to see his mam because she hadn't been well, which was true. So then after a bit longer he said he couldn't wait any more, and he'd call another time. He said to tell Alan George'd been, that was all: and then he went.

That was the first time ever, that night, that Alan didn't come home. The next night when he did, he said the job he'd been on at Portrush, they hadn't finished till very late and then they all went and had a few drinks and he didn't feel he ought to drive home, so he'd stopped the night at one of the other men's house. I told him then this man George'd been the night before.

Then what happened was something that astonished me, it really did. Because it seemed like to slip out before he'd time to stop himself. Alan said 'I don't know anyone called George.' So I said to him 'Well he seemed to know you Alan, he knew Robert and Tina's names.' He looked puzzled for a minute, really you know sort of confused. I said 'I thought he might be somebody from work', and it was like he grabbed hold of that: he said 'Oh yes' he said, 'Yes, that George.'

It sounds ridiculous. But it is, it's true: that's all I know, just those two little incidents that's all. I've been over it and over it, and that's all I know. And then five months ago now, one Tuesday it was, he just didn't come home from work. And I've never seen him since. Not seen him, not had a phone call from him, or a letter – not anything. Nor his mother, she's not heard anything from him either. No one has, not at work, the police who I've reported it to, nothing, no one, anywhere.

The only one I'm not absolutely sure about is his mother. I can't explain it, but somehow she doesn't seem . . . I mean she's upset all right, but she did once say to me a little while ago 'I know he's alive.' That was after I told her about the telephone call. She said 'I know he's alive.'

That was eight weeks ago now. The telephone rang and I picked it up and this voice said 'Tell him we know where he is.' And I started to shout, I said 'Well tell me where he is!' but then it clicked and they'd rung off.

So what's it all about? I don't know, I really don't. I tell the kids Daddy's working over in England. But I don't know what's happening, I don't know where I am, I don't understand. The doctor's given me something, some pills, they help a bit but not much, and I don't know how long I can go on. I'll tell you though: when it comes down to it, I do, I really do – I hope it is another woman. I really do. I'm sorry, I can't go on, I'm sorry.

Rose Murphy

A dark rainy night in December. The palely lamplit street made the house difficult to find among the others in the terrace, since few had numbers on the gates or doors. In the small and furniture-cramped front room she spoke quietly and formally, almost as though she was apologising for herself at first. Her hair was scraped back from her plump face and held with an elastic band.

– You're in west Belfast and you're talking to Rose Murphy. You could say you're in a house in the Whiteshaw Road which is in the Ardoyne, but don't say any more than that, not its number or anything, not exactly where it is. And Rose Murphy isn't my real name, but it's near. I'm a Catholic woman who's thirty-eight and's got six children, and whose husband's in hospital with a bad illness but I'd sooner you didn't say more than that. This is my house and I moved here with my children six months ago, and I hope I'll be able to stay here. If they leave us alone I will, but if they don't then I'll have to move again, which'll be my third move in two years.

I asked you to come this late, eleven o'clock at night, because I didn't want anyone to know you were coming. I know you're all right because I've been told you're all right by people whose word I can trust. But all the same you can't be too careful. If someone knew you'd been here and I'd been talking to you, it might be someone who knew you were a writer who was writing a book, and they could come to me afterwards and say to me what had I been talking about to you and what were you going to put in your book. If I told them they might say they were going to make things awkward for me. Or they might say they were going to make things awkward for you, they could say that as well. You can't be too careful, because

they don't care what they do, these people, they think they're a law
unto themselves, and so they are.

Yes I'll try and start at the beginning, but I'm not very good at
talking so you'll have to help me with asking me questions. If there's
anything I say that doesn't seem clear and make sense to you, ask me
more questions about it. I don't mind because I want people to try
and understand, and you'll know what's the best way to do it. Right,
start at the beginning. Do you mean the beginning of what
happened, or the beginning of my life? Beginning of my life, all
right, yes.

There isn't much to say about it. I'm an ordinary person, an
ordinary Catholic woman today in west Belfast. I was born in west
Belfast, I've lived all my life here, I've never been anywhere else and
I'd never want to go anywhere else. No, not even after what's
happened, I still wouldn't want to go and live anywhere else. I
suppose because it's the only place I've ever known, all my family are
here, it's where I belong. I can't put it any other way than that. Your
friends, your family, it's what you're used to isn't it? Nowhere else'd
ever be the same, it's where you belong, it's your home.

My mammy and daddy have nine children, and I'm the third
youngest. My daddy used to be in the docks, he was a dock worker.
But he's on the brew now, he hasn't worked for nine years. I'd say I
had a happy childhood, I'd describe it as a normal childhood. I don't
remember anything in particular about it, nothing unhappy at all, I
was just an ordinary girl. All I did was the things all girls do, played
in the streets when I was young, went out a bit with boys when I was
older and things like that. I wasn't good at school especially, I don't
remember anything I was good at. I went to the Catholic primary
school in Beechmount, then I went to the secondary school, the
Catholic one up at the top here. I didn't have any ideas of doing
anything after I left, I just wanted to do what all the other girls did,
get a job and work for a bit and then get married and settle down and
have kids.

I left school at fifteen. First of all I worked in a factory in the
canteen, doing general kitchen duties. Then after that I worked in a
box factory where they made cardboard boxes. The thing I liked was
it meant you had a bit of money of your own, you could go to the
cinema or a disco without having to ask your parents for the money

for it. I had a regular boyfriend, he was the boy from next door, he was a boy I'd known since I was eleven. I think we always knew we'd get married to each other, we knew it and everyone took it for granted. For a brief time I went out with someone else when I was sixteen or seventeen, but it was nothing serious, we were just friends that's all.

In fact that boyfriend was a British soldier. The British army hadn't been long here and in the beginning they were friendly to us, and we were all curious about them, I mean all we girls were. It was a big thing at first to have a boyfriend who was a British soldier. I've forgotten his name now, Eric it was I think, something like that. I thought he talked funny and he thought I talked funny and half the time we couldn't understand what each of us was saying. It wasn't serious between us, and then one day my mammy told me I shouldn't go out with British soldiers. They were getting very unpopular, people didn't like them, so that was more or less the end of it. But as I say it'd not been serious at all anyway, and after that I got married.

I don't know what it was with the British soldiers, why it was people liked them at first and were glad to see them, then they became our enemies. I could never understand what happened. I didn't know anything about politics and I still don't, it's not something that's ever been in my life at all. My daddy wasn't a republican or a nationalist, nor my mammy. There are some households in west Belfast where those things count for a lot but they didn't in ours, leastways not with my parents they didn't. As far as I know they never voted in their lives, not for any party. I don't think they did, and I know I never have. Nor my husband, none of us, we've never been political at all. That's what makes it horrible: I mean we're not anybody's friends but we're not anybody's enemies. Leastways not until two years ago I wasn't anybody's enemy.

The only person I know that had in any way ever been mixed up in anything of that sort was my brother Rory. He's been interned, when they brought in internment, he was one of the first they lifted. But he wasn't ever charged with anything, and he's not been in prison since for anything, so I don't think he can have been much involved in anything at all. All I've ever heard him say once was when he was in the kitchen sitting at the table having a cup of tea with my husband Jim. I was making some sandwiches or something, and as I was going in I heard Rory say to Jim 'It's all wrong, there shouldn't be British troops on the streets of Belfast.' That was all, I remember Jim just shrugged his shoulders and didn't say anything. His attitude was that they were here and we couldn't do anything about it, and one day they'd go and that'd be the end of it. That was all there was to it to Jim. He's no more political than I am, Jim and me just get on with our lives, that's all.

You wouldn't have thought that'd be too much to ask. That's all my eldest boy John wanted to do too, to be left alone and get on with his life. I'm sure that's all he's ever wanted. Last year I went to see Rory, and I said to him 'Rory, I want to know. Is my John into something that I don't know about? Because if he is I want you to tell me Rory please.' And Rory said no John wasn't, as far as he knew he definitely wasn't. I think he would have told me if there'd been anything: he's my brother and he's John's uncle, so I think he would have told me. It was something I couldn't imagine, but you do hear of cases where parents don't know what their kids have been up to, there are cases like that. But I asked John to swear it to me whether he was: and he did, he swore to me he wasn't into anything at all.

I've gone on a bit too far ahead. But I get emotional about it, I get so I can't think. It's hard for me to keep it all in order in my mind.

I'll go back to my husband, I'll go back to Jim again. He's got one of those illnesses where they don't seem able to say for definite what it is: sometimes they think it's what's called sclerosis, other times they say they're not so sure. It gives him a lot of pain and he can't work and he's classed as permanently disabled. He's been in and out of hospital, as a patient, and he's had hundreds and hundreds of tests. Sometimes when he's at home, he can't walk: it's tablets and tablets and more tablets, and sometimes injections. Then other times it seems it goes away for a while, for as long as a couple of months sometimes: but it always comes back. It's been going on ten years now and he has bad depressions with it. He says 'I'm only forty and my life's over, I'll never work again.'

John's our eldest, he's just on twenty now. I had him when I was eighteen, the first year after Jim and I got married; then we've five others, two of them twins. The youngest's Paul, he's eighteen months. From when he was ten, John's only known his daddy as someone who was ill all the time. Jim feels that, sometimes he says if being ill hadn't happened to him, he thinks somehow he might have been closer to John. He blames himself for John getting into trouble in the first place. I think that's wrong, I don't think parents can stop their kids doing things, not everything that they do they can't. I know I used to do things my parents didn't know about, I know Rory did and Sean and Peter, they're my older brothers. But Jim feels it very much, he gets very down about John when he's depressed.

He was just turned seventeen John was, the first time he got into trouble. We were living then in Oldpark, in one of those houses up near the top: the council've pulled them down now and built new ones over the other side. The police came one night very late, about midnight or near, they said they'd got John at the RUC Station and they wanted us to go down. Jim couldn't because he was bad, so I went on my own. They had John there, and two of his friends a bit older than him who I didn't know. The three of them had taken a car and been joy-riding in it, and they'd been stopped at a road block.

You know about joy-riding do you? It's something there's a lot of here, not all the kids do it but most of them: well anyway perhaps not most but a lot. I suppose they do in other places too, and people don't take it very seriously usually do they? They say 'Well it's just kids', don't they? Only here it's more serious because it's much more dangerous you see, there've been a lot of bad incidents and young people have even been killed. The police and Army at night set up road blocks everywhere because they're looking for the IRA. And if you don't stop they shoot – and in some cases even when people did stop, they've still been shot. Or that's what the police and the Army've been accused of, and you don't know the truth of it. You never know what's the truth.

When it's ordinary people, youngsters like John and his pals, normally the police don't want to be bothered with them: they're after the IRA people, not silly kids. So they told me they weren't going to take any action against John this time, but if they caught him again he'd be in bad trouble. John said he was sorry, and he looked sorry. He said he'd not do such a thing ever again, he told me that and he told his daddy too. We warned him, we said never mind anything else, it was such a stupid thing to do because it was dangerous, and he ought to know better.

Then it'd be about a month after that, one night I went through to
the kitchen to make some tea or something, and two men were
standing there. They were only young, about in their twenties, and
they were wearing overalls. How they'd got in I don't know, I
remember thinking I must have forgotten and not locked the door.
But there they were, not with their faces covered or anything: and
they stood and looked at me without saying anything for a minute,
then one of them said 'Tell your John to stop it or else there'll be
trouble.' I couldn't speak for a minute, my heart was up in my
mouth. Then I said 'Stop? Stop what?' One of them said 'Cars.' That
was all, 'Cars' very quiet, then they both turned round and walked
out.

John wasn't in, but the other kids were, they were only in the
other room watching the telly, and they hadn't heard any of it. I
went back where they were and my heart was beating so hard I
thought I was going to faint. I was very frightened, because I knew
who they were and what they did. I don't mean I knew them as
people, I didn't, I'd not seen them before. But I knew what they
were, that they were IRA.

When John came home I went crazy with him. I told him they'd
been and given him a warning, and he knew what that meant, he
must swear he'd never do it again. And you know, he laughed. He
just laughed. He said 'They've made a mistake mammy, they can't
mean me, I've not been in a car since that night the police took me
into Oldpark.'

Then only two weeks after that there was a knock at the front door
and it was the police. They said 'Mrs Murphy your boy's been shot,
he's in the Royal Victoria. He'll be all right, they've shot him in the
legs. But we want you to come with us and see him and tell him he's
got to tell us who it was who did it to him.'

When I got there John was white, he'd lost a terrible lot of blood
and he was in a lot of pain. As soon as I went to the side of his bed,
before I could say anything he said 'Mammy they made a mistake,
they hit the wrong one.' And these two policemen, they just looked
at each other and they didn't say anything, they just turned round
and went.

That was all John ever said. I talked to him, his daddy talked to
him, but none of it made any difference, all he'd ever say was only

that they'd hit the wrong one. The surgeon at the hospital who'd operated on him, he said he had eight wounds in his legs and at first they thought he wouldn't walk again. But he was young and strong, he made a good recovery and after three months he was walking again, though he had a limp. I went to the housing people and they were very good: they said we were overcrowded which we were, and they moved us to another house which is this one here. And I thought at least that was that.

Then last January . . . I'm sorry, I can't help it my hands start to tremble, I can't stop them. Last January one night I'm here with the five kids, and Jim's upstairs in bed, and we're all watching the telly, then suddenly there's this big crash. It was the front door coming down, and the next minute that door there opened, and they came into this room. Three of them all wearing overalls and all with these black knitted hoods on. They stood there as though it was their own house, and all the kids were sitting with their mouths open looking at them. The tallest one, he stood there by that chair and he said 'Tell John he's forty-eight hours to get out. He's to be gone by Saturday or we'll be back.'

That was all. Thirty seconds to smash somebody's front door down and come in and say that in front of me and the kids, and then they've gone. I wake up at night I do, I can see them standing there. Smashing the door down, you can't believe it would happen to you: how can it, how can something like that happen to you in your own home?

I ran round to Rory's house, he lives only up the road, and he came back with me straight away. He was still here fastening up the door at past midnight, which was when John came back. And he started to laugh again, John did. But Rory stopped him: he said to him 'Look John I'm telling you son' he said, 'even if it's so that they've picked the wrong one, it doesn't matter. You go John – all right? Tomorrow – you just go.'

That was January. Five months ago, and he's been over the water with my sister in London ever since. Once a week I go to Rory's and I make a phone call to him, and he says he's all right. One time about two months ago he said he thought he'd be all right now, he'd come back. So Rory spoke to him, and told him no he wasn't to. He said he'd find out when it'd be all right for him and he'd tell him then, but until then he was to stop where he was. Rory said for my sake and the others, his brothers and sisters, stop there where he was.

I don't know when he'll come back. When Rory says it's safe for him, that's all I know. I don't know when it'll be and I haven't asked. But who do these people think they are? They make laws for other people about when they can live in their homes and when they can't, how can they do that? Rory says from what he understands they say what lads like John are doing is called 'anti-social behaviour', and it gets all of us in west Belfast a bad name. So what do they think going round shooting people in the legs and breaking into their homes does? Isn't that anti-social behaviour, doesn't that give west Belfast a bad name? They must be sick, really really sick, mustn't they?

Doreen Prescott

A sunny early spring Saturday morning, the sky clear and blue. Her house was in a newly-built row, set back behind a low wall close to the edge of the main road which was busy with buses and shoppers' cars. Neat and precise in manner and speech, she sat on the settee with her feet together and her hands resting lightly on her knees. She had short dark hair and blue eyes and wore a plain dark brown woollen dress. High in the blue sky over the distant west of the city a stationary police helicopter hung, faintly droning. The Saturday morning traffic whirred busily past, outside her house.

– I'm the widow of a paramilitary. Well I'm the common-law widow, if you can have such a thing: we weren't actually married but we lived together and I was known as his common-law wife.

I'm forty-two and I've two daughters: the eldest's thirteen and the younger one seven and their names are Margaret and Mary. They weren't his, they were my first husband's. He died too. So I'm twice widowed, in my own mind at least I am, Edward was as much my husband as my first husband Harry was. If this sounds a bit cold to you in the way I'm talking about it, it's because I am cold, I'm a cold person, life has made me cold. Underneath perhaps not, but on top I'm definitely cold, I need to present myself like that.

As a job I'm a receptionist-telephonist: I'm on the reception desk and the switchboard for a firm in central Belfast. I'm a Belfast person, I was born here and I've always lived here: I was born where my parents lived which was on the Shankill Road, so from that you'll know I'm an Ulster Protestant, an Ulster Loyalist. Very much so.

At school I think I was quite bright, I was a grammar school girl.

All I ever wanted to do was be in the services, I never had any other ambition except that. My father had been in the Air Force through the war and I wanted to follow him on and do the same. I had a brother and a sister younger than me, but they didn't want to do that, they weren't interested. I was, not so much because of my father, but because it seemed to me an independent life, especially for a girl. There was a kind of adventure about it. A lot of northern Irish girls are what you might call fixed, on the idea of home and marrying and having children. I don't know why I was any different, but I was. And I was very patriotic British, I still am: my father had fought in the war for his King and country and I'm very proud of that. So was he: towards the end of his life his health wasn't good and he couldn't work, but I remember him saying to us many times the best part of his life had been in the war. 'I can always say I fought for my King and country' he'd say. I don't think he was romantic about it: he hadn't been a fighter pilot or something glamorous like that, just an Air Force mechanic. But he'd done his duty, that was the important thing.

He was very pleased when I told him I'd put my name down to join the WRAAF, the women's Air Force. It wasn't long before he died. When I told him he smiled, he said 'You're my girl Doreen', I think it gave him a big feeling of pride. My father was the sort of man he always felt there was a clear difference between what was right and wrong. You knew what it was, you didn't need anyone to tell you, you didn't need to read books about it, you knew without having to think about it. In the war, we were right and the Germans were wrong so they had to be stopped, it was as simple as that.

I went to England for my training, Scotland actually it was, a place near Glasgow. I was a clerk, a telephonist. The thing I wanted to do most was come back to Belfast in my uniform and let my father see me. I sent him a photograph, but I didn't get back in time for him to actually see me: he died two months after I'd joined. I got compassionate leave to come for his funeral, and I wore my uniform then, but that was the nearest I got to him seeing it. My mother said she thought somehow he'd know.

I enjoyed my time in the WRAAF very much. I liked the life, I liked the discipline, you made lots of friends, and I thought it was great. After Scotland I was posted to Germany, and I went for a few weeks on a special training course to Gibraltar, and also I went to Cyprus. I thought that wasn't bad for a young girl of twenty as I was then, an ordinary young girl from Belfast to go to all those different places. When I came home on leave, other girls of my same age all seemed to me to be leading very dull sort of lives. I was well paid, well travelled, I'd got independence, I wouldn't have changed places with any of them.

Altogether I was four years in the WRAAF, then I came out because I wanted to get married. I'd met a man, he was a Flight Sergeant and he was ten years older than me. The idea was we'd marry and have living quarters and wherever he went I'd go too, but I wouldn't actually be in the services. The idea appealed to me because it would mean I'd still be half-and-half in the service life. He came from Belfast too, it was funny: he'd been born and brought up only a few streets away from where I was, but we'd never known each other. The first time we met was in Germany.

After we'd been married a year I got pregnant which we hadn't really intended, and after we'd had a talk about it we decided I'd come back here and we'd get a house. And he'd see if there was a chance of him getting some sort of clerical job in northern Ireland in the RAF because of his health, and not have to go abroad. They were good about it, I think the RAF have always been better than the Army about families and things. After only a little while he was more or less permanently back here. His name was Harry, and we had nine very happy years. There was our first daughter Margaret, and then we'd another girl Mary, and we had a quarter in Lisburn. Everything seemed as though there was going to be a good future for us.

The worry though was Harry's health. He had a slight heart attack, then he had another, then he had another after that. It was obvious he wasn't going to be able to stay in the RAF, he'd have to be invalided out, and that's what happened. Before we could really settle and discuss what the future was going to be though, he had yet another heart attack and he died. I suppose it sounds hard of me to say it, but by then I won't say I was expecting it, but it didn't come as a terrible shock, not like a bolt from the blue or something like that. Margaret then was nine and I had talked to her about it: she'd known for a year or more daddy was ill and one day he might be taken from us. Like me, she was prepared, well as much as a young child can be. Mary was only three, so she didn't know very much about it. Even now four years afterwards, it doesn't seem she recalls him much in any way.

Well as I say that was four years ago. Within a year after that I was living with Edward. I'd met him once or twice through friends before Harry died. There wasn't anything between us. He was separated from his own wife, and it could have been, I don't know but I think I ought to say it, I think it might possibly have been that even if Harry hadn't died, Edward and I might have well developed into something. I think you can usually tell with a person more or less as soon as you've met them, whether there's a possibility of something there or not. With Edward I was aware there was, and so was he too, I'm fairly sure, I think. Well as I say we started living together. The good thing was both the girls liked him, especially the older one Margaret: she was very fond of him, Edward could make her laugh.

People might find this hard to believe, but right up till the time Edward moved in to live with us, I never actually knew what his job was. He said it was to do with selling computers on a freelance basis. Some days he had to go off to work and sometimes he'd be away two or three days at a time. Other days he seemed to have nothing to do and stayed at home. There were phone calls now and again, and he'd say 'I've got to go and see someone' and he'd go. We had quite a lot of friends between us and we did a fair amount of socialising, and on the whole life seemed to be improving then as far as I was concerned. I wouldn't say I'd resented it, but the last year or so of Harry's life had been pretty hard, he was never well enough for us to go out anywhere, so it hadn't been all that easy.

And then there came the big shock. A friend of Edward's, somebody he liked very much and been very close friends with, was killed: he was shot. I asked Edward why, why the man'd been shot, but he didn't give any explanation. I thought it was because he was too upset to talk about it. We went to the funeral, we went to the man's house, and there was a crowd of people there, a procession, what do they call it, a cortege. I suddenly realised from everybody there and what they were saying that the man was a paramilitary, a member of the UVF.

When I got over the shock of that, naturally a couple of days later I realised something else too. Edward was a paramilitary also, he was in the UVF as well. I'd have thought if anybody'd told me, that if I'd ever suddenly found out something like that about my husband – and I thought of Edward as my husband – I'd have gone crazy about it. But I didn't, for some reason I could understand how a lot of people felt there was a need to be ready to protect northern Ireland if it came to it, because we wanted to stay British. My father had always said 'British and proud of it' and things like that: so had Harry while he'd been alive, and of course being in the WRAAF I felt it too. I still do to an extent.

About a week after the funeral I sat down in the evening with Edward one night, and I asked him to tell me honestly how much he was involved and what he did. So he came out with it: he was an intelligence officer in the UVF, quite high up in the chain of command in Belfast. He was in it right up to here. I asked him to tell me everything, or as much as he'd be allowed to because of military secrecy and so on. He told me he was responsible for all the file-keeping and indexing and cross referencing and so on, for one particular area of Belfast. I can't tell you much about the system because I don't know it myself: but things like files on known IRA people, where they lived, what their movements were, where they went, which pubs they drank in, who were their friends, their car numbers, everything. Yes and what they were suspected of having done, yes: and what they were definitely known to have done, yes that too. They're very thorough.

I asked him for one promise. I asked him would he promise me, for the sake of the girls, he'd never bring guns in the house. Immediately he said no of course he wouldn't, he wasn't into that side of things, his work was purely intelligence gathering and clerical. What he meant by that was he wasn't a member of what they call a death squad. That still didn't make what he was doing not dangerous of course though: he was helping target people, and you took it for granted if he was doing that, the other side would be targeting him if they found out.

But what I didn't know, and this makes me bitter, is that someone else was targeting him as well. The law, the police, the people we'd every right to think would be on the same side as we were, they were

watching him and waiting to catch him too. They came one morning
in a dawn raid at six o'clock and arrested him and took him away.
Up till then they hadn't seemed to be being too severe on
Protestants. They picked up some of the actual death squad people,
they had to because they were killers: but they didn't go much
further than they had to, as a rule.

The morning they came for Edward, it was the first of a new lot of
swoops as they call them, against Protestants. I heard later they'd
arrested altogether about forty people I believe it was, all over Belfast
and surrounding areas. They took them in and held them all on
remand in Crumlin Road gaol. There was a mass of charges against
them: murder, conspiracy, possession of firearms, explosives,
offences against the person, even not having dog licences some of
them said. They were making an example, trying to show they were
impartial again, as much against Loyalist paramilitaries as they were
the IRA. That was why Edward got taken in, because he was one of
the top people.

It was all based on the evidence of an informer, a man who was a
so-called supergrass. They put as many charges against him as they
could: there were three of conspiracy to murder, they were the main
ones. Regarding three different people, and two of them were
persons who'd actually been killed. But Edward had a good defence
team: he was very important to the organisation, and if he'd been put
away on life sentences, which was what he could have got, it'd have
done great damage to them. He was on remand a long time waiting
trial in Crumlin Road gaol, nearly a year. Then, I don't know the
technicalities of it, but one day in court the prosecution announced
they weren't going to proceed in his case: the supergrass's evidence
wouldn't stand up.

You'd have thought that was cause for celebration. He was
discharged and let free. But there'd been publicity and too many
people knew things: he'd been identified, which meant he was a
marked man to the IRA. I feel very bitter: the police should have
given him protection and so should the UVF. They said they were
going to, both of them: they said they'd see he was all right for
money and we could go away and start a new life. That's what we
were intending to do, but there were things to arrange, where we
should go, the girls' schooling especially Margaret's, she was just

starting secondary school. You can't choose a new name and a new life for yourself overnight just like that. We needed more time, and that was what we didn't have. Edward stayed in the house for three days, then we decided it was too dangerous to stop in one place so he went to a friend's. But he'd only been there two days when he decided to risk going down to the corner shop for some fags. That was it, they were waiting outside the house for him in a car. Three men in it and it never stopped, they said: it drew alongside him and they put fifteen bullets into him, then they were away. It all took less than thirty seconds, so they said.

I've always been strong, in a way this has made me stronger. Stronger but not in a nice way: much harder. I know where I stand now. I'll not forgive the people who did it, but I won't forgive those who didn't help him either. I think I forgive them even less.

5 *To try and explain some of it for you*

Father Michael Brown

Tea in the high-ceilinged dining-room of the modern single-storeyed presbytery, at the back of the old red brick church; bone china teacups and plates, and ginger biscuits. A bald powerfully built man with a ruddy complexion, he talked animatedly, sipping his tea rapidly, brushing crumbs fastidiously away from his chin.

– Oh it is Tony, it's terrible difficult. Two men shouting to each other across an abyss in different languages, you know? A priest and an Irishman, born in County Mayo – and an Englishman from over the water. Different from each other as chalk and cheese aren't we, eh? Yet under the skin, in our hearts, in our blood, we inhabit the same planet. So somehow we've still got common humanity, mm?

You've asked me to speak frankly and so I will. History's against us, that's the thing that separates us most. You know, to me and most Irishmen, history is the story of how your people for hundreds of years have oppressed mine. This is what makes it so difficult, because you see we do, we like the British. In many ways we're very close to them, we always have been. Whether it's that we envy them and want to be like them I don't know, but there's been this kind of bond of liking and affection. Like a child's for its father, that's the nearest I can get to it: however cruel, however dominating its father is, the child always loves his father in his heart. He wishes he'd be different and kinder to him, but he's the only father he has.

That's not so good an analogy, but I think it's the only way I can put it. We can't separate ourselves from the British: however much we want to, we can't tear ourselves away. And yet in many of our hearts there's an unforgettable memory, of all the cruelty and wickedness that's been done to us. We have to live with this sort of eternal sadness and regret at what's been done to us. And you know, all the time we go on and on wondering why you've done it. There's over a million Irishmen today living and working in Britain, bringing up their families and living in British society, so there can't be irreparable hatred between us, not if so many of us co-exist with you. All we want – I'm sure all you want – is for us to live together in peace and harmony, for us to treat each other with dignity and respect.

There've been good times and bad times in our relationship. It makes me despondent that at this present time it seems to be one of the worst for many many years, you know. To hear young men talking, as I do and you will yourself – to hear them talking of 'the war' they say they're carrying on against the British, I can't tell you how sad it makes me. I visit them in prison, and that's how they talk you know, to themselves and to me. War, killing innocent people, men women and children, bringing explosives into the city and destroying it, it's terrible. They seem to me like sadly desperate and desperately sad young people, who've lost all sense in their lives. Yet to them and many of their families too you know, they're heroes, carrying on this tradition of war against the Brits.

But how can they talk like that? Last year alone the IRA killed five British soldiers, forty-five of their fellow Irishmen who happened to be Protestant, and twenty-three or twenty-four I think it was as well who were Irish Catholics. So how in the name of God can that be called carrying on a war against the Brits? It's insanity. But these young men when I talk to them, they say what's the alternative? Can those of us who're in the Church, or anyone else, promise them justice without there having to be violence used to get it? We've failed them you know, the Church has failed them, that has to be said. Not just in Ireland but worldwide: revolutionaries in the end always take up the gun. Only the trouble is you see, isn't it, that once you go down that path, the end of it is gangsterdom? Taking the law into your own hands, tit for tat killings, beatings up of your own side who step out of line, and all the rest. Violence has an appeal in itself, and that easily takes over from the idealism you might have had when you started.

But I'll go on. I said I'd speak frankly to you, and so I will. What I must say to you as well you see, is what goes with it, which is the

violence is very far indeed from being all on one side. The Royal
Ulster Constabulary and the British Army, they indulge in hideous
violence too. When a young man sees those who are called 'the
Security Forces', the upholders of law and order – when he sees them
doing the same thing, to him that justifies his own actions. The
whole might of those who're ranged against him, all their equipment
and their armour and their technology – they're practising violence
far more indiscriminately than he is. They too shoot innocent
people, blind and maim and kill women and children – and it's been
going on for twenty years, many of these young men have seen it
going on all their lives.

And there's one difference too you see, one very big difference. If a
young man, what they call a 'Volunteer' of the Irish Republican
Army is caught, he'll be put in prison for a very long time for what
he's done. And sometimes you know to be honest, it must be said for
what he hasn't done: these recent celebrated miscarriage of justice
cases such as the Birmingham Six and the Guildford Four, they've all
too clearly shown that. On the other hand though, someone in the
RUC or the British Army, if they kill an unarmed civilian, nothing
in the way of punishment happens to them at all. In all their lifetimes
these young IRA men have known many hundreds of people the
same as themselves, put away to languish in prison for years. But not
one, not one single one, of those he sees as members of an occupying
army has that happened to at all. I say not one, but in fact that's what
there was I think: one British soldier and one only who was found
guilty of murder, and served time in prison. And he was let out after
only two years.

It's true isn't it, it's more than true it's a truism, to say that
violence begets violence? But I fear it has to be said that the record
of the Army and the police in northern Ireland doesn't bear
examination when it comes to dispensing justice to them for it. On
the flimsiest of evidence, on confessions which have undoubtedly
been beaten out of them – young Irishmen, misguided and
undoubtedly guilty as many of them were – they've gone to prison,
and those they see as their oppressors have been let free. I've said
enough to you I hope, to make it clear I don't condone the IRA. To
say I understand some of their feelings though, well that's a different
thing. If violence is ever to cease here, it has to be ended completely
by both sides together. To my mind there's no hope otherwise.

It's difficult to talk entirely reasonably about this, because naturally it raises in me feelings I'm sure are common to all Irish people, men and women both. They're the feelings that are rooted in our past history I was talking about: the history of both our countries, yours and mine. Because we, you see, we've never done anything to you like you've done to us. We've never exploited you, or oppressed you. There's no single instance in history of us having invaded you: nor come to that of doing it to any other country in Europe, so far as I'm aware. The French, the Dutch, the Scandinavians, the Germans of course – they've every one of them at some time been your enemies, invaded you, robbed and killed and pillaged and taken your goods and your land. But not us, the Irish: we've never done that to you.

But what have you done to us? Not only what we've never done to you, but much worse than you've ever had done to you by anyone else. Massacres, transportations, gaoling, starvation, driving us off our lands, dividing them up in parcels and giving them as presents and rewards to your ruling nobles and men at court. The history of the British in Ireland over hundreds of years is beyond description it is, indeed it's almost beyond belief. It's an appalling story.

And the terrible thing you know, is that never at any point in the history of our two countries has it been any different, ever. There's never been one time when you could put your finger on the chart of history and say 'There – then – that was the time when the British treated the Irish people as fellow human beings.' You took away our religion, our history, our education, everything that we had. You appropriated it as though it was yours by divine right, and you never gave it back. And when we tried to fight you for it, you visited the most ghastly and inhumane treatment upon us that one people ever dealt another. You behaved towards us as though we were a subhuman race, just as the Germans regarded the Slavs and the Jews.

You could say this was all old history, all in the past and should be forgotten. But I don't think it can be and I don't think it will be, because it's there as what you might call the backcloth to all our relationship. Feelings of anger, feelings of resentment: they're deeply inbred in the Irish people towards you, much much more than your people understand. But in our dealings you never sufficiently take them into account. You look down on the Irish as figures of fun, stupid half-witted people of little or no account. Irish jokes, Irish jokes: sometimes we think that's all the British know about the Irish. Jokes about Paddy and his stupidity, how he cuts one end off a ladder to put it on the other to make it longer, and thousands more like that. The idea of the Irish as a cultured and civilised people is one that's hardly ever seemed to enter the British mind.

And the tragedy of it all – the biggest tragedy ever I think, certainly of recent times – was when the troops first came back in 1969. I said earlier about there never being a moment in history when you could say the British behaved towards the Irish as though they were honourable people. And I mean as though both of them were. But that was a moment, it really was – a Heaven-sent opportunity when they could have done that. When the troubles began and the Labour Government sent over the British Army to protect the Catholic population here – that was the moment when hundreds of years of history could have been reversed. Tens of thousands of Catholics, don't forget, had been driven from their homes and were in fear for their lives. So the British soldiers were welcomed with open arms by them and the nationalists as saviours: and for a very short time, it seemed as though out of the sufferings of the Irish people there might come something at last which was going to be good. A coming together of the British soldiery and the ordinary common Irish people – it seemed like the beginning of a miracle. It was scarcely credible it could happen, surely it was too good to be true: and I wasn't alone in thinking that I assure you.

Well – it was so, yes it was too good to be true. For a few months there was hope of a new friendship between us, a chance to forget all the things that had happened over hundreds of years before. It was one of the most terrible tragedies in our joint story that it didn't last. Truly I don't think there's anything other than that can be said about it now.

What and when and above all why? Those are questions that have a multiplicity of answers, and none of them's simple. Most of them are true to some degree and false in some degree as well. The only fact of the matter is that it went wrong. Blame the soldiers, blame the politicians, the fanatics, the religious bigots, whoever you like: everyone has to bear some responsibility. But most of all my feeling is that you have to blame the Church. I'll say that plainly. I blame the

Church. Not the Protestant Church or the Catholic Church: both of them. Utterly and completely, the Church failed its people it did, on both sides.

If ever there was a time for coming together, for denouncing sectarianism and bigotry, it was then. The Church leaders should have been just that – leaders, they should have announced from that moment on they'd work together to build bridges, and make the presence of armed forces on our soil to keep the peace unnecessary. It was a matter of shame they had had to come in the first place – shame to us all, whichever side had been most at fault. And the moment was there then for both our churches, I'm convinced of it, if only we'd had sufficient humility and compassion towards one another – to make all the movements towards each other that needed to be made, and would have brought us all to live in peace.

Well, we didn't do it. Within a short time the British Army was put in the position of supporting the *status quo* – that being the dominance of the Protestant community. I don't think that was what was intended to happen, but that's what did. And for evermore afterwards, for more than twenty years now since, the Catholic community – which after all is a third of the population in the north – has come to see the British soldiers not as their protectors after all, but as the hated symbols of domination they've always been in the past.

Of course it's said that these young boys, these British soldiers, they don't know what it's all about; they're caught in the middle between two warring factions, all they're trying to do is keep the peace. But when the British say that, if they do see it like that, I'm afraid they're deluding themselves. Because it's very far indeed now from how the Army are seen by the Catholic people here. By their loutish behaviour – that's a very strong word but I use it because I think it's so very often justified – by their loutish behaviour the soldiers alienate a very large section of the population. I've heard them myself on the streets of west Belfast, shouting oaths and abuse at men and women old enough to be their parents and their grandparents. 'Fenian bastard', 'Irish whore' – these are terrible things for young boys to be shouting at citizens of their own country. And the shouting, sadly, is of course only a part of it: the killings, the brutality, the breaking into peoples' homes goes on too.

The British people, I think, would be deeply ashamed if they knew one half of the behaviour of their own sons, over and over again, on the streets of Belfast. At least I hope they would.

6 Three men

Pat Taylor

Joe Maloney

Sean Kelly

Pat Taylor

He brought in a tray with two mugs of coffee with spoons in them and a packet of sugar and a half empty milk bottle, and put it down in the tiled fireplace in front of the old gas fire. Heavily built with a neat beard and curly dark hair, he wore an open-necked check shirt and crumpled corduroy trousers. His voice was gruff, almost surly: sometimes his chin sank down on his chest as he talked.

– It's ten years now since my brother was killed. He was twelve. I don't think there's been a day ever since he died when he hasn't come into my thoughts one way or another, whatever I was doing or where I was. Often, you know, it'll be the first thing registers in my mind when I wake up, especially if it's near Christmas time, or if it's his birthday anniversary coming up. 'Paul'd have been fifteen next week', I'll find myself thinking, or eighteen or twenty or whatever. Or I see a lad of that age that he'd be, in a bar perhaps, you know having a drink and chatting-up a girl: and I think 'That could be Paul now, sitting there doing that.'

There were four of us children. I was the eldest, then two girls, then Paul and he was nine years younger than me. Whether it was because he was the youngest, the baby you know, and I was the eldest, I felt sort of protective towards him. Or it might've been because he was the only other boy besides me – you never know things like that consciously do you? But they're there, it doesn't greatly matter to you much why. And somehow there were a lot of times when neither of us was aware of the difference in our ages – say when we were playing football, when we went out to the Lough fishing in the little rowboat we had, or if we were only sitting talking about nothing: that feeling, you know, it was always there. All the time from when he was eight or nine, and me seventeen or eighteen, it was always there: it wasn't only that we were brothers but we were good friends together as well.

My mother broke down crying you know, when I was talking to her about it once, it'd be a couple of Christmas times ago. I was trying to tell her about all the feelings still inside me about what had happened, how I was going to spend the rest of my life if necessary getting to the bottom of it; I was telling her about the anger of it, the bitterness, and that I wasn't ever going to let go. She burst into tears, she did: she said it was poisoning my life, I'd got to make myself get over it and start trying to come to terms with it, like she'd had to do herself over losing one of her children. But you know that was the point of it: she had three other children to think about, but for me all there was was the loss of my only brother. You know, it was the circumstances more than anything else, the manner that he died in: that's what's left me with all my unresolved feelings I suppose you'd call them, that's been the hardest part.

Well I ought to try and go back to the beginning, and tell you about it from there. But it'll still make no more sense to me than it's ever done. I expect it'll not do to you either: you see it leaves so many questions hanging around unanswered. Like I said to my mother that Christmas time, until I know what some more of the answers are, I'll never feel I can get on with other things in my life properly at all.

I suppose perhaps I should start first with a bit about myself now. I'm thirty, not married, and I live here in a flat just off the Malone Road on my own. I don't have a regular job, but I'm a qualified teacher, I have an English degree. All I use it for though at the moment is I tutor a night-school evening course for mature students, grown-ups who want to get themselves an 'O' level for one reason or other. I teach two evenings a week to earn a bit of money, and as well as that I do freelance proof-reading and some copy-editing from time to time. I don't smoke, I don't drink, I don't go out except to the cinema now and again: this is a one-room furnished flat with shared kitchen and toilet, so living expenses are low and I earn enough to get by. I've no particular ambition to achieve anything at all at present: it's a disappointment to my parents but they're getting over it now I think.

I'm their eldest son and I was considered to be bright when I was younger, so naturally I suppose they had high hopes for me. They're working-class people, ordinary Belfast people: the only unusual thing about them is my father's a Catholic and my mother's a Protestant. Coming from the sort of born-and-bred backgrounds they both did, it must have been a brave thing to do for both of them, marrying across the divide. But neither of them's got any strong religious feelings, and they've never been interested in politics either: so I don't think there was much in the way of big doubts or questioning themselves over it at the time. I believe they met at a dance in a club near the Shankill Road, though what my father was doing in that sort of area when he was a Catholic I've no idea. Mind you, this was over thirty years ago: there was nothing like the sectarian feeling then that there is now.

I think even the firm my father worked for as a storeman was Protestant, so they can't have exercised the total one hundred per cent discrimination that a majority of employers did then. And from what I remember people who knew him have told me about him, he was a quiet sort of man who everybody liked. His health was poor and he died not long after Paul was killed: he'd not been well for a long time, and I'm fairly sure that happening contributed to it.

He'd lived long enough though to see me get my schooling and start university. It was typical of him and my mother to say when I told them I'd got a place offered me at a university in England, they thought going there would be a good idea. Nothing was said out in the open as it were: but I think both of them felt it would protect me from politics and religious sectarianism. It was beginning to look then like it does now, that it was going to send Belfast and most of Northern Ireland all up in flames. I believe they were even considering moving away then themselves: not emigrating to another country, I don't mean, but perhaps moving down to Dublin or somewhere in the south. I think it was only my father's health that was holding them back, they knew that wouldn't make it easy for him to get a job.

So anyway I went to this English university, a red brick one in the Midlands. The way I looked at it mainly was that if you were going to study English, what better place to do it than England? So off I went: and did the first thing I should think nine out of ten young chaps do when they go to university, met another student, a girl, and fell madly in love with her. She wasn't the first girl there'd been, but it was the first time I'd had that sort of relationship or anything like it: it was the sort where nothing else matters for you except to be with that other person morning noon and night. Your books and your studying all go out of the window, all you want to do is just lie with your arms round each other looking into each other's eyes.

Her name was Sandra: she came from Durham from a mining family background, she was doing philosophy and economics, and she was very left wing. There were times it was quite humorous really: she'd be carrying on about the presence of British troops in Northern Ireland, or about the historical justification for Republicanism and all the rest of it – and there was I, the young boy from Belfast saying I hadn't really thought about it much, but I supposed one day it'd all sort itself out, and it was a cold winter's afternoon so why didn't we go to bed again? She was a very genuine girl and very patient with me. I think in that respect I was a big disappointment to her, and she'd have liked it more when we were lovemaking if I'd worn an IRA beret and black gloves and maybe a balaclava helmet as well. Well no, I shouldn't say things like that, but it's only looking back you see things don't you in a different light? It wasn't Sandra's fault I was like I was and it wasn't mine: it was the difference between our upbringings. Hers had been one where you stood up and fought as best you could, mine had been you kept yourself as far as possible away from confronting things, do you know what I mean?

As it came up towards the end of the first year, we started talking about what we were going to do in the summer through the long vacation. We had various ideas: one was to go off with a pair of rucksacks and a tent, and bum our way round Europe. Neither of us had travelled much, so setting off into the unknown together as you might say, it had a big romantic appeal. But she wanted to take me to her home in Durham first and meet her people: and she wanted to come here to Belfast and meet mine very much as well. I dragged my feet about that, but I couldn't explain to her properly why: it wasn't I wanted to hide my parents from her, or them from her or anything, it was just I didn't have the same kind of feeling about my background as she did about hers. I said I'd sooner that we went first to Durham, then around Europe, then ended up here. I suppose I was postponing it really for some vague kind of reason I wasn't even clear about in my own mind. I'd told my parents about her and said I wanted to bring her with me at the end of the holiday to meet them. They were as I'd have expected them to be about it: excited at the idea of me bringing a girlfriend home, and more than ready to make her welcome.

I had a regular arrangement with them I always gave them a phone call once a week on a Sunday night. We didn't write letters much to each other, we kept all our news from one weekend till the next. So when I got this message about seven o'clock on a Friday evening to phone home at once, I knew something pretty serious must have happened. I thought it must be something to do with my father: I won't say I'd been expecting it, but it was always there at the back of my mind that something could happen with him.

I went straightaway to the call box in the entrance lobby of the students' union building, put the money in and dialled, and I heard my mother answer as though she'd been standing waiting right by the phone. I said 'It's Pat mum, what is it?', and I thought the line must have something wrong with it and she couldn't hear, because she didn't answer, she didn't say a word. So I said again 'Mum can you hear me, it's me, it's Pat, what is it, what's wrong?' There was still a silence, and then she said 'Can you come home Pat?' I said 'Yes mum, yes, but what is it, what's happened, is it Dad?' I couldn't really grasp her reply: she said 'No Pat, come home, it's Paul.' I said 'What do you mean, what? What about Paul?' She said she couldn't say any more, something about an accident I think she said, and I should come as quickly as I could.

I went to Sandra, she had a flat she was sharing with a couple of other girls, and I said I wouldn't be able to have a meal there that night like we'd arranged, something'd happened at home to my brother and I'd got to go straight over to Belfast. We rang the airport at Birmingham and they said they still had a seat for the last flight that night. It was a hell of a price but everyone could tell it was serious and they had a scrape round to raise enough money for me for the ticket. Sandra said should she come with me, but I said no I wanted to go on my own. I couldn't explain why, but I knew I had to, it wasn't the right time for her to be there. I promised I'd ring her the next night, and depending on what it was about and what the situation was, perhaps she could come on over the day after.

I got back here to Belfast airport I suppose it must have been about half past ten, eleven o'clock, came on the bus down to the city centre, and then from there I more or less ran all the way home. I'll always remember a funny little detail, though it didn't seem odd at the time: when I got there the front door of our house was wide open and all the lights were on, so I didn't have to ring or knock or anything, I just walked straight in. My mum was standing in the hallway by herself as though she was waiting for me, which she was. She didn't hold out her arms or touch me or anything, she just stood and looked at me. Then she said, quite flat and without any emotion or anything 'It's Paul, Pat. He's been shot with a plastic, he's dead.'

I don't remember a lot about the rest of that night. My father was there, my sisters, one or two aunts and uncles, some neighbours and people: and two uniformed policemen, RUC. For a long time I couldn't understand why they were there, why they were behaving the way they were doing, and talking like they were. I'd always thought when there'd been an accident and someone'd been hurt or killed, the police were supposed to be sympathetic, saying things like they were sorry to give you bad news and so on. But these two, all they were doing was asking my mother questions, going on and on and on. What time was Paul usually allowed out until on a summer's evening? Where did he go playing, did she know he'd been over at The Glen near the park? Then another one came, a man in plain clothes: he may have been RUC or he may have been something else, I've never been sure. And he started going on the same way too.

I still didn't properly know what had happened. Every time I asked a question to try and find out, they said 'We'll come to you in a moment sir, all in good time.' 'What's happened?' I kept saying, 'What's happened to my brother, what've you done to him, why's he been killed?' When they eventually finished questioning my mother and father, then it was my turn and they started on me. Where had I been, why'd I come home so late, where did I live? I was at university in England, which university, had I any papers to confirm it? And so how had I got to Belfast from there at that time of night? Well did I still have my plane ticket, could I prove it? And after that, it got more unbelievable still. What organisations did I belong to? Not organisations at the university, organisations in Northern Ireland: was I a member of Sinn Fein, did I belong to the UDA, to the Workers' Party, or what?

My young brother, twelve years old, had been shot dead earlier that evening by a plastic bullet in the head. Who'd fired it, they couldn't tell us or they weren't going to say. They said they didn't know if it'd been the Army or the RUC, it'd been a ricochet and until there'd been an enquiry into it it wouldn't be right for them to comment. A gang of youths had been rioting and throwing stones in the street: some plastic bullets had been fired to disperse them, and unfortunately yes, some people had been injured or killed. They weren't in a position to make any kind of an official statement about it though. Paul's body was in the mortuary at the hospital, his mother and father had been taken to see him and identified him. If I wanted to go and see him as well, they'd make arrangements for me to do it the next day.

I didn't feel anything you know really, only cold. I was cold inside me I mean, in a way as though it was me that life had gone out of, not only Paul. I was angry, but with the sort of anger that was about them being there and asking all their questions: I wanted them to go away and leave us alone. I can only describe what they were doing and how they were doing it, it was as though they were trying to find someone they could put the blame on. My mother for letting him out late to play, or me for perhaps being somebody someone had a grudge against and they were wanting to get even with me. There was not one single time any time that evening when any kind of sympathy was expressed: in some kind of way it'd been our own fault, that was the impression they were trying to give us.

In all the years since, there's never been any kind of explanation given us in detail about how it happened and who was responsible. There was an inquest, it was adjourned, then adjourned again, and again, and again after that, I've lost count now of how many times. The final verdict given was it was an accident: it wasn't anybody's fault, no one was really to blame. So we still don't know, and we will never know now, whether it was the Army or whether it was the RUC. The RUC I think myself, because they were the ones round at the house all that time that evening, trying to find someone else to blame.

Sandra never did come over and meet my parents. I went back to England a couple of weeks later after the funeral, and stopped a few days with her and her people. They were very nice: but it was all somehow very embarrassing, for them and for me. I didn't want to talk about it and they didn't want to question me about it. Before long I said to Sandra I was sorry, but I didn't want to go off to Europe with her: all I wanted was to come back here. I said I'd see her in the autumn at the start of the new term. But I didn't mean it, and she knew I didn't. I didn't go back to university, and I've not seen her since. She wrote me a letter after a while saying she wanted to try and help us get back together like we'd been before. But I didn't reply. A couple of years later I finished off my degree course here.

That's about all there is to it really. The unresolved feelings I said to you about, how long they'll take to go away I don't know you know, perhaps they never will. Every time I see an RUC man on the street, I look at him and think 'I wonder if it was you?' And I think 'Even if it was, I wonder if you know it was you? Do you ever let the thought enter your mind you might have killed a twelve-year old boy with a plastic bullet you once fired, when you were perhaps not even aiming at him?'

Only you know I still do want to get to the bottom of it somehow if I can, find out who did it, who it was. Even if it's only to discover which RUC were there in that area that night, and which of them fired plastic. That'd bring me a bit nearer to it all somehow, and something might lead on from there. You don't always know with these things do you, you just never know. I'll make some more coffee shall I, that'll be cold.

Joe Maloney

On a cold rainy afternoon he was sitting at a table in the corner of the deserted members' bar in the social club above a parade of shops on the Falls Road: from across the room the flickering lights of a silent fruit machine threw coloured shadows in sequence across his face. A frail gaunt-faced white haired man, with a cough and a rasping voice: he chain-smoked, his fingers stained deep brown with nicotine.

– When I was a young man, it was something to be proud of as you know, to be able to say you were a member of the IRA. Sinn Fein was the Republican political party, but to be a member of the actual Republican Army itself, you were following in the tradition of those brave men who'd fought for Irish freedom at the time of the Easter Rising in 1916, then on through the 20s and after that. You were a soldier, a volunteer who was fighting the old enemy, the hated Brits. Of course they called you a criminal and a terrorist: but those were their terms for you, not your own. For Irish people, you were a freedom fighter.

And it's always been like that all through history so it has: Britain was a colonial power, an occupying power, and that was what it always called the guerilla fighters who opposed it. I think they forget you know, or at least the people of Britain forget, the number of times in the past the British have done that. They've clung on to power and clung on to power, always saying they were never going to negotiate with terrorists: always saying until the violence stopped they were never going to negotiate. They always said that: the abandonment of violence was a prerequisite, it had to stop before talks could begin. And then what did they do, what always happened in the end? They finally woke up to it, to the fact there was no way they were ever going to subdue the people's resistance. So they sat down and talked, got the best deal out of it for themselves that they could, then they withdrew and went away. Usually leaving the country impoverished of course, into the bargain. That was British imperialism and its legacy.

You only need to talk to any Republican or any IRA man, he'll point to example after example for you. Cyprus, Malaya, Rhodesia that's now Zimbabwe, Kenya – everywhere you can think of, the Brits started by saying they were never going to negotiate with those who were fighting against them, the ones they dubbed terrorists: then in the end they turned round and did. I've forgotten where I read it now, but someone was quoted in this book or newspaper article not long ago and he said 'The British'll never give you your freedom, the only way you'll ever get it is by taking it from them.'

That was what I grew up to believe, and that was what I grew up to learn. It wasn't I was influenced by one particular person no, or anything in particular I'd read. My parents really weren't all that political at all. It was just being born and growing up as a boy in west Belfast: it did, Republicanism seemed to be in the air you breathed. Even at your school with your school friends all you talked was Republicanism, so it was. And it wasn't you got it from your teachers: don't get me wrong, I'm not saying that. The school I went to was run by the Christian Brothers: if you've heard of them you'll know what they were keenest on teaching you was discipline and obedience. They tried to beat and bully it into you every minute of the day: they were ferocious and sadistic almost, many of them, you could say. Yet you'd have to grant on the education side of things they had a high standard, even if their methods did leave a lot to be desired. You learnt nothing about politics though from them, and little of your own country's history either. But like I say, in west Belfast you couldn't escape coming to know about them from outside school: and in my opinion that was much the greater influence on you, it was.

What sort of young man I was was a socialist: a Marxist even, I'd not object to being called that. I believed in social justice, in rights and fair play for the deprived and under privileged: and there were plenty of those around the Falls Road area where I lived. Particularly among the Catholic people, they were very much discriminated against in housing, in jobs, in representation, in every way. In a lot of ways I think their own church, my own church for that matter as it used to be, I was born a Catholic, I think they've a lot of responsibility for the present situation, they must share the blame. They spent too much of their time offering the faithful redemption from sin and eternal glory hereafter in Heaven, and not enough time on standing up for better living conditions for them. It was no surprise many of the flock decided if the Church wasn't going to help them here and now, they'd no alternative, they'd have to take matters into their own hands.

Only I didn't want to be just a starry-eyed idealist, you know: I wanted to do something practical as well. In the time I'm talking about it was the late 1940s and 50s: and however much there might have been a socialist Labour Government in Westminster, it wasn't doing much for the poor of west Belfast. The only way thing'd get better, from your point of view if you were a Republican, was the old old story: get rid of the Brits. Because it was clear Labour had no more intention of leaving Northern Ireland than the Tories had ever had: so it was very simple, there was nothing else to do but to go on with the fight.

My mind's rather hazy these days about exact dates and so on, but I'd say I joined the IRA was about 1950 or 51 or so, when I was nineteen or twenty perhaps. Our operations in those times were concentrated very much against the British Army: you had hardly any at all of these shootings and killings of civilians for sectarian reasons that there is today. I had quite a high position in the Republican Army command structure, and after the border campaign started being stepped up in 1956, the British brought in internment without trial. I was well-known so I was one of the first they lifted: at the age of twenty-five, without any trial or charges against me. I was interned for four years. It didn't make any difference to my ideals or beliefs of course: I regarded myself as a prisoner of war. When I was released, in my own mind I was still a soldier and the Brits were still here so of course it's only natural, what else does a soldier do, he resumes the fight.

Only by then you know things were changing. Through the 1960s there was a great movement towards change: the civil rights marches, fighting between the different religious and political factions and all the rest of it. The whole picture altered, we got to a state almost of civil war. Came August 1971 so once more they brought in internment without trial and because I was a known IRA man I wasn't surprised to be taken in once more.

But this time you see they made a mistake. I was one of those in the IRA who was beginning to think by then the violence had got out of hand: as I saw it, the two communities of the north were more concerned with fighting one another than they were with getting rid of the British. A different way'd have to be found. The Republican Army Council felt we had to be realistic, we had to recognise that in the foreseeable future there were going to be three different parliaments involved: Dublin, Westminster and Stormont. So it was decided to offer recognition to all three of them, and see if something could be worked out that way.

And well, there were those who that wasn't good enough for. They weren't willing to give up the armed struggle, so they split away and formed a separate section, calling themselves 'Provisional IRA'. They used that word in the name they took because it had the echo to it of 'The Provisional Government of the Irish Republic', which was declared on the steps of the Post Office in O'Connell Street Dublin by Patrick Pearse, at the time of the Easter Rising in 1916. The rest of us remained as what was known as 'Official IRA'.

And you know, what went on after that, well it was, it was a tragedy. There was rioting, there was Bloody Sunday in Derry when British Army paratroopers shot dead thirteen unarmed civilians taking part in a protest march, there was murder and mayhem and sectarian killing, everything you could think of. It played right into the hands of the Provos it did, there can't be any doubt about that. The men of violence were the ones who were in the ascendant everywhere, so they were. I don't mean just the Provisional IRA, I mean the British Army, the Ulster Defence paramilitaries, the RUC, all of them. Ever since then they've been the ones in control: and none of them has any reason to be proud of themselves, they haven't at all.

I mean you take the RUC. No society can function properly unless it has a police force that has the support and respect of everybody, and who everybody looks to for protection. So you need say no more about the RUC than that the Catholics don't look on it as their protector, and it isn't. Catholics only see it as an oppressive paramilitary force, made up of Protestants and only serving the interests of Protestants. Or the British Army, look at them. They were put on to the streets of Belfast by a British Labour Government, and they're still here over twenty years later serving the Tories, with only one aim in view – holding down the Catholics and letting the Unionists carry on exercising power.

So when they got desperate, like they've been for years now, who do some people turn to for hope for a better future but the Provos? They're the ones who've never compromised about insisting you'll never get anywhere except by using force. They're wrong, wrong, absolutely wrong: and if they ever won their armed struggle and achieved power, that'd be the end of democracy in northern Ireland. They terrorise and they enjoy terrorising for its own sake: the last thing they want is agreement between the opposing factions or a progression towards peace. If that happened they'd lose their whole reason for existence and it'd be the end of their power.

As for those who call themselves Ulster Loyalists and shout about how they're British and they're going to fight to the death to remain British, even if it means fighting the British themselves – well all you can say about them is the only idea they're loyal to is the one of maintaining their own power and privileges, and they'll never allow those to be taken away from them. They're not going to share that with anyone: 'No Surrender' is their cry, and it means no surrendering of anything they've got.

I'm sixty years of age, I haven't changed my socialist principles, I haven't lost my desire to see a better fairer society for everyone, and I don't mean just in Ireland but everywhere in the world. I'd like to think I'd seen some improvement in my lifetime in the way things are, especially here, but I can't. All I see is more and more hatred, more and more lives being lost, more and more despair. I don't see any hope myself, not anywhere: not in five years' time nor ten nor twenty, nor long after I'm gone.

The people I feel it for most you know is the young ones, they're the ones it's hardest for, so they are. So much unemployment for a start: what's a young man to do when he's like so many of them now, nothing to look forward to after schooling except hanging around on street corners and drawing the dole? When some of them feel the only thing they can turn to is violence, that's not something should cause anyone much surprise is it? The Provisional IRA, INLA, the IPLO, and then on the other side the Ulster Volunteer Force and the UFF – they're all senseless frustrated young men hitting out at everybody and everything without giving it a thought. Violence for the sake of violence, that's all it is, because it's the only thing gives any sort of point to their lives.

Or these young soldiers you know, walking the streets in their uniforms, swinging their guns about and menacing passers-by with them, like they were expecting them to attack them any moment: to me it's a terrible sad commentary on our society it is, that you can see such a thing every day on the streets of Belfast. You know, I've read some of the soldiers have even been quoted as saying they like doing it, they enjoy it: they say they think that's what soldiering's all about.

It's sad, it is, it's terrible sad. It's sadder still even when some of those young soldiers become involved in something like they sometimes do, when they really are attacked, they're blown up or shot and lose their lives. If you were to have the chance afterwards to ask them what it was they'd given up their lives for, they'd only be able to say something vague to you you know, about dying for Queen and country: they wouldn't have the faintest notion in their heads of the history of it all and how it'd all come about. When you hear about it you think about their parents too, their mothers and fathers back in England. They're told their son's lost his life here for his Queen and country: and they don't know anything about it all either, they don't know how and why. Once they had their son, now they've lost him, and what was the point?

I know how they feel you see, I really do. Where are we now, January is it? Well, five months ago this week I lost my own son, so I did. He was twenty-four, and he was killed: one more victim of this senseless meaningless violence. He was gunned down in broad daylight in the transport yard outside the depot where he worked. He was the youngest of my three children, a decent hard-working young man: and I say with my hand on my heart, without a word of a lie, he wasn't involved in politics or anything to do with anything political at all. He wasn't even interested in them: it's always been my principle never to try to put my own views or beliefs into my children in any way. I've always wanted to let them come to things themselves in their own time and their own way, like I did myself. What he died for, why he died: I can only say truthfully I've no idea. Whether it was because he was my son, and in some way those I've opposed thought they were striking at me, I don't know. Or perhaps those who did it thought he was somebody else, that's something that happens from time to time that you hear. But all I can say again is I don't know. Who killed him and why, they're two terrible questions for me, and the answers I'll never know.

Sean Kelly

As the afternoon darkened, he sat on the sofa in the neatly furnished sitting-room of his small modern semi on the vast modern estate on the outskirts of the city. Short, sturdy, brown eyes, with a soft lively voice. He was thirty-nine, and he smiled gently from time to time as he talked. Beside him he had a small pile of papers, neatly arranged.

– She was a lovely girl my daughter was, I think anyone who knew her would tell you the same. There was something about her, she had a way with her that seemed to draw people to her somehow: people liked her and she liked them, whether they were her own age or older or younger, that didn't seem to matter if you know what I mean. I'm not saying all this just because she was my own daughter, I'm not trying to give you the impression she didn't have faults or failings like everyone else. But there was this sort of quality she had, it was what you might call a kind of warmness and friendliness, that made her a special sort of person somehow. I'm not saying either she was brilliantly clever or above average in any way: she wasn't, she was ordinary, no different from any other young girl of her age. This's her picture that I've got out for you, it's a photo of her taken two years ago on her eighteenth birthday, it'd be about three or four months before she died.

While I talk about her to you I'm going to try hard to keep bitterness out of what I say as much as I can. I feel it enough, but that'll not bring her back, she's gone. In a kind of a way I feel I owe it to her to keep myself calm, try and speak plainly and truthfully about what happened to her and keep her memory alive in a way that she'd have liked herself. I'm not by nature a bitter person and I'm not a vengeful person: all I want is for the truth about what happened to be known, and for the authorities to deal as they should with those who were responsible. So I'll wait patiently with all the determination I have till eventually justice is exercised on her behalf. I've been told it might take a very long time to happen: so, well if it does, I'm not an old man, I'm not even forty yet, I can take my time as long as justice is done in the end. I'm an ordinary person, not someone with a lot of money or education or an important position in society: but a lot of people are helping me, people who believe a wrong should be set right. When you know you've got people supporting you and fighting on your behalf, it gives you strength.

I have four children – well three now, but I had four, and my daughter Linda was the eldest. Like any other girl of her age her chief interest in life was going out at the weekends with her friends. They went round the shops in the city, looking at clothes, buying things she could afford, or saving up two or three weeks for something she specially liked. She went to discos on Saturday nights, and she liked being in the company with her friends; every way, she was an ordinary normal girl. When she left school I remember asking her not long after if she'd any special ideas about what she wanted to do. She just smiled the quiet little smile she had, and she said no. What she most wanted to do was work till she was nineteen or twenty, earn a good enough wage so she could go out now and again with her friends, and then when she was old enough marry and settle down and bring up a family of her own. The way she said it though, it wasn't what you might call in resignation or something of that sort: she was happy at the prospect and she didn't feel she was missing out in life or anything.

She wasn't interested in politics even though she was born and brought up here in west Belfast. To someone from outside that might sound a strange thing to say: but you have to say it, because to a lot of people these days, saying you come from west Belfast is almost like saying you're a member of the IRA. Falls Road, Catholics, Republicans, to a lot of people they're all one and the same thing. When you try and point out not everyone's like that who lives here, it doesn't really convince them. And the people least of all who'll believe you if you come in contact with them are the police. Show them your driving licence with your name and address when they stop your car, and you can guarantee every time you'll have to give them a long explanation of who you are, where you've come from, and where you're going to. I'm an ordinary working man, a roof tiler and that's what I've always been: certain policemen know me well enough by sight to know all about me and who I am. But that won't stop them tomorrow if there's a vehicle-check in the city from having me recite it all to them all the way through again.

No one in my family's ever been at any time connected with Sinn Fein or even Republicanism, never mind the IRA. I won't say politics doesn't interest me because it does: it's bound to if you're an Irishman and you read anything about your country's history. But what I am if I had to describe myself, I'd say I was a nationalist. I'm someone who hopes one day there'll be a united Ireland without the border, and we'll settle our differences and all live peacefully together. I don't agree at all with those who want to try and make it happen by violence: that's something I'm totally against. If unification's going to come, it's got to be done democratically by political negotiation and adjustment: never through bloodshed, and it'd not be worth having if it did. That's something all my family's always believed: and it's what I've brought up my children to believe too. I did talk a time or two about it with Linda, like I would with anyone else, only it wasn't to convert her to my way of thinking. I knew she'd no strong feelings and wasn't greatly interested in politics, not at her age.

I've wandered a bit from what I was saying, haven't I? It was only I wanted to make it clear to you I'm not one of those who has strong ideas about the British having their troops here, or at least I wasn't. I didn't like the idea any more than most Irishmen would: I thought we should be let settle our own affairs without interference from a country outside. And I still think British withdrawal's got to come about politically, not because of fighting them. I think talking about carrying on a war against them only makes things worse: if they're ever going to go, it'll have to be by their own decision. They can't let themselves be seen as giving in to force, not really can they?

All this you see, it's all part of what makes it so hard for me to accept there was any justice or justification for what happened. All it was was a totally unnecessary loss of a young person's life, or two young persons' lives in fact: for no good reason at all, and out of a situation that shouldn't ever have been allowed to occur. That it did occur, that it happened, well it tells you something about northern Ireland today: you can't believe it'd be let happen anywhere else in the United Kingdom. I don't mean just Linda and a young lad being killed, but that still two years later no one's been brought to justice for it. I think that's almost even more wrong than what took place.

It was a Sunday evening in late September last year. Like she usually did at weekends Linda got herself dressed to go out and be with her friends. Saturday was disco night, but usually on Sundays there wasn't much else to do except walk about and talk, go to different corners and places on the estate where you knew others'd be. She was just going to go off when her Mam asked her if she'd go down the newsagents for some fags for her: she did that and brought them back, then she went off very bright and cheerful and saying she'd not be late back.

You might think because of what I'm going to say, because I can tell you all the detail of what happened after that, that I must have been with her myself each step of the way. Well I wasn't of course, but I've talked with every single one of her friends who saw her or was with her that evening even if it was only for one minute, I know every detail of it.

She went up to the top of the estate, and there was quite a few young people there, all standing around and talking. She was with them for perhaps an hour or more, then some boys drove up in a car. They were what's called joy-riders: they'd stolen the car, but not to sell it or anything, just to ride around in it a while. I'm not saying it's right of course: it's not, they shouldn't do it, but there you are they do, so do a lot of these young people nowadays. When it runs out of petrol or they scratch the paintwork or something, then they jump out and leave it somewhere and run off. More often than not no more's heard about it: the police can't be bothered with petty crime of that sort, there's so much else more serious they've got to deal with. The only people I've heard of who ever do anything about joy-riding are the IRA. If there's too much of it in some particular area, they start to issue warnings about how they don't approve of what they call 'anti-social behaviour'. There's not much of that goes on on this estate though. I've not heard of anything of that sort round here.

Anyway these lads stopped by the group of youngsters Linda was with, and they asked did anyone want to get in the car with them and go for a ride? No one did, not Linda or anyone: so they drove off again. I don't think anybody knew them, they were from somewhere else. Then a bit later along comes another car: there was a young lad of seventeen driving it, and he had his girlfriend with him, who Linda knew. When they stopped one of them asked her did she want to join them, so she said yes all right she would, and she jumped in the back seat. They drove round for a while, and Linda was sitting on like it would be this side, behind the driver. Her friend, the girl in the front was turning round like this now and again, and chatting with her. They had the car radio on, they were listening to some programme with the latest rock and pop songs, with all three of them joining in singing the words of the ones they knew. Linda'd not long broken off with her latest boyfriend, the last thing her friend remembers them talking about was she asked her was she going to go back with him and Linda said no, definitely she wasn't.

It's very hard for me to go on from here but I'll do my best. Excuse me. By this time it was dark, and Linda's friend said she saw nothing ahead because she was turned round talking. She couldn't hear much either because of the noise of the music on the radio: but she says suddenly there was this terrible sound of repeated shooting. The car wasn't going fast but it started careering about completely out of control, because the driver'd been shot, and then it crashed. The lad was dead, and so was Linda: she'd been sitting right behind him.

There's two versions of what happened. One is the official Army one: they said a road block had been set up and the car'd stopped. Then they say it revved up and drove towards them at full speed, hitting a soldier and injuring him, and that was when they opened fire. The other version is the one by Linda's friend, the girl who'd been the front passenger in the car: and it's confirmed by several eye-witnesses who saw the incident and have given statements since. They all say there was no road block and the soldiers were a foot patrol standing in the road. All they were doing was waving a red lamp, and the boy driving couldn't have seen them till the last minute, and he was swerving to try and avoid them when they started to shoot.

I've puzzled and puzzled over it night after night ever since, when

I've not been able to sleep. If there was no road block, and the eye-witnesses said there definitely wasn't, why did they open fire? The soldiers must have panicked, it's been said: so well yes, perhaps they did. I think I might almost have come to accept that and somehow learned how to live with it. I don't know, I think I might. But not with what happened a short time afterwards, I can't live with that. Something came out: it shouldn't have, but it was in one of the newspapers. Two months later, Neil Kinnock came over to Belfast for a visit, and one of the places he went to was an Army barracks where those same soldiers were. At the end of one of the dining-halls he went into – I'm not saying it was meant for him to see, and I'm not saying whether he did see it or not because I don't know – but up on the wall at the end was a full-size cut-out of a car, with bullet holes marked all over it. This newspaper published a photograph of it. Under the cut-out is a big hand-lettered notice. It says: 'Vauxhall Astra. Built by robots. Driven by Joy-riders. Stopped by 'A' Company.' And I won't ask you to take my word for it. This is a photocopy of that page of the newspaper that printed it.

*

(Ten months afterwards, six soldiers were charged in connection with this happening. One with murder, the rest with malicious wounding and attempted murder, and all with attempting to pervert the course of justice. Two years later they have not yet been brought to trial.)

7 *To do justly, to love mercy, and to walk with my God*

Revd Martin Smyth MP

In his small first floor office in an east Belfast side street, he asked his secretary not to put through any phone calls for an hour, closed the door behind her as she went out, and pulled his swivel chair away from behind his desk so he could sit informally at its side. A slim quietly spoken man with greying hair, his manner courteous and relaxed.

– I think sometimes you can't help but suspect quite strongly certain sections of the media are engaged in something that could almost be called conspiracy. I've really no wish to be unkind to him, because he does have some good qualities I'm sure, but the Reverend Ian Paisley gives a quite awful impression of what northern Irish people are like, particularly churchmen and politicians, and especially those who are a combination of the two. Yet whenever a comment on any situation concerning here is required, he's inevitably the first person asked for his opinion, and doesn't hesitate to give it so that it's widely disseminated via radio and the television. It's a well-known trick and the media people know it: if you want to discredit an attitude or stance, the best and most effective way of doing it is not to present someone arguing against it, but vehemently for it in the most extreme and unreasonable manner you can find.

There's a great deal of very carefully and cleverly orchestrated propaganda in favour of those who support the Republican cause, and one of their most successful methods is to present the opposition in that way. I very much regret how often the Reverend Paisley is used, and allows himself to be used, like that. So I'd like to make clear at the outset that he's a member of what is called the 'Democratic' Unionist Party, a considerably smaller one than my own which is the Official Unionist Party and the largest political party in Northern Ireland. And also that his church calls itself the 'Free' Presbyterian Church, which is a small break-away group from the very much larger and longer-standing orthodox Presbyterian Church, of which I am an ordained minister.

It's necessary to make this clear to English people and to people in the rest of the United Kingdom in general. I discover repeatedly when I'm in Westminster carrying out my parliamentary duties there, there seems to be not so much an unwillingness as more an inability on the part of very many people to make this important differentiation. As a result the differences which there are between us and you, and equally importantly the very real points of unity and agreement which there are, do tend to become obscured quite often in discussions because of this misunderstanding. I hope our conversation will contribute something towards clarifying this situation.

That said, yes willingly I'll talk about what might be called the two strands in my life, the church and politics. They're not mutually exclusive: I'd say in some senses as far as I'm concerned they're a continuing of the same sort of activity, but on different planes. I come from a Belfast artisan background: my mother was a shop assistant and my father was a plumber. He'd been gassed in the First World War, but he was involved with many aspects of life within the Protestant community and things like the British Legion. I'm the youngest of five children, and even as a young lad I always had a sense my destiny was to become a minister: I think somehow everyone else in the family did. Then at the age of sixteen or seventeen I had a clear experience of Christ as a saviour: I was still at school, and I then made a bargain with God that if I passed my Senior Certificate as it was called in those days, I'd take it as a sign I should go on from there into the ministry. It was necessary for me to retake part of the examination because my initial results weren't good enough, but I did eventually pass, and after that I went to Magee College in Londonderry for four years.

Magee's a Presbyterian foundation, but it's open to anyone. It's not so much a theological college as a university liberal arts college, now completely secular and part of the University of Ulster. Tragically the Church of Rome has always refused to recognise it or for that matter any other similar institution of its kind: I say tragically because I strongly believe that by so adamantly keeping themselves apart so far as education's concerned, the Catholics have greatly added to the division in our land. Over the years in our educational system you've seen children going to state schools walking on this side of the road, and those going to Roman Catholic schools on that, and both eyeing each other suspiciously. And in many English colleges, and certainly in the United States of America, you'll always see the flag of the nation plainly on display. But you don't find that here in any Roman Catholic school: the Church of Rome is adamant that they must always control their children's education.

However, to resume my own story, after I'd left McGhee I worked for two years as a full-time assistant in a Belfast church. Then to my great joy I had a call to be a minister of a church of my own, in a rural area fifteen miles outside Belfast. I spent six very happy and delightful years there: I was married, and my wife and I had three daughters. But I think I was always conscious even then that that was only what might be called a staging-post on my journey. Then, at the age of thirty-six, I had another call: this time to a much larger church, and in Belfast. I wrestled in my mind about responding to it, and I recall that I found the challenge to accept the call in the Book of Jeremiah. The words are to the effect, I believe, 'Go and preach to the north', and I took that as a direction for me to take the call.

I was at that church for over fifteen years, and I enjoyed it immensely. It was taxing work but very varied, and I suppose if circumstances had been different I may well have remained there until this day. But by then I was also an officer of the Ulster Unionist Council and naturally a firm believer in the importance of maintaining the Union. As the political situation developed in the 1970s, and as you might say with some justification worsened, I felt increasing responsibility of a personal kind, that I should not only encourage others to serve the community in the political field, but also do the same myself. Things came to a head when a parliamentary by-election became necessary, owing to the death of my predecessor, our constituency MP. It was also being felt too by my party that we were losing ground to the Democratic Unionists:

they were anxious to have an agreed candidate, but one who would do their bidding, and things had in a sense got out of hand. So when finally I was asked if I personally would stand, as I saw it I'd no alternative but to agree. I'm happy to say that then, despite being opposed by the Democratic Unionists who put up their own candidate even though in doing so there was a danger of splitting the vote, I retained the seat for the Official Unionists, and I've remained as the constituency's MP ever since.

It meant there couldn't be any question though of my continuing my church ministry. People were kind enough to suggest it, but it didn't seem to me it could be satisfactory if someone needing pastoral care were to telephone for instance, only to be told by my wife I was away at Westminster until the end of the week. I believe a pastor's place should be first and foremost with his people: and so, reluctantly, I resigned my post.

In some ways as I mentioned earlier it could be said that politics might be looked on as a continuation of my work in the church. I'm a Unionist politician and a Christian Unionist politician, and my principles and my ideals are still the same: they are to do justly, to love mercy, and to walk with my God. That means trying to be helpful to people whatever their background, without of course being so naive as to accept every hard-luck story that I hear without question, and trying to improve the living standards of our community. I don't believe in a vague socialist idea of dividing all we've got equally between everyone, because we all have different gifts: what we have to do is use those gifts to help one another.

I also regard myself as a pragmatist, and that is why I'm a Unionist. Great Britain is a union of four nations, the English, the Irish, the Welsh and the Scots: there are more of course, but basically that's the composition which has existed for hundreds of years. I want to see it maintained: I regret very much that for religious and other reasons, some elements in the Republic of Ireland, as it's now known, should wish that part of the country to be separate from the British Isles. I think it would be fundamentally anomalous, not least for example because of the fact that there are more southern Irish people living on the British mainland than live in the Republic of Ireland. And their numbers are continuing to grow: something like twenty thousand people a year leave from there and go to the UK mainland.

I see the only answer for the future being in some form of federalism, with a smaller Parliament in London dealing with central issues such as international relations, defence, Treasury matters and so on and setting national standards. But I think there should be regional assemblies, properly elected, which would give people more say in their own local affairs. Also there are minorities in every country of course, and they should have representation too: under the system I'm advocating they'd have a better chance of attaining this than they do with things as they are at present. And I'd like to see, very much, a greater emphasis on co-operation between groups of people with different aspirations: rather in the same sense as the old trades union idea of conciliation between workers and bosses: better conditions for the former and fair profits for the latter. You'll never get them to agree with one another, because their aims and objects are so different, but I think you could get them to work together for the common good. There has to be mutual tolerance and a real desire to understand the other person's point of view.

Some people may say this is idealistic and oversimplified; but I think that with goodwill and a realistic approach, it could work. I'm aware, as many other people are, that there'll have to be considerable changes of attitude, however, before it can happen. The Government of southern Ireland, for example, will have to abandon its claims that the north is part of the nation of Ireland. There are points where the interests of the north and the Republic are in conflict yet there could be negotiation; but on a fundamental issue of that kind I feel there can be none. Unfortunately the British Government made a grave error in negotiating the Anglo-Irish agreement: and when she was Prime Minister Margaret Thatcher denounced us for calling people on to the streets to express their opposition to it, even though what we organised was a completely peaceful demonstration. Yet she herself enthusiastically endorsed the actions of the citizens of Moscow not long ago when they took to the streets to protest against government by the Communist Party. But, proportionately, if you compare their respective populations, more than twenty times as many of the people of Belfast demonstrated than did the citizens of Moscow. I still feel, however, that there can be conciliation between national and political aspirations and parties – with, of course, one exception.

That exception, naturally, is Sinn Fein. I believe that a definite and final decision has to be taken to proscribe a party such as that, that seeks to impose itself and its views only by violence and terror. It obviously can neither expect nor be given any democratic legitimacy or standing. No political system admits people who say that if they can't convince by argument, then they'll force their opponents into submission. It's probably too well-known to require repetition, but no one should ever forget what their Publicity Director Danny Morrison said publicly ten years ago at one of their annual conferences. He said 'Who here really believes that we can win the war through the ballot box? But will anyone here object if with a ballot paper in this hand and an Armalite in this hand we take power in Ireland?'

That should never be forgotten, ever, because it clearly illustrates, spelled out in their own words, that we're not dealing with just another political party. I believe most politicians are honourable at heart: they seek to argue their cause, and they can be relied on to continue to do that whatever degree and extent of opposition they encounter. But Sinn Fein adherents are not of that kind. They wish Northern Ireland to be separated from the United Kingdom, and to become part of the Republic: and they'll adopt any measures they can to bring it about. And this despite the fact that the Republic itself opposes their way of trying to bring it about.

Sinn Fein can't claim they are disenfranchised, and have therefore turned to violence as a last resort, because that manifestly isn't the case. What the true situation is is that they cannot convince enough people to support them by reason and argument, and therefore they've taken to terrorism to achieve their aims. You may sometimes hear them being described in some such terms as 'the political wing' of the IRA: in my opinion a more exact word would be they're a political front for the IRA. Until Sinn Fein categorically and unequivocally renounces the use of violence and dissociates itself totally from it, and can demonstrate it honestly means it, then I've no time at all for those who suggest we should try and reach any kind of accommodation at all with them. Not only do no Protestants agree with them, but they've not even been able to convince a majority of Roman Catholics to follow them. They represent no one at all except an infinitely tiny minority – and I mean not only here in Northern Ireland, but in the Republic as well. In recent times we're always hearing from those who call themselves libertarians, protesting that through the media of radio and television the voice of Sinn Fein is no longer allowed to be listened to. What they omit to mention, and many people in the United Kingdom apparently don't know, is that a ban on Sinn Fein broadcasts has been in existence in the Republic for many years, and it has had a devastating impact there in preventing the spreading of their views.

As far as Sinn Fein and the IRA are concerned, it is bestiality which is at work. There's no other word for it, and it has to be recognised and confronted. It would be less than honest of me not to admit that in some instances it has brought out similarly bestial behaviour on the part of certain elements on the Loyalist side: but that it has had that effect only adds strength to my argument. I know of no evidence at all anywhere in history that shows you can successfully deal with a bully by trying to placate him. You have to deal with him rigorously and unhesitatingly, and in the only way he understands: he has to be stopped, and there's no alternative to using every method of doing that you can command.

He must be stood up to, and shown that people are not afraid of him. My conviction about it, by the way, was another and most compelling reason for my decision to allow my name to be put forward as my party's candidate for Parliament in the original by-election which was the result of the sitting MP's death. He, you see, was assassinated by an IRA murder gang in a local community hall where he was holding his weekly surgery for his constituents.

I'm glad to have had the opportunity for our talk, and hope something of what I've said may be of value for you.

8 *The educators and the uneducated*

Terence Flanagan, Principal, Lagan Integrated College

Sister Maria, History teacher, Catholic school

Ann Douglas, History teacher, Protestant school

Pupils: Marian Darley, 17

Kevin Roche, 16

Neil Garside, 16

Cheryl Goddard, 15

Rebecca Jordan, 16

Alan Hart, 15

Terence Flanagan,

Principal, Lagan Integrated College

Because they all felt religiously integrated education for children between eleven and sixteen was desperately needed, in 1981 a group of Belfast parents wrote to a number of well-known charitable Trusts asking for funds to set up a school. Rowntree and Nuffield were among those who offered support, and within six months what was to become Lagan College had opened in a scout recreation hall with 28 pupils and staff. The issued prospectus said 'We hope to have purpose-built accommodation within three years.'

It was an optimistic estimate. But meantime mobile classrooms were added to the site, and a semi-permanent block was built containing science laboratories, an assembly area and a staff room. The number of pupils and staff grew so rapidly that after five years the premises had to be extended to incorporate the annex of a nearby primary school. But it was not in fact until ten years after its original founding that the whole college finally came together in newly-built and permanent buildings at Lisnabreeny in east Belfast.

There are now 740 pupils and 47 staff. Terry Flanagan, the Principal, is a dark-suited bespectacled man in his late forties, quiet and direct in manner, his voice and his convictions both equally firm.

– Well, whatever I said at the interview must have been all right, because they offered me the job. I came here five years ago; before that I'd been senior master at another school, and before that I'd been teaching in Kenya for two years. Why Kenya? A complex of reasons, I suppose. I was educated at Magee College in Derry and was in contact there with some of the early Civil Rights movement people, and then I went on to Trinity in Dublin for another two years, doing philosophy and English. But in common with many young people when they're around that age I hadn't given much thought to what I finally wanted to do. Gradually the idea of teaching became more and more appealing, so I then went to Queen's University Belfast and did a post-graduate diploma. Idealistically, by then I wanted both to broaden my own horizons and, if I could, contribute something to one of the developing countries. So I went off to teach on the Equator for a couple of years.

That was at the end of the 60s. The troubles as they call them hadn't really begun here but they were starting: and as news of what was happening reached Kenya, I found the children I was teaching asking me questions like 'What's happening in your home country sir?' The way I could best explain it to them was in terms of tribalism. Let me say here quickly I'm not suggesting our own divisions can be explained as simply as that: but in Kenya, after Mau Mau and the Kikuyu and Jomo Kenyatta and so on, tribalism was a concept children could grasp. As often happens when you try and explain things to other people, it gave a new perspective to the subject to me as well.

I married when I came back to Northern Ireland, and my wife and I did seriously consider starting our new life together somewhere else: but in the end we decided to stay. With the street rioting and bombing and killing, Belfast then was a very grim place, grimmer even than it is now. And as our family came along and started to grow up and go to primary school, the inevitable and unavoidable questions began: 'Daddy, why do we go to a different school to our friends Peter and Anne who live in the house opposite?' 'Mummy, what's the difference between Protestants and Catholics, and which are we?'

You'll notice that so far I've been assiduously avoiding identifying my own religious origin, treating it with the same lack of emphasis as we do throughout the school. I'll just say that in fact I was brought up among the Plymouth Brethren, and it in many ways made me very conscious at an early age of religious divisions because at my own state primary school, like the Catholic pupils, I had to leave the classroom when certain subjects were taught. That however's an aside: I only say it to illustrate that even from a very early age I was aware of sectarianism. I continued to question its effects after I returned from Africa and began my own teaching career: and as the years went by, I became more and more convinced that while there might not be anything morally wrong in educating children of different faiths separately in a society which could afford to do so without harming itself, Northern Ireland wasn't yet ready for that luxury. I still believe that: if anything more than ever, and that's why I'm now here. Our society can't afford an education system that supports or fosters division: and we'll continue to reap the resulting whirlwind so long as we continue to divide children's education, as we do, from the age of five. Some progress has been and is being made, but not much. There are fifteen integrated primary schools, but so far only two of them beside ourselves are in the secondary sector. Unquestionably there have to be more, not only because of the fundamental rightness of the idea, but also and most importantly because more and more parents are seeing themselves trapped in ghettos and having no choice. Over and over again parents who want their children to come here say to me how much they object to the fact that when it comes to the age of eleven, they have to choose between a Catholic or a state Protestant school for their child. You can't compel people with long and opposing historical traditions to integrate: but you shouldn't have to deny them the opportunity to have their children differently educated if they wish to do so.

And many do, there's no doubt of that. We have a long waiting list: in the past year alone we've had to turn away over a hundred applicants who applied, as their first choice, for their children to come here. There are no fee-paying pupils: the school's grant-maintained by the Department of Education and admission is discriminatory, for which I make no apology whatsoever. We try to keep a half-and-half balance in numbers between boys and girls, but at the moment there's a slight preponderance of boys: and then there's a further division again within those two numbers, of almost equally Protestants and Catholics. It's not quite exact, because roughly five per cent of the total number of pupils are from other religious backgrounds, or ones whose parents have stated themselves specifically to be of no religion.

Each year's prospective intake is divided into four groups, Protestant and Catholic boys, and Protestant and Catholic girls, and we select separately from within each group, so that we maintain a continuous balance of half Protestant and half Catholic from each group – which, by the way, doesn't represent the population balance of Belfast. Nevertheless that's what we do, and we do it deliberately.

Only one part of our activity is not funded. It's that as well as teaching religious education, as we have to, we also employ six part-time chaplains – one Catholic, one Church of Ireland, one Presbyterian, one Methodist, one Baptist and one non-subscribing Presbyterian. We find the money for them ourselves, and the reason for our having them is quite specific: we want to reassure both parents and children that their denominational identity will always be preserved, whatever it may be. Our commitment to the Christian ethos is to embrace all denominations and cherish their different traditions, and not in any way to weaken ties or responsibilities to different churches. This means that at any time they wish, or their parents wish, children may meet in small groups with their own chaplains, all of whom are freely available to them.

From time to time, perhaps monthly and additionally at Christmas and Easter and so on, we have whole or half-school assemblies: these are interdenominational, and we alternate between different forms of worship. For example the Protestant way of saying the Lord's Prayer incorporates the doxology 'For Thine is the kingdom, the power and the glory' and so on: sometimes we use it and sometimes we don't. Equally, most Catholic forms of prayer include the words 'In the name of the Father, the Son and the Holy Spirit'. Sometimes we use those forms, saying to begin with where it's appropriate 'Today we're using the Protestant form, and please all join in' or 'Today we're using the Catholic form but shall not include the doxology.' Also we encourage the Catholic children to bless themselves when they wish to, so that they and the Protestant children will come to regard it as natural for them, and not a matter for embarrassment or even comment.

In certain areas, such as the teaching of history for example, there tends to be division and divisiveness: mainly Nationalist history is taught in Catholic schools, and British history in state schools. The new core curriculum now defines a programme which is the same for every school: so we try to concentrate on the context in which the programme's taught. Two dates for instance, 1690 and 1916; they're not just past events to people here in Northern Ireland. The first was the Battle of The Boyne, in which William of Orange defeated the forces of James the Second and confirmed the Protestant ascendancy; the second is that of the Easter Rising in Dublin, which led to the founding of the Irish Republic. Each of them is part of the stream of consciousness almost from birth to members of our two communities, so in one and the same class you'll have pupils sitting together who have completely different attitudes to those events. What we try to do, and we have to do, is teach all the children to study the significance of both, and recognise the importance of them to each other. You need very sensitive teachers for this: I'm not saying you don't get them in other schools of course, but nevertheless it's a particularly important area.

These matters, which I've only briefly touched on, are of course fundamental in the Northern Ireland of today, but I don't want to give the impression that the school concentrates on them to the exclusion of everything else. Academically Lagan College is as good as – or in some respects we like to think even better than – any other secondary school, and offers a very full and wide-ranging curriculum. We now have pupils up to the age of eighteen, and we're unique in that our seniors, instead of doing A levels, take the International Baccalaureate exam. Naturally we'd like to extend our scope still further, and in a number of different directions: I'm sure in the future we'll develop quite considerably, but whether we'll do all the things we hope to do, we can only wait and see. Undoubtedly I think the original aim of the founders has been achieved: a great need was identified, many steps were taken and much hard work was put into meeting it, and I think it can now safely be said that Lagan College will thrive. In the beginning the concept of it was greeted with a considerable degree of scepticism: that I think's now vanished, and it's been conclusively proved that such a school can succeed. But being an integrated school doesn't just happen, it has to be constantly worked at, and I mean by both pupils and staff.

The most important question of all, of course, and the one we're most frequently asked, is 'Does it work?' By this is meant, I suppose, 'Does it remove sectarianism?' And if you're talking in terms of the whole of Northern Irish society, the answer naturally has to be 'No'. We are, after all, as yet only a tiny drop in the ocean, and what history will eventually say of us, who can tell? Another associated matter that's also often raised is when people say, as they sometimes do, that it's not the sort of parents who send their children to a school like this who are the ones we need to reach. I can only answer that by saying what I referred to earlier – that nobody knows how many parents there are, in both the tightly exclusive Protestant and Catholic communities, who feel they've no option for their children but a continuation of sectarian education. Therefore we must continue to provide it and make it more widely available. I don't know if you're familiar yourself with the areas or whether the names convey anything to you – but we do actually have here now, in this school today, children who come from both Annadale Flats and from Divis Flats, one of which is renowned for its one hundred per cent Protestantism and the other for its similarly entrenched Catholicism.

I think it's fair to add too, on this subject of whether we're reaching the people we need to reach, that it's my belief that education, of itself and on its own, is not and never can be the cure-all nostrum some would have us believe. The prisons of Crumlin Road, Long Kesh and Maghaberry all contain people, many of them unfortunately still quite young, who went either to Catholic or Protestant schools where they were taught – I've no hesitation in saying this – that terrorism was absolutely and totally wrong. I don't know of a single school anywhere that teaches its pupils anything different to that. But they got nowhere: other influences were stronger. You can't expect or demand of any educational establishment or system that it should accept sole and total responsibility for its products.

To revert to the more positive aspect, about whether Lagan 'works', I'm not going to make extravagant claims. Sectarianism is frowned upon whenever and in whatever way it manifests itself; every single member of staff, whether they're teachers or clerical or maintenance workers, is committed to that, and sectarian behaviour or expression is regarded as a very serious offence throughout the school. Perhaps the best measure of our progress so far came a little while ago when we invited a researcher from Queen's University to devise a questionnaire and come into the school to study different aspects of this 'whether it works or not' area. Among a number of interesting things he found, one in particular seemed to me to be very significant. It was that when children first came, their five best

friends they identified were, naturally, from the same school they'd
been at themselves. Therefore they were almost entirely of the same
religious denomination. But with the seniors – those who'd been
here five years or more – their 'best friends in school' came randomly
from across the different religious communities. They were also
asked a series of open-ended questions about their own political
and religious identities: whether they considered themselves
Nationalists, Loyalists, Republicans, fundamentally Protestant or
Catholic or whatever. And the researcher found, surprisingly to
some people I think, that they had a strong sense of who or what
they were and their origins, and this kind of schooling hadn't in any
way confused them about that. But – and this was the important
thing – they seemed to be more aware than pupils in other schools
that their friends and colleagues were similarly conscious of their
identities and didn't necessarily share the same points of view. And
they nearly all thought solutions to political problems should come
from tolerance and compromise, not from 'We must win, they must
lose' attitudes.

I thought that was important, and very hopeful. If children can
grow up to understand that change has to come in so bitterly divided
a society as ours, but only through great efforts of understanding
before harmony can be achieved, then progressing towards that
attitude means what we're doing is worthwhile. So I've really no
doubts or qualms at all about what we're doing: I'm absolutely sure
it is right. It's a journey, we all look at it like that – and journey's end
will be when consciously integrated education of Catholic and
Protestant children is neither controversial nor necessary.

Sister Maria,

History teacher, Catholic school

– I've been teaching here at this Ursuline College for girls for oh my goodness almost thirty years now, all my teaching life. My mother was a teacher here herself, but I went to a different convent school. Because of her connection I always knew a lot of the staff and pupils, and after I'd finished my degree at Queen's I straight away applied for a vacancy which had just arisen, and I was accepted. I was delighted. I never wanted to go anywhere else, this is my particular rut and once I was in it I've stayed in it.

Our girls range in age from eleven to eighteen, and we've 800 pupils: I teach other subjects as well when required to, but my principal one is history. With different classes I cover from Norman times up to the present day, including both Irish and British history. In years past teachers were free to teach what they wanted and in their own way without regimentation. But that idea's now out of date and there's much more standardisation, quite rightly I think. As we all adapt to the new core curriculum we choose our own programmes within it, and pick optional aspects to concentrate on as well. Here all teachers in my department discuss them and agree on what they should be, so that we're all going in the same direction, or at least we hope we are.

Northern Ireland has its own national curriculum, and considerable emphasis is laid in it on the teaching of Irish history. Pupils doing A levels can do the period between 1912 and 1923 as a special subject. Personally I feel that period's too short, and with the younger classes we have an option covering modern Irish history up to and including the present day, but obviously in less depth.

The greatest problem you face is that of your own bias, but once you recognise it you're moving some way towards keeping it in

check. Whether we succeed or not I don't know, but we do try to be
moderate in the way we teach certain aspects. Obviously sometimes
it's difficult: it's hard to be moderate about Cromwell and his
religious fanaticism, but you're constantly being surprised by the
mature attitudes pupils themselves will express in discussion of
things like that. The Great Famine of 1846 and after is another area
which arouses strong feeling; I don't myself see it as genocide as
some people do, and I teach that it was a result of the British
government's policy of *laissez-faire* rather than a determined attempt
to wipe out the whole Irish race.

I don't think you'd get agreement anywhere, not just in Northern
Irish schools, about how exactly history should be taught so that it
was completely what should we call it, 'neutral'. I forget who it was
now, but I remember somebody once said that no one under the age
of forty should ever even try to study history, and I think there's a lot
of truth in that. And here in Northern Ireland of course history's
constantly in the making, in a way that it isn't to such a dramatic
degree in many places elsewhere. I remember a girl in a class I was
taking just a few weeks ago which wasn't even a history class, I
remember her commenting about when she was born and saying just
in passing that her father hadn't been there because he was interned:
and it brought it home to me that what for me had been a historical
event in the past, internment, would always for that girl be a
significant event in her memories of family life.

And we get even more poignant things too now and again that we
have to try and deal with as best we can. All the time while you're
teaching you have to think before you say certain things, or stop
yourself from phrasing them exactly as you were going to. Because
there in front of you in your class is, to choose an example we have at
this very moment, a girl whose father was shot dead three weeks
ago. Perhaps by the IRA, perhaps by the British, or by the RUC –
you don't know all the details, only that the slightest chance remark
by you or one of the pupils could wound that girl most terribly. I
won't say it happens every time, but certainly it's always in your
mind when you notice that someone's suddenly absent, to wonder
whether it's because she's ill or if it's because of something much
worse that you haven't yet heard about.

All in all, we can only do the best we can. I was saying earlier about trying to maintain a moderate approach: and I think it's worth saying that one of the things that indicates to us we come near to achieving it is when we get complaints from parents, which we sometimes do, that our history teaching isn't Republican enough. Quite a high proportion of our girls come from for example the Turf Lodge area: and while of course not everyone who lives there is the same, it is a place where Republicanism is widespread and strong. When discussions arise as they do in the classes studying modern Irish history, about what the IRA did in bringing about the British withdrawal and the setting up of the Irish Free State in the 1920s, the subject of violence and whether its use is justified inevitably occurs: and then the discussion of course spreads to the present day activities of the IRA. Most children, I'm glad to say, seem to feel that what's happening now is wrong; but there are bound to be some who feel still that the tradition of fighting the British has to be continued. As far as we can, we consider all points of view, and we certainly don't try to sweep certain subjects under the carpet.

Integrated education? Well, whether that will one day become widespread I don't know, but I personally doubt it. The Catholic Church is often criticised for its opposition to it, and I know to some people the idea of integrated education is a high ideal. I don't really think it's possible, just on practical grounds alone, because in some areas the population balance is so much to one side or the other that you'd have to think in terms of things like bussing children to school in other parts of the city to maintain a balance, which would be nonsensical. And to many Catholics too, Catholic education is just as much an ideal as integration is to others, and very much worth preserving. I think it'll stay, and I think it should, it's not as divisive as some people say, or at least that's my personal opinion. If after all these years two such previously historic enemies in Europe as France and Germany can get together as they are doing now, economically and militarily and in every other way, then there has to be hope for the Catholic and Protestant communities of Northern Ireland finding a way of living together, don't you think?

Ann Douglas,

History teacher, Protestant school

— I've always been fascinated by history, it's been my favourite
subject as long as I can remember, I don't know why. Even when I
was a young schoolgirl, to me there was something about it that was
very special. I remember once having to stay in bed because I'd got
flu or something, and being very upset about not being able to go to
school for a week or more, and then suddenly finding out that on the
radio every morning there was a schools broadcast about I think it
was the Tudor period, and immediately cheering up and listening
every day to it avidly. I mean I even read historical novels for
relaxation, still. We must have had good teachers of history at school
too, that will have had something to do with it: they can make or
break a child's interest in something can't they?

I never thought though that I'd one day be a teacher of history
myself: or even a teacher of any kind, come to that. I did the usual A
levels at school, but I knew there was never going to be any question
of going to university because my parents were poor and on top of
that my father was a permanent invalid, so it was a case of having to
find a job and contribute to the family income. I did that, but then I
got married fairly young and I had three children: but it wasn't until I
was in my mid-thirties in fact, when the kids were all beginning to
grow up a bit, that I really gave much thought to any other or
different kind of future.

I wasn't unhappy, I enjoyed being a housewife and mother: but
one day I happened to make a remark about sometimes getting very
bored with housework, and saying something like I was wondering
whether to start looking for a part-time job just to stimulate my
mind a bit. My husband was himself a teacher, and he said well why
didn't I look into the possibility of going to college as a mature

student and taking a degree? And rather to my own surprise, I think, that's just exactly what I did, and in four years found myself with a Bachelor of Education degree. I'm in my nineteenth year at this school now, and head of the history department, and I'm a very very happy person indeed. It's a large modern secondary school with 500 pupils, boys and girls between the ages of eleven and sixteen, and we teach up to GCSE level and I shall stay here, I hope, until I retire.

Being a state school it has only Protestant children, or perhaps more correctly I should say that the pupils are almost entirely non-Catholic. Personally I think this is a bad thing: I do very much favour the idea of integrated education, and hope one day it'll be universal. I don't believe that it would be the solution to all of Northern Ireland's sectarian problems; it wouldn't, because parental and family influences are always stronger than anything education can do on its own. But I think it has to come and it will come, and the sooner the better, especially at this level, because there's nothing like as much mixing between the communities as there should be. It's a sad fact of Belfast life today that the majority of children get very little chance to mix socially with others of different religious upbringing. Over and over again you'll hear a young boy or girl say that until they went to university they'd never met a Catholic or a Protestant as the case might be – and you have to remember it's only a few, and the brighter ones at that, who even get to university. So all the others go on living lives that are segregated right into adulthood.

I think I'd agree with the suggestion that teaching history is probably like walking in a minefield, and that a lot of what we say and how we say it presents particular difficulties, or challenges if you like to use a fashionable word. Always taking into account what I've already said, that family attitudes probably carry more weight than anything put forward at school, I do think that something can be done to open a few windows or shed a few insights here and there. One of the things that's helping, and is probably going to help in the future, is the new core curriculum thing, which means that in all schools, both Protestant and Catholic, at least in the very broadest terms the same subjects will be taught. With this in mind, a series of conferences are going on now throughout Northern Ireland which are attended by all teachers, at which we discuss our mutual problems and try to reach some kind of consensus regarding our approach. And I must say that so far at least, I've found history teachers in Catholic schools have been very ready and willing to discuss the subject with those of us in Protestant schools.

Cromwell? Yes well obviously this is a very dicey aspect isn't it? But you know I think you'd find very few Protestant teachers who were going to talk about him and his actions here in Ireland, as anything other than an example of religious fanaticism at its very worst. You can say as much as you like about him being a product of his time and all the rest of it, which I know some Protestant teachers do: but even they won't go so far as to try and justify his ordering the massacre of the citizens of Drogheda in 1649, or fail to denounce it as the butchery which it unquestionably was. But one of the traps you can very easily fall into is the one of giving too much of an impression that that was all back in the past and people aren't like that any more. I don't know if all my colleagues would agree with me, but I personally use something of that kind as an illustration of how badly human beings can behave when they let their own fervour run away with them.

It's not difficult, of course, to draw parallels between an occurrence like that and what's going on in the present troubles, where you have sectarian killings going on and on. And it's not difficult with children to get them to see that in things of that sort, there's not much to choose between the behaviour of both sides. What is very difficult though, I find, is to try and get them to see that because the IRA for example kills Protestant Loyalists, they haven't to some extent brought it on themselves when the UVF or the UFF retaliate. This comes back yet again you see to home influence: I should think it's absolutely certain and without question that when innocent Protestants are murdered, the atmosphere of outrage in Protestant homes is different in quality as well as in degree to what it's like when Catholics are killed. There'll be head-shaking and tut-tutting about that, but not the same kind of incandescent fury which murder of Protestants arouses. And children sense this and know it, and I'm sorry to say carry it on in themselves.

So summing up for you I'd say that I think history teachers, or at least those who I know and work with in a Protestant school, and those who I meet in our regular conferences who are from Catholic schools – we're all very conscious indeed of our responsibilities, and we do all try not to give fuel to sectarianism. But I don't think any of us at all feel that we can make much impression on deeply ingrained family attitudes. I think I must say too that I don't know what ever will: I'm afraid I feel fundamentally that we're all like Sisyphus, trying to push a boulder up a hill and having it roll down to the bottom again just when we think we're getting to the top. A bleak prospect, I feel: yes, very much so.

Marian Darley, 17

– I'm a pupil at an all-girls' Catholic school: I've been here since I was eleven, and I like it very much though I think it'd be better if it was a mixed sex school. The thing I'm best at is languages: at the moment I'm doing French and Spanish for A level, and if I get them I'd like to go to Queen's University. Ultimately I hope to get work as an interpreter or translator, or perhaps with a business company which has branches in France or Spain. I've been several times to both those countries and I wouldn't mind working in either of them: in fact I think I'd like to live somewhere else in Europe for a few years before I finally get married and settle down. It's not that I don't like Northern Ireland: I do, I like it very much and I wouldn't want to live permanently somewhere else. But I'd like to see a bit of the world first, and in a few years' time perhaps Belfast will be a more peaceful and hopeful place.

I think most young people are like me, what they want most is that all this fighting and killing and sectarianism should stop, and every one should get on with everyone else. It makes me sad to see British troops out every day on our streets: as far as I know, no other country in Europe lives like we do with quarrels and shootings and woundings going on all the time. French and Spanish people have asked me about it often, why it's happening and when it's going to stop, and I feel really embarrassed about it when they do. I try to explain that the majority of people, both Catholics and Protestants, don't hate each other. But of course when you learn about past history, you realise it's been going on for such a long time now that it's difficult to know how it could be brought to an end.

I've not so far seriously thought about the future much. Eventually I'd like to marry and have a family, and I certainly wouldn't let religious difference stand in my way if I loved someone who was a Protestant. My sister has done just that, and I know that at first they had a problem in deciding where to live, because in certain parts of Belfast it matters very much what religion you are, and it's looked on as something dreadful if you don't marry someone from the same faith. I think it's ridiculous, but all the same it's a fact. I've talked with my sister about it, and she says that it has happened with both her and her husband, that they've met people who they thought would be tolerant but haven't been. So it's still a fact of life, and one you'd have to take into account yourself when the time came.

Kevin Roche, 16

– I go to a Catholic boys' school in west Belfast in the Falls Road area near where I live. My main ambition is to leave school and start work: most of all I'd like to have some sort of business of my own, say a handyman's or decorator's or something of that sort, because if you're going to go round looking for a job you don't really stand much chance of getting one. My father's been out of work for over five years now: he used to be in the docks, but he got laid off and hasn't been able to find anything at all since then. As well as the high unemployment there is in Belfast, it's much harder too to get something if you're a Catholic, because most of the big employers are Protestant and there's a lot of discrimination. I've two brothers older than me, and neither of them is working either.

If I had the chance I'd like to go to England. I know there's unemployment there too, but from what I hear from those who've been, it's nothing like as bad as it is here. Most of all though the place I'd really like to go is America: four years ago I went on a three-week holiday with a school party to a children's farm camp near Boston, and I've always had the idea since that if I could once get to America, I could get forestry work or something like that, and get away from Belfast for ever.

That's something that I'd do in a split second if the chance ever arose, I wouldn't even stop to think about it. I can't see any future here at all, except civil war. I think one day the British'll decide they've had enough and they'll go, and then I think the Protestants will take over the running of the country again, and do everything they can to keep themselves in power. They've got too strong a grip on the country for anyone to be able to make them let go: I don't agree with the IRA and the violence and all the rest of it, but I can see their point of view. I'm not old enough to vote yet, but when I am it'll be for Sinn Fein because I think they're the only ones who are for the working people. If the British Labour party put up candidates here I'd vote for them, and so would a lot of other people too.

At the moment I've got a Protestant girlfriend, but I wouldn't like my parents to know that, and she hasn't told hers. Neither of us thinks religion's very important, but all the same you have to be careful about who you tell, because to some people it's all that matters.

Neil Garside, 16

– I'm at a big state school in east Belfast: it has 600 pupils, mixed boys and girls, and I'm in the sixth form. Next year I'll be doing A levels: my best subjects are physics and biology, and my ambition is to go to university to study marine biology.

I live in a Protestant area, my family are all Protestants but not fanatically so: they don't make me go to church, and I don't go very often. I think people's religion is their own affair and I certainly don't think there ought to be discrimination against anyone because of their religious belief. I don't actually know any Catholics because there aren't any at our school, or at least not that I've come across: and as I say, where I live is a Protestant area so I don't know anyone of my own age who's Catholic. Occasionally at a weekend I'll go to a disco with some of my friends, but as far as I know no Catholics go there to that one: I think a lot of people don't understand this sort of thing, they think it's religious prejudice but it isn't. It's just you don't get the opportunity to meet many Catholics, because they keep themselves to themselves and we keep ourselves to ourselves. I couldn't ever see myself going out with a Catholic girl, for instance, because I don't know where I could meet one.

You'll get the impression from television and newspapers that in Northern Ireland Protestants and Catholics are at each other's throats all the time, always trying to murder each other and so on: but it really isn't like that at all. On the whole I'd say it was a good country to live in, and I think that's because it's part of Great Britain. I've never been south to the Republic, but from all I hear they've nothing like as high a standard of living as we have here, and in addition the Roman Catholic church interferes far too much in people's lives, on matters such as divorce and birth control. I think most people in

Britain wouldn't like to live in that kind of a society at all, and I think
that Sinn Fein and all the rest of them who talk about having a united
Ireland should go and live in the south if that's what they want, but
not use violence to try and bring down the Government here. After
all, Northern Ireland has been British for hundreds of years, the
majority of the people who live here are of British origin, and
nothing's ever going to change that.

Cheryl Goddard, 15

– When I met you that day in the coffee-bar place where you were talking to my Mum I was a bit cross actually, because I'd had a letter that morning from a school pen-friend I've got in Belgium. It said she wasn't going to come after all for her holidays because her parents wouldn't let her. She didn't say why they wouldn't, but it's easy to guess: she's a Catholic actually, and one of the very good things our school tries to do is get us to take up pen-friends in schools on the continent, and where possible do it with Catholic schools because ours is a Protestant one.

I do sometimes think people think we've all got two heads or something, but we're just ordinary normal people and we don't get any anti-Catholic teaching at our school, in fact it's quite the reverse. We're always trying to get out-of-school activities that are joint things with Catholic schools – not just sports and football matches and things like that, but also music groups and play readings. I definitely do get the feeling though that it's the Catholic schools who aren't as keen on it. My school is a big secondary school in north-east Belfast, and we do have a few Catholic pupils in it. They're just like everybody else and there's no discrimination against them or things like that: but they can't take part in religious services like assembly and stuff, and I think it's a shame they keep themselves separate like that. I could go into a Catholic church any time I wanted to, but they can't come into ours, so I think all the prejudice is on their side, or most of it.

I think all the troubles in Northern Ireland would be solved if people just got together and were sensible. I think the IRA are terrible: I know there are some Protestants who are fanatical, but not many, and it's mostly because they're taking revenge for what Catholics have done. I don't agree with it but you can understand it.

And I definitely think the British Army should stay here. After all, Ulster's part of Britain and they're here to protect us and I think that's good. I'd be very worried if they were ever to be taken away, like some people who don't know much about it sometimes suggest they should be. I don't think people are grateful enough to the soldiers, after all they're risking their lives so that we can be safe, and I think that's good. All our family are on their side, and most of the people I know are too. People ought to just think what would happen if they weren't here. There'd be war, I really believe that definitely.

Rebecca Jordan, 16

– Daddy is a Minister of the Gospel, and we came to Ireland from Scotland just before I was born, because the Lord had called him to come and preach here. He had been a minister in the Baptist Church first I think. He and mummy and my two sisters and myself, we're now members of the Free Presbyterian Church and we go to an Independent Christian School, which is a fee-paying private school belonging to our Church. It's a very good and nice school with a lovely atmosphere there: it has about a hundred pupils, both boys and girls, from the ages of eleven up to sixteen. I'm studying English and history for A level, and what I hope to do eventually is be a nurse.

Each day we begin with an assembly where we have readings from the Gospel and instruction about the word of the Lord, and we have prayers before we begin each class. We all give our lives each day to the Lord: all the teachers and most of the pupils have been saved, which is what makes the school special. Unfortunately it is discriminated against by the government and doesn't get the same amount in financial support and grants that other schools do, but we pray to the Lord for him to provide and he always does. Our school motto is 'The Lord Giveth Us His Wisdom', but he gives us much more than that, he gives us help when we are in need, and peace of mind when we are troubled. I myself had a religious experience when I was four years old: it is called being born again as a Christian, and it is a very wonderful experience.

One of the people who comes regularly to our school is Mr Paisley, and he is a very nice and kind person indeed. Also sometimes mummy takes me to his church on about one Sunday a month, and after the service Mr Paisley speaks with every single person who is there. It doesn't matter who you are, high or low, he treats everyone equally and I think he is a very fine person. He has even been to our house because he is a personal friend of daddy's, and when he comes he remembers all my sisters' names and mine, and what point we are at in our studies, and talks with us in a very nice friendly way.

It makes me sad that there are so many people in our country who have not given their lives to the Lord, and that evil men are allowed to escape being brought to justice. We must keep praying that soon everyone will experience the power of the Lord's love to heal all divisions, and so bring lasting peace to our country. It says in the Bible that one day this will happen, and so it will if we maintain our faith.

Alan Hart, 15

– My mother's a Catholic, and my father who died a couple of years ago was a Protestant. Neither of them was ever very strongly religious though, and they never put any pressure on me or my older sisters about it. I remember my father saying once he thought nobody could ever really decide what they were until they were in say their 20s or 30s, and had had a bit of experience of life and could form their own conclusions. As far as I was concerned I'd say I hadn't decided yet, and leave it at that. 'No fixed religion' would describe me, I think.

I came here to Lagan College when I was eleven: it was a conscious decision on my parents' part, but of course at that age I didn't really understand why. I had an older friend who'd been at my earlier school: he was here, he said it was good, and if he said that then it was good enough for me. Another thing my parents told me was that if I found I didn't like it and didn't want to stay, they'd let me go somewhere else. That's never arisen though, I've always liked it very much: it's a good atmosphere, most of the teachers have a good approach and treat you politely, and as a result you behave in the same way back to them.

From time to time you hear criticism of Lagan on the grounds that it's a bit snobby and middle-class and thinks it's a cut above other schools. Against that I'd say that I come myself from a working-class area and a working-class family, and I don't think it's middle-class at all. Everybody's the same here: Catholic, Protestant, middle-class, working-class and upper-class too, whatever that means. It doesn't matter where your home is or what your parents do, or how much money they've got or haven't got. What matters is what you're like, what sort of person you are, that's all. You can have religious or political beliefs of whatever sort you choose; people might disagree with you or have arguments about it, but they won't think any the less of you if your views are different from theirs.

I suppose the best example I can give you of that is not a religious one but a political one. My mother's a Sinn Feiner, and has been all her life: a socialist, a very keen Republican, a believer in a united Ireland and all the rest of it. Even though he was a Protestant my father was an Irish Nationalist, so I suppose I'm naturally rather what you might call a left-winger myself, with definite leanings towards Sinn Fein. In some company if you say that, people start asking you daft questions like 'Oh, you support the IRA do you?' or 'You want to overthrow the Government by force' and so on. Even people who ought to know better have that attitude as well: the other night there was an SDLP Member of Parliament on TV, and I don't remember his exact words but there'd been a killing by the IRA and he said something like 'All ordinary decent people will turn their backs on Sinn Fein after this.' Well my mother's an ordinary decent person and so are other people I know who are in Sinn Fein: in fact they're more ordinary and more decent than some I can think of who are in other political parties. But what I'm getting round to is to say that when we have discussions here in class, or outside for that matter, everybody listens to your point of view with respect, and the result is you do the same with them. I can even see the Loyalist point of view, or anyway I can accept they have one.

I suppose about the only thing I would criticise about Lagan is that from my point of view, which is just my personal one, is that because it has to be very careful not to offend any religious denomination, every denomination has to be given its share of the curriculum or timetable, and as a result there's rather too much of it in total. We have chaplains from all the churches, except the Catholics who send a nun instead of a priest: and they all want to make sure they're given their fair share of time. I think it'd be better if we didn't have any, and left religious upbringing to parents at home. But of course you'd never get anyone to agree to that in Ireland, none of the authorities I mean.

But on the whole I'd say Lagan's a good school, and there ought to be more like it. If and when at some time in the future I get married and have children myself, I'd want them to come here or to somewhere similar. By that I mean to an integrated school, because if there's going to be any future at all for the people who live here in Northern Ireland, they've just got to find a way of getting on together despite all their historical differences, and the best place to start learning that is when you're young and still at school.

9 *The obdurate and the obstinate*

Alec Friel, University lecturer

Margaret Anderson, University lecturer

Joe Austin, Belfast City Councillor, Sinn Fein

Sammy Wilson, Belfast City Councillor, Democratic Unionist

Alec Friel,

University lecturer

– I'd prefer it if you didn't give very much description about me, or say where we met and where we are now as we talk. It would be best, I think, if you describe me in no more detail than saying I'm on the staff of one of the departments of the University of Ulster.

– You see when you ask me the question you've just done – 'Are you an Ulsterman?' – I have to say that's a highly political question, and the term isn't one I'd ever use. I was born in the historic province of Ulster, yes: but in Northern Ireland such terms as 'Ulster', 'Northern Ireland', 'the Six Counties' and so on are all value-laden: they all have specific meanings to different people. For a start, the description of 'Ulsterman' is almost exclusively used by Protestants and Unionists, and people from a Nationalist background don't accept such a term. Historically 'Ulster' was a province of Ireland and comprised nine counties: then six of those nine were partitioned off in 1921 and called 'Northern Ireland'. So the answer to your question is therefore 'Yes I am an Ulsterman in that I come from the historic province of Ulster, but I am not an Ulsterman in the sense that it's used by Loyalists or Unionists or the British.' They use it to try and give a kind of historical legitimacy to the idea of the present six counties: but Nationalists in the north think of themselves as 'Irish' rather than as 'Ulster' people. Another expression not liked at all is 'The Province'. To Nationalists it means ancient Ulster, one of the four original provinces of Ireland: but in its usage by Unionists and Loyalists, it's referring to Northern Ireland as a province of the United Kingdom and Nationalists don't like that at all. Instead they prefer to talk about 'the North' or 'the Six Counties'. I always think it demonstrates the lack of confidence of the Loyalists, that they try to make such a term as 'Ulster' mean the Six Counties, which is what they're doing when they resurrect that old term.

'Am I a Nationalist or a Republican, and what's the difference between them?' Well that's another difficult question. I suppose the difference is similar to that between Unionists and Loyalists. All Republicans are Nationalists, just as, I think, all Loyalists are Unionists. But the reverse isn't necessarily true. When I say I'm a Nationalist, I mean I'm from the Catholic population: because to me Catholic and Nationalist are to all intents and purposes synonymous. But when it comes to whether I'm also a Republican or not, I think at this point I have to ask you for a most explicit assurance you won't use my name. This is because of where I work: in my section of the University of Ulster, for me to describe myself as Republican could greatly affect my standing in the department, because it's a very political term. The short answer is 'Yes I am'.

I think of myself as Irish, not British: my identification is with a place, a land with its own history and culture: and in my case the majority religion of that land too, which is Catholicism. I'm from that background and I'm descended from people who've lived here from as far back as anyone I know. I love Irish culture and language, I identify it with the experience of my ancestors: and that means, I must politely point out to you, the conquest and colonisation of us by the British, and our subsequent resistance to you.

A sense of identity isn't something you acquire consciously of course: it's not as straightforward as taking out a passport or deciding to follow a particular football team. One's whole upbringing socialises one into it, and I can't separate the influence of my parents, the influence of my school, or the influence of reading about the past. I grew up in a milieu totally identified with Ireland and its history and culture. My father was an ardent Nationalist, but not a Republican in the sense of being a socialist. And he didn't believe in violence, he didn't think that the way of the IRA was correct: not I think from moral grounds, but because he didn't feel it was necessary. He was only a working man, but like many Irish working men he studied and was very knowledgeable about Irish history. Reading was the great thing in our family, I always remember books in the house throughout my childhood.

Books? Well those which stick in my mind as being the ones I enjoyed as a youth were the stories of Charles Dickens, and everything by P. G. Wodehouse. Dickens because he was aware of the social problems in his time: and I found Wodehouse intriguing because although he was writing about the English upper classes, he always did it in a very irreverent way. He more than anyone else showed just how funny the English look to other people, without being in the least bit conscious themselves of how ridiculous they are.

Well, if we can't avoid it, then I'll say yes, I do think there are sometimes certain situations when violence is both necessary and justified. My father didn't: I do, perhaps because I'm a generation on from him. I feel if everything else has been tried, and undoubtedly everything has been tried, and nothing has succeeded, then I do think people are entitled to resort to violence. For an English person to understand the mentality which is bred into people like me who've been brought up in Northern Ireland would take a considerable leap of the imagination. The nearest analogy I can come up with for the moment is to suggest for example that if Germany had won the last war, and came to an agreement whereby it occupied the south-east of England, imagine how people who lived there would feel if they saw German police and troops in their streets every time they went out. I have a strong gut-reaction when I'm stopped by a British soldier when I'm driving my car in my own country and asked to produce my driving licence and other proofs of identity. I am an Irish person driving from one part of my country to another, and there is someone with an English accent and a gun who has the right to stop and question me. That makes me feel very much a Nationalist, and sympathetic to any Republican who'd want to consider using violence.

One million Protestant people in the population were born here and have the right to live here. But does that mean the other half million of the population who're Nationalists and Catholic have to live like refugees in their own country? It's one of the things I never understand about the British left for example, how they get much more worked up about what goes on in El Salvador or Chile than they do about what happens here in Northern Ireland. The bilateral policy of both Labour and Conservatives won't do, it's ignoring the situation here.

But I suppose it's presumptuous of me talking to you and trying to suggest there are certain things English people ought to understand. To put it bluntly, I don't think it's anything to do with you really. The people of Ireland must solve the problems of Ireland, so the sooner the English get out of the picture the better. Their only concept of Ireland seems to be a mass of Paddys who fight amongst themselves about religious questions. Nothing's further from the truth: nobody's killing anybody because of disagreements about transubstantiation or the Virgin Birth. What people are concerned about are political issues, not religious squabbles belonging to the days of Cromwell.

It's inevitable British troops will have to be withdrawn. I think it'll occur not for moral reasons – the British never do anything for moral reasons if you don't mind my saying so – but for economic ones. With the cost of security and the much reduced revenue now coming out of Northern Ireland, the British aren't making any money out of this country, and I can't see the situation continuing because of that. Return on investments is nil, and there's no other reason now why the British should stay.

I don't agree with those who say there'll be a bloody civil war if the British go. What happens will be a matter of negotiation between Catholics and Protestants in the north, and to some extent the Republic of Ireland will have a say. Minds will be greatly concentrated by the announcement of an impending withdrawal, and people who live here will simply have to decide between themselves how they're going to live together. Sinn Fein hasn't been invited to any discussions yet: but I think any talks will be pointless if they exclude a party which has the support of a sizeable part of the population. There's no point in people talking only to those they agree with: the extremists on both sides have to talk to each other.

In my position as an academic, one thing that depresses me is that our contribution to discussion of problems and possible solutions has so far been minimal. Both our universities have tried to portray themselves as above the conflict, and they've appointed their staffs deliberately to contain a low proportion of native-born people. There are far too many English academics here: and they all pretend there's something rather superior about being above politics. I find it extraordinary that almost all our intellectual output about our problems is only to be found in a magazine called 'Fortnight'. It's the only place where discussion and different intellectual analyses are found. But the universities really ought to take more responsibility about this, because no society in any country can do without the involvement of academics.

Finally I'd like to say I'm no different from anyone else in being unable to talk very long about the situation here without expressing my personal beliefs. I didn't intend to, but I did. I have them and I don't see there's anything wrong with that. But it irritates me to see and hear Unionists on the university staff trying to pretend they have only a lofty independent point of view. That's why I want to be completely anonymous and unidentifiable. As I said, it'd damage my standing if I were known to be a Nationalist, and damage it even more if I were known to have marked Republican tendencies. At English universities there are academics who are well-known as Marxists: it doesn't affect their work, the seriousness with which it's discussed, nor the readiness of people to listen to them and consider their point of view. But here in Northern Ireland today there'd be immediate dismissal for anyone who admitted he inclined one way or another. It's ludicrous, it's wrong, and it's dishonest.

Margaret Anderson,

University lecturer

A tall grey-haired woman in a green skirt and white blouse, she sat straight-backed on the settee in her comfortably furnished sitting-room. From time to time she gave a small grave smile, polite and proud.

– Well I'd describe myself as an ordinary Belfast woman. My husband is a teacher, he's at one of the large secondary schools near here in east Belfast, and we've lived here more or less all our lives. My husband is an Ulsterman, my mother was English and my father Ulster, he was in the British Army and wounded in Italy in the Second World War: and we have three grown-up children.

I think I'd also describe myself as someone very much from the Province: I mean by that that I was born and brought up in this area, I went to school here, and then I went on to the University of Ulster where I studied English. So I've never really moved very far away from Belfast. But I do go occasionally to England to see my brother and sister, both of whom are married and live there: one in Yorkshire and the other in London. Politically I'd describe myself as a Unionist: but I'm not a member of any particular party nor is my husband, and we both like to think of ourselves as moderate.

I'm a perfectly ordinary Ulster woman, by which I mean that I'm British and proud of it. It might sound strange to say to someone coming newly here from England that I enjoy living in Belfast, but it's true, I do, very much. I think an exaggerated picture of the troubles is given by the media: for all of that, nevertheless Belfast's a fine place to live, and its people are fine people. They have a tremendous integrity and courage, and great readiness to put up with difficulties and sometimes danger. I can't ever see them allowing themselves to be incorporated in the rest of Ireland, they're too much independent for that. I hope I'm not sounding too prejudiced if I say the Catholic church doesn't really like independence of thought at all. I regard the idea of full integration between the north and south with a mild amusement: it really wouldn't ever work, because the people are so different. Ulster people are British people and Irish people are Irish, and never the twain shall meet as they say.

But that doesn't mean I think that here in the north, there's no hope of future *rapprochement* between the two-thirds of the population who are Protestant and the one-third which is Catholic. I genuinely believe, or perhaps it'd be better to say I sincerely hope, that one day all this dreadful factionalism and sectarianism will gradually disappear, and people will all live happily together. There are a surprising number of mixed marriages you know. I can't quote the exact numbers, but I understand that they're increasing all the time between Protestants and Catholics: and I do think this is good. In fact one of my own children, my oldest son, has married a Catholic: she's an extremely nice girl and I think it isn't unusual nowadays for this kind of thing to happen. I was a little surprised when my son agreed any children they had should be given a Catholic upbringing and education, and we have from time to time discussed it. But my daughter-in-law Evelyn is not what one might call a bigoted person, and I'm sure anyway as they get older, the children will probably re-think a lot of the ideas which the Catholic church does tend to try and instil as dogma.

I also think great strides have been made in recent years about anti-Catholic discrimination. It did occur, everybody admits that: but rapid progress has been made in such areas as housing and employment, and there's now a far more equal and fairer situation. I don't think it's a great help to anyone if politicians go on talking about anti-Catholic discrimination any more now. There are Catholic people with bad housing, but there are also Protestants in the same situation: and anyway, there are a lot of people on the mainland with bad housing, and no one can point the finger there and say it's due to religious discrimination can they?

I think one of the most important things that would contribute to an improvement in the situation is an absolutely firm and irrevocable statement by the British Government that they intend to keep the

Army here. Protestants do want to be reassured that the extremists
and terrorists are never ever going to achieve their aim of uniting the
north and the south. There's really far too much mild speaking by
the British Government about this: I think it does nothing but give
support to Sinn Fein and the IRA. And I honestly don't know what
their idea is, because certainly no one in the south, or no responsible
person in the south, is all that anxious to take on the economic
problems of the north. We have a much higher standard of living
here than they do in the south, and this is something which the
Republican or Nationalist elements, whatever you want to call them,
don't seem to want to try to understand, or pretend not to. Belfast
Catholics would very quickly find out which side their bread was
buttered on if Northern Ireland were taken over by the Republic:
their standard of living'd drop very sharply indeed.

You can't help but suspect sometimes that terrorists have never
really given much thought at all to their own political ideology, if
you can call it that. They want to force a united Ireland not only on
the north but on the south as well. But the south doesn't want it,
that's the fact of the matter. So I don't think there's any point in the
argument that there'll be no peace here until all the political parties
including Sinn Fein get together round the table. I think that would
be deeply insulting to the Protestant people of Belfast. They've stood
up for years against the most appalling acts of destruction of
property, not to mention the loss of hundreds and hundreds of lives:
so then to be told they had to sit down and try to reach agreement
with those who'd done such things to them is unthinkable. At least
until Sinn Fein makes an irrevocable commitment never to resort
again to violence of any kind, that is. But even it they did that, I
think the majority of people wouldn't trust them, and with good
reason. And you know, to ordinary people like me there's a great
danger that Sinn Fein and the IRA may feel that if they continue their
campaign of intimidation, and indeed step it up which they've been
doing particularly during the last year or so, the British Government
might feel it's no longer worthwhile them staying here and leave.
But that really would be a terrible letting-down of Northern Ireland
people. The British Government mustn't give any sign or indication
that it's weakening in its resolve to crush the terrorists.

I don't know what your own particular views are, so you must

forgive me if I assume incorrectly your attitude towards the situation
here is probably the same as that of the majority of British people on
the mainland. You seem to give the impression at times you don't
want to know what's going on here: you want us out of your hair as
it were, and you're impatient with the lack of progress that's being
made. In my personal opinion that's because you don't properly
understand the situation: and you don't understand because, to be
honest, I think you don't want to understand.

You'll hear a great deal I'm sure, if you haven't heard it already,
about the Battle of the Somme in 1916, when so many men from
Ulster lost their lives. And you may be tempted to think 'Good
heavens, that was how long ago, eighty years?' So it was: but one of
those hundreds of thousands of men who died was my grandfather:
and the memory of that is part of my family's history. It can't just be
dismissed as obsession with the past: my grandfather died for
Britain, my father was wounded in the Second World War for
Britain, so surely this deserves respect and most of all some loyalty?
You must forgive me if I sound angry about this: but the fact of the
matter is I am angry. And I'll continue to be for the whole of my life,
unless the British Government assures me – not just with words but
with actions – that the sacrifices those men and many others made
really do still count for something. How can you betray us? We feel
we're being left on our own to fight fanatical bigots who want to
take us back to the dark ages and the ruthless oppressiveness of the
Roman Church. Our fathers, our brothers, our sons, they all
sacrificed themselves for you in two world wars: so how can you do
this to us now, and show us no feelings of loyalty or gratitude?

I'd say over and over again to English people: 'Look, please
listen to me. You're British, I'm British. We have the same
background of history and culture. I'm Anglo–Saxon, just as you
are. I was born British and I want to live British. I feel under
threat from those Irish people in the south, and if the border went
I'd be terrified, because I feel the south is a male-dominated and
church-dominated country. We fought with you and for you in
the last war. We gave you submarine bases and air bases: and
without question, we gave you the lives of thousands of our men
just as we did in the First World War. But what did they do in
southern Ireland? They called themselves 'neutral' and they didn't
lift a finger on your behalf. There are stories and rumours that

I won't go into, but you must have heard them yourself often enough, of the extent to which they went to give aid and succour to the Germans. Not to us, their neighbours, but to the Germans. You were being bombed, and we were being bombed: we were in battle together, and when the war was over we suffered the deprivations of rationing and everything else. We never demanded that we should be given freedom from you, in fact we insisted we were with you by your side.'

That's what I'd like to say. I'm sorry, I'm afraid I've let my feelings run away with me, but I think such feelings – and they're not just mine – are not properly understood or appreciated, and they're certainly not respected. Just to give you one small example, I can't tell you how angry it makes me on the occasions when I go to London and do something like offering a Northern Irish banknote to a taxi-driver and he refuses to accept it, and says like one did when I was there last year: 'Sorry lady, I don't take foreign currency.' I can't tell you how that makes me feel: rejected, hurt, neglected, they're only a few of the words that come to mind.

Look, I'm sorry, do forgive me. Rationally I can't deny the Nationalists have their own history, and when they learn about what the British have done to Ireland, it rouses very strong feelings in them. It was dreadful, nobody could say it wasn't. But I think it should be remembered that when the British were imperialists and colonialists, as they were for hundreds of years, their behaviour towards all the people they subjugated was terrible. It wasn't just the Irish – it was towards the people of India, and everywhere else you can think of: Africa, south-east Asia, Scotland, Wales, China, everywhere the British were terrible. And the British ruling class were terrible to their own people too: they made them live in poverty, they sent women and children down the mines, they massacred people at Peterloo – you name it, they did it. The British ruling class were always cruel and arrogant, they didn't behave in that way just towards the Irish. But the people I've mentioned from other parts of the world, they're not still fighting the British, they've got over what was done to them, they're not still carrying on terrorising the British in their country who've stayed there.

And lastly I'd like to admit I'm not really very proud of all my prejudices: I know they're the result of my emotions and not my intellect. I mean, whenever there's an atrocity, I always find myself thinking 'The bloody Irish!' And intellectually I know very well the Irish aren't any bloodier than anyone else. Some of them are good and some of them are bad, but I have an uncontrollable emotional reaction which comes from my background and upbringing and everything else. I'm surprised though at how quickly the emotional reactions come to the surface. Perhaps it's because I'm getting old.

But it makes me angry when I see slogans painted on the walls in streets saying 'Brits out'. It's the unthinkingness of it that annoys me so much. Two-thirds of the population of Northern Ireland are British, so what on earth does some idiot with a spraycan mean by 'Brits out'? That's the sort of trivialisation Nationalists and Republicans indulge in that upsets me. It's not a matter for slogans, it's how people live together: they should do it and they could do it, in peace and with respect for each other. I honestly don't believe the troubles in the north of Ireland are the responsibility of anyone except the Nationalists and the Republicans. They simply won't accept the historical inevitability of the situation, the situation of the north of Ireland being British and staying British, and its people preferring to die rather than be taken over by the Republic. Surely they can see that, surely it can be accepted as fact, and a way be found for us all to live together as civilised people? Instead of talk of 'Brits out', it's the Nationalists and Republicans who should go out. If they don't like living here under the British Government, if they won't accept it and don't want it, then they should go peaceably down to the south, and leave the north to us.

Have I sounded like a tub-thumper? I hope not. As I said to you at the beginning I'm just an ordinary Ulster woman. An ordinary Ulster woman's what I am, and an ordinary Ulster woman's what I want to stay.

Joe Austin,

Belfast City Councillor, Sinn Fein

A small quietly spoken man wearing a dark suit, a pale blue shirt and a red tie: while he talked he sounded self-assured but at the same time diffident in expressing his views. Sometimes he gave an ironic smile, self-deprecatingly: at others when he spoke of his deep convictions he narrowed his eyes, focusing on the seriousness of what he had to say.

– I'm a Republican yes, naturally I am as a member of Sinn Fein. The difference between Republicans in general and Nationalists, well I think you could best describe it as being one of final intent. Basically I think general agreement – if there ever could be such a thing as general agreement between two or more Irishmen – might be obtained for the statement that Nationalists want to see a united Ireland free of British or anyone else's involvement, and Republicans want that plus a radical change in the way society is structured. Republicans are bound to be socialist, I think that could be said: Nationalists are not necessarily so. Republicans believe that the way forward for the Irish people has to be based on the unity of everyone, but in a non-sectarian and secular way. To many people the Republican movement is inevitably associated with the IRA and violence and that is partly due to the influence of the media in portraying them that way. But it's incorrect and it's very misleading. If you've not already come across them, you'll meet many people who go so far in condemning Sinn Fein as to say we all support the IRA. There's a difference though in supporting an organisation and not condemning it: the two things aren't the same. I'm only speaking for myself of course, but as I see it Sinn Fein would like to see a peaceful solution to the Irish situation which exists at present.

Unfortunately though if that's to happen everybody will have to agree to give up using violence, but so far the only calls for this are that Sinn Fein and the IRA should do it unilaterally. It's hypocritical, I think, for the British Government to issue statements to the effect they won't even begin to talk to Sinn Fein unless Sinn Fein disavows violence. It can't disavow something that it doesn't advocate, and Sinn Fein as such doesn't embrace violence. Equally the British Government should disavow violence, should disavow using its troops, and should condemn the violence used by the RUC. Otherwise such demands are just meaningless, or that's how they seem to be to most ordinary people at least. Only all the time, please, I'd like to emphasise I'm speaking for myself and not on behalf of my party. I may well be saying things most people in Sinn Fein wouldn't agree with. We don't have a very rigorous orthodoxy about our statements: as far as possible we try to allow individual members to speak as they see things themselves.

Most of my personal philosophy? Well, if you can dignify it with as grand a name as that, it came from my mother. Both my parents were Catholics and I was one of eleven children. My father was an ordinary working–class man, very hard-working and very devout Catholic. He saw his way of life, indeed his main purpose in life, to help his family to climb a small way up the social ladder. My mother worked in a garments factory and she was very active in union activities there. I won't say that religion took second place to politics for her, but certainly politics were a practical affirmation and extension of her religious belief. She influenced me towards Republicanism in teaching me the need for social change and social development. She wasn't exactly a crusader, but she had a great pride and dignity about her which she instilled in her family. Like many Catholics when the troubles began, she saw how the police and then later the Army always seemed to be on the side of the Protestants.

I myself witnessed a lot of the street riots and fights when I was only a child: and another great influence was television. We saw civil rights marches in the USA, we saw and heard men like Martin Luther King, and we saw that ordinary people if they banded together had a great strength. The State learned the same lesson too: and so they attacked many of the marches, which they genuinely believed were threatening the stability of the State. One of the slogans of the protestors when they marched was 'One Man, One Vote'. I can't help thinking that if the authorities had had the sense to address that demand and promise to satisfy it, a great part of the problem would have gone away. But instead of trying to defuse the situation by doing that, they preferred to try and suppress the people who were making the reasonable demand. The Loyalist ethos was in that well-known phrase used by Lord Craigavon: he said Ulster was a Protestant state for a Protestant people.

Besides being provocative and inflammatory, the remark wasn't true. Ulster was only a section of the island of Ireland which belonged to all the Irish people, Protestant and Catholic. So the Catholics weren't simply trouble-makers: they were only trouble-makers to the Protestants who were oppressing them, who then said they wouldn't do anything to make conditions better until the violence ceased. It's always puzzling that those who want to retain power and privilege aren't more subtle in the way they go about it, isn't it?

Anyhow I'll get down off the soap-box. Yet it's not really just a soap-box, it's rather more serious than that. People may see me and others like me as stirrers-up of trouble, but we aren't: we're symptoms of trouble, and can't be suppressed and kept quiet in any other way except by removing the things we're protesting about.

These two things, the views of my mother and what I saw for myself was going on in Northern Ireland, they're both what led to me becoming a Republican. I suppose it could be said they were wrong reasons, because political theory shouldn't be reactive: but I think it has to be accepted that these things exist as a real force in the lives of people here, and one which can't be stamped out by being called just ' terrorism'. It has to be thought about more deeply than that.

I know I'm regarded by some people as an agitator, and I'd like to think I was as dangerous to the fabric of the State as I'm supposed to be, but realistically of course I'm not. But I see my own society, and it's mine as much as it's the society of any Protestant, being ground into subjugation by the forces of the State. What am I supposed to do? Run away? There've so far been five attempts on my life, shootings at me in the street and places where I've been such as clubs or pubs. But none of them has had the effect which presumably was

intended: and if any'd been successful and I'd been killed, or if I'd
been so terrified I'd run away and given up political activity, straight
away others with more courage would have come forward in my
place. Nothing disturbs me or deters me.

Only one thing could ever dampen my Republican faith. It's
happened once, and if something like it happened again, I don't
know what I'd do. It was the Enniskillen bomb explosion at the
Remembrance Day ceremony in November 1987. The reaction
amongst all the Republicans I knew was enormous, and people were
looking at me as though I was going to try and defend the
indefensible. When you're accustomed to being on the receiving end
of violence somehow sometimes it gives you a sense of moral dignity
because you're the oppressed. But when you yourself are the
oppressor, when you're associated with those who've inflicted
suffering as happened that day at Enniskillen, then the dignity goes.
I've a deep sense of shame that people I thought were of high
principle should perpetrate an act like that. If Republicans claim
responsibility for good things they do, as they do, then they've got
to accept it for bad things done in the name of Republicanism too.
After Enniskillen, I was left feeling totally sick, and very conscious
of the same feelings of many of our people about it. They were
disgusted and rightly so. And I'd no time at all for 'What aboutism' –
you know, people who said 'Yes, but what about what's been done
to us? What about Bloody Sunday in Derry, what about the shooting
of three defenceless people in Gibraltar by the SAS?' That had
nothing to do with it, and if you got into it you were defending the
indefensible.

And perhaps one other thing might make a difference to me.
Perhaps. I feel we Irish have never had what could be called a normal
relationship with England. Your country's only twenty-two miles
from here, and we share a lot of history and heritage: but so far it's
always been on the basis of your country dominating ours. So if only
somehow we could get on to some kind of level in our relationship,
one of equality and respect for each other, I think there's a chance so-
called firebrands like me might not have such an easy time of it. But
until we do, I and people like me are ready to die in the struggle for
independence and a united Ireland. People will know why we died,
that we made our choice to do so, and it was a matter of conscience,

and belief for something we thought was worthwhile. It makes me very sad for their sakes when I see your young soldiers on the streets. Some of them have come here only a couple of weeks ago and they haven't the first inkling what the situation is about: and when I look at them and think some of them will undoubtedly be killed before it's all over, I can't help reflecting they won't have the same reason for their deaths. Nothing they've ever done will enhance the future way of life of their families, their descendants, their friends or their neighbours: their deaths'll be quite pointless, and all they'll result in is greater bitterness and greater hatred between us. And that doesn't seem to me to be something worth young men dying for.

Sammy Wilson,

Belfast City Councillor, Democratic Unionist

The phone conversation was welcoming.

– Yes of course you can, come round to my house one evening when I've got a free one, we'll have a chat for as long as you like. A lot of nights I'm away on council business but we'll fit it in somehow during the time you're here. I like talking. You'll have a job to stop me once I start.

Mugs of coffee, biscuits, chocolates, coconut cake, on a neatly-arranged low table by the settee. A well-built smiling man with a direct and friendly manner.

– I'm thirty-eight and I've been involved in local politics all my life: since I was two or three, do you know how I mean? I've always been aware of it, conscious of it all the time.

I was born around here in east Belfast, in the shadow of the City Hall. My father was a clergyman, but the church wasn't something I wanted to go into: with a thing like that you either know it's for you or you know that it isn't. In my case it wasn't. Although my parents were strong Unionists, there wasn't any political influence on me through them. When I was a youngster, it was more a case of following behind the vans in the election parades you know, being attracted to all the razzmatazz. It wasn't till I went to university I really became much involved, which was in the 60s and 70s when the troubles were starting. I was then at Queen's, studying economics, and my intention had been to go into town planning. But my political conscience was developing: because at Queen's there was a strong Republican element among the students. I think I reacted

against that because of my family background. Anyway, I lost
interest in town planning. I went on instead into teaching at a
grammar school, and that's where I still am. Only I've no particular
vocation for it: as I say, I was and still am much more interested in
politics.

After university I came to live here, in this house: or rather where
this house was, this was a slum clearance area. I began to understand
how frightened the local community was of what was going to
happen to them. So I became involved in housing groups and things
like that. But obviously if you want to channel any kind of social
concern into action you've got to do it through the established
political parties: that's how I became a Unionist. Now I'm a
Democratic Unionist which I suppose would be regarded as being on
the right of that. You know, if you've been brought up all your life
in a working-class Protestant area like I have, you're bound to have a
conscience: and the whole community round here was really under
threat. Not far from here people were regularly being fired at by
gunmen from the Short Strand area, so I don't think anyone who
lived through that period here wouldn't have gone in the political
direction I went. I'm now Ian Paisley's press officer in fact.

If you go back historically to medieval times, or indeed even
earlier than that, you'll find this north-eastern corner of Ireland has
always identified strongly with Scotland, and with what we call
mainland Britain, much more so than it has with the rest of this
island. Most of the trade, and most of the population, it's always
tended to go back and forth in that direction, rather than down
towards the south. And another thing that's always motivated
people here to regard themselves as British is that over the years our
bond has always been with Britain. We fought in Britain's wars, and
our history's coloured by that. Not fifty yards from where we're
sitting now, in this very street live people whose parents fought at
the Battle of the Somme in World War One in 1916. In one morning
there, 5,000 people from Northern Ireland died in the battle. So over
the years loyalty to Britain has always been very very strong, and
isn't something that will ever be forgotten.

Going back though to what I was saying earlier, since 1641 when
there was a massacre of the Protestants in this part of the island,
there's always been a siege mentality here: after all it's reckoned

about 150,000 Protestants were killed then. And again in 1690 you got the same kind of thing looking as though it was going to occur: King James came with his Catholic army, but people were prepared to starve in the city of Londonderry rather than surrender to him. You can look up all this historical background if you're interested: and it's something very real to us Protestants in the north. This is something that people in the rest of Britain just don't understand.

We're afraid of the Republic because of the commanding position that's occupied there by the Roman Church, and the way its influence permeates the whole state. I've no objections to people in the Republic wanting to lead their own way of life: in fact, coming from a religious background myself, I can understand why people accept things they've been taught from childhood by their own Church. But I don't want Catholic doctrine nor do the rest of us Protestants. To me, being a Unionist means keeping all that stuff out of our lives and living the way *we* want to.

And personally, British as I am, I feel that in my lifetime there's been a considerable betrayal of Northern Ireland by Britain. I'm not by any means the only person who feels this, it's something you'll come across very often in the Unionist community. As one of their elected representatives I speak for nearly all of them when I say we feel successive British Governments are not much interested in what happens here.

The prime example is the security situation: I don't believe any British government would accept the level of violence we have here if it were happening on the mainland. There'd have been greater political will in winning the fight against terrorism. Can you imagine, two Sinn Fein members of Belfast City Council, if they flew to London they'd be stopped by the police at Heathrow and put back on the plane because they are deemed to be a threat to public safety? So they get sent back here. On the mainland those men are not tolerated, yet you send them back here though we're part of the United Kingdom too!

These people are actually trying to destroy the state: there's no point whatsoever in even trying to have dialogue with them. Ten years ago Danny Morrison said at Sinn Fein's annual conference 'Who here believes we can win a war through the ballot box? Will anyone here object if with the ballot paper in this hand, and an

Armalite in this hand, we take power in Ireland?' That word he used
– 'war' – you've seen it yourself in the last few weeks, all these bomb
attacks on property in the centre of the city. Yet some people still
seem to believe you can talk to those responsible. What I say is, if
you're ready to listen to them they'll feel their bombing campaign is
changing your point of view. It's like giving them a green light. If
somebody said to me when I was engaged in a fight with them 'I'm
ready to talk to you, I don't think I can beat you', that wouldn't
discourage me from going on fighting would it?

The terrorists have totally excluded themselves from any
democratic process. The security forces should be allowed to go after
them and take them out of circulation, by internment or any other
method, so we have a period of respite. They say they're carrying
out a war, so we should carry out a war against them too. And what
are war's normal rules? You don't catch the enemy and put him in
prison for a short time, you eradicate him, and I firmly believe that's
the only way we'll ever beat terrorism.

I know these views won't be well received in many parts of the
Catholic community. But I'd like to emphasise something: which is
my view's only a selective one. I own this house where we are now:
and in it, I rent a couple of rooms to two people who are Roman
Catholics. We've great debates about their point of view and mine,
and they don't agree with me and I don't agree with them. But we all
live in the same house. So I can't be the bigot some people say I am,
can I?

– I think most English people don't understand there's a fight going
on here between people who are Democrats and people who are
Fascists: it's between people who wish to express their preference
through the ballot box, and people who are trying to gain their
objectives by force. I'm appalled when people from England come
here and say 'You're all just as bad as one another, you're all to
blame.' That's simply not the case and it shouldn't ever be said. And
another thing I'd like people in England to understand is that we
Unionists are not monsters, we're human beings. Our loyalty to
Britain is strong, and no one could argue that we haven't
demonstrated it. There's hardly a village in Northern Ireland where

people were not bereaved by what happened in both the first and the second world wars. Hundreds of the finest of our young men died for Britain. So it leaves a bitter taste in our mouths now when it seems there's no gratitude due to us from Britain. We want to remain British, it's as simple as that: and we need your help to do it.

I've enjoyed talking with you, and I hope something of what I've said makes sense. I don't expect your book to reflect purely the Unionist point of view, because I accept that wouldn't give a full and complete picture: but when I come to read it, I'd like to be able to say someone looked at the situation, asked people questions, and tried to show the issues were not entirely black and white. Too many books are written about us which tend to suggest that, and those who've usually been shown to be black are the Unionists.

10 *Everyday lives 1*

Fergus Notley, gateman

Norah Smith, seamstress

Deanna Joyce, teamaker

Billy McFadden, bus driver

Gerry Peel, delinquent

Brenda Ferguson, refugee

Anna Whitely, waitress

Fergus Notley,

gateman

The collar of his old anorak turned up against the rain and the wind, he sat in the doorway of his little wooden hut at the gate of the goods yard behind the prefabricated concrete building near one of the motorways. A ginger-haired man in his sixties, he chain-smoked roll-ups.

– Us caught in the squall sir, ordinary people like me, all we want to do's get on with our lives. Bring up the families, have a drink of a Friday night in the pub and a bit of the craic* blah blah blah, nothing in particular, know how I mean? I'm an old man now, I'd like to have been retired, stay at home and have a bit of peace and quiet. That's all I always looked forward to when I was a young man. My father always used to say to me 'Son, it's only looking after yourself and the family, and all the rest of it's blah blah blah.' Don't know how it's come about these days, I don't: can't look forward to things any more can you? And the young people've nothing to look forward to either. Them politicians all they talk about's blah blah blah. It's no meaning for anybody no more, I don't know what the world's coming to I don't for sure.

But I'm one of the lucky ones sir, know what I mean? You will, but these youngsters don't seem to know what you're talking about do they? Tell them they don't know anything of what life's really like and they don't want to know. All they want's this terrible blaring music all the time, pop songs they call it. This week the number one's this one, next week number one's something completely different. And that Sinead O'Connor eh, what about her? Jesus it's cold today sir isn't it just?

* 'Craic' is pronounced 'crack'

I've eight children myself sir, five of them girls but only three boys, thanks be to God. Yes indeed I do mean that sir, if God'd had given me five sons that'd've been five unhappy men. The girls see, they'll be alright: find husbands for themselves or go across the water to England and work. Always work for women you see, but not so easy for a man. I worry about my boys. I don't worry about my girls but my boys I do, I worry about them. You never know you see sir: no work for them, standing around talking with their mates all day blah blah blah. Never know where they're going to end up sir do you? One of these days someone's going to come and see me from the police, and tell me I'm in trouble. Not me myself, I don't do anything: but one of my sons I mean, he's had something happen to him or done something to somebody else. You take my Brendan now, twenty-four years of age and's never had a day's work in his life. All the time on the brew he's been. What sort of a life that's for a young man? So who'd be blaming him if someone offered a job to him that he didn't make any enquiries as to what it would involve? Said he'd just take the job whatever it was eh? They'd tell him this and they'd tell him that and blah blah blah, before he knew where he was he'd be driving a van wouldn't he? Somebody else didn't want to drive it because of what was inside it, you know what I mean? And the police'd stop him and ask him who he was and where he came from, what was he driving that was in the van and where was he driving it to and blah blah blah, and what then? He's a good boy, they're all good boys so they are, all of them. But they don't know what work is, they don't know what opportunity is, they don't know what a future is. They're like the rest of us, all caught up in the squall.

The end of it? Well sir I wouldn't have no ideas about that. I'm just an ordinary ignorant uneducated man, us people've no say in what happens to us. It's only the clever ones, the politicians, the ones who've got themselves into good jobs and sit around all day and talk, blah blah blah. And people dying every day here on the streets of Belfast, people dying and killing one another. And what for? I don't know, only for blah blah blah. Catholics killing Catholics and Protestants killing Protestants, so it can't be for religious reasons can it sir? This is what I don't understand.

Come in and out of here with their lorries and their trucks they do, to and fro, and so long as they've got their authority-passes I open the gates for them. I don't know if they're Catholic or Protestant, I've no idea and I don't ask. If they've got their authority-pass they can come in or go out, that's all I'm worried about. That's the way I look at life, that's how I think life should be altogether. If you're reasonable and respectable who the devil cares, if you'll pardon the expression, who the devil cares whether you're Catholic or Protestant? Your living to earn, your family to keep, that's all that matters: so's at the end of your time you can say you've done no harm to no one. I think it should all be like that.

I'm not a thinking man though, to be sure I'm not. If I was sir perhaps I wouldn't be here. I would have gone in the year 1950 when I was twenty-two: my wife wanted us to go to Canada where her brother was. 'Fergus' she'd say to me, 'Fergus, there's no hope in Ireland for decent people like us.' I used to wonder what she meant, so I did. I used to think, she might know something I didn't know, you know what I mean? I think now maybe she did. Eight children we had, and all of them brought up decent and good. A good wife to me too she was until the day she died. Another thing she always said to me was 'Fergus, I've had a good life. You've been a good husband to me, and I've tried to be a good wife to you.' I'm glad she didn't see the worst of things, God rest her soul. 'Why are people killing each other?' she used to say to me. 'Fergus, why's all this happening?' I couldn't answer that then and I can't answer it now.

I've been doing this job five years now sir. I was a driver before I did this, driving for the council. I drove people from here to there, or from there to here if that was the way they wanted to go. I had a smart car, I kept it clean as a pin, I was driving that for fifteen years. It was a good job so it was, and I lost it through foolishness. After the death of my wife, God rest her soul. A bit too much to drink one day, you know what I mean? They said because of my good record they'd give me another chance so they did. Only I wasn't wise enough to take it was I? Well I'll tell you, I did a foolish thing. I borrowed the vehicle which was the council's and I took it home with me. When they asked me to explain for why, all I could say was it was the drink. I had to go up to the offices up there and explain myself. These five fellers sat at the table and listened, and I said this that and the other, and blah blah blah. 'Fergus' they said, 'you've been a good servant to the council but we can't let you drive for us no more.' So that was the end of it. I had a whole year or more I just sat around in the home: no wife, no job, nothing at all.

And then Patsy my daughter came and told me she'd been to the council, someone there'd said they'd put a word in for me because they wanted a gateman here. So I was very lucky sir like I said at the beginning eh, if you know what I mean? Many a man would give his right arm at the chance, there's little work now to be had. And it's not hard, you know what I mean? Twice a day a man'll come down from the main office up the top floor there, and ask me if I've anything to report. I never have anything to report so I don't. I just do my job, open the gates or close the gates, and don't talk to anyone because nobody comes to talk to me.

Norah Smith,

seamstress

In the morning the community centre hall was bustling with the noise of mothers and toddlers who'd come to play and talk and have cups of tea. She was sitting by herself on a bench near the door, embroidering a cushion cover. A frail woman in her eighties, wearing a shabby black skirt and an old blue cardigan.

– Yes of course dear I'll talk to you if you like. An old woman like me won't have much to say of interest though. I just like sitting here and looking at everything going on. I come here every morning if I'm up to it. It gives me an interest you know, watching all the wee bairns.

Aye, yes it's a Scottish word yes, that's where I come from, I was born in Glasgow. Folk tell me I've long since lost my accent, but that wouldn't be surprising considering Belfast's where I've lived most of my life. A wee girl asked me a few weeks ago where was I from, and when I said Glasgow she said was that north Belfast, south Belfast, east Belfast or west? They say such funny things don't they sometimes, the wee ones?

We came here when I was a baby, I don't remember anything before. I was the youngest of five, my mother was a widow and my father'd died when I was very young. I'm not sure at what age, when you get old you forget things easily, you do.

The first thing I remember clearly was our shop. We sold cigarettes and sweets and newspapers, and it was on the corner of Mercer Street and Shankill Road. It's all knocked down now, Shankill Road was this way and Mercer Street across it here like that. All this side of us was Protestant, and all this side was Catholic. We were Catholic ourselves, only in those times that never came into it:

your customers were from both sides of the road, and what was important was you kept the goodwill of them all. My mother always did, her name was Alice, and she was very popular with everyone she was.

I'd have liked to have worked in the shop myself you know. But my older sisters had precedence and the amount of business we did wasn't enough to support us all. I left school when I was fourteen and went to the sewing factory up at the top of Stuart Street. It was a Protestant concern in the middle of a Protestant area, but in those times if you did your work satisfactorily, that was all that was important. I had a lot of friends there, all girls of my own age: some from this side of the street, some from that and it made no difference. On Friday nights we all met at the dance hall down by the bus station. We were all happy you know dear, we really were. Do you see that pretty young woman there, making the tea? Deanna, the very pretty one? Sometimes I wonder if she's as happy as I was when I was her age. Those dances at the dance hall, they were like fashion parades you know. In the factory you learned a lot about embroidery and seamstressing and things, and you always tried to go looking as though you were a princess. You'd find a dress and you'd put bows and decorated hems with little flowers on it. You could do it so quickly and easily, it was never necessary for you to look as though you were wearing the same thing twice.

I was a very quiet girl, not much of a one for boys myself. When the war came our factory was re-located to near Bedford in England, we were put to work making uniforms and overalls for the Army there. And oh I found the English girls so sophisticated and worldly in comparison with us. I was very very shocked the first time I ever heard one of them say 'bloody': I thought it was a terrible thing for a young lady to say.

At the end of the war, I didn't want to come back to Belfast, I was earning much better money in England and enjoying myself more. My mother kept writing to me saying she needed me back to help in the shop: but I held it against her she hadn't wanted me before.

I wrote to her and said I was not going to return: and gave her as reason the one thing I knew she'd understand, which was I was getting married. I'd met a soldier who'd asked me: I'd refused him twice, I should have refused him the third time as well, but because I needed free of my mother I didn't. It was a grave mistake it was. In three months he was free demobilised, and with a small sum of money we'd saved between us we set up home in a furnished flat.

Do you want to know how long we stayed together? All right then, I'll tell you: eleven days. After he'd come home drunk the first five nights of our marriage, then not come home at all for the next three and wouldn't say where he'd been, I walked out. He didn't seem to mind, he told me he didn't like me much and was going to live with another girl instead.

I soon found I had something to remember him by though, which was I was pregnant. I couldn't live on my own in England with a baby coming, so I had to come back to Belfast and my family.

My mother and sisters welcomed me, they didn't condemn me, it wasn't as though the baby was going to be illegitimate was it? Anyway it's not unusual in Catholic families for a girl to have a baby and there be no father present. We came to a financial arrangement that my mother and my sisters'd keep me till after the baby was born. And then I went back to work, though it wasn't easy to get: it was things like scrubbing and cleaning often at night, so my son could be looked after by my mother. I worked hard, and I was happy enough. There was something about it, I don't know what it was in those days, but you had that feeling of security, of belonging, with your family and friends all round you. Like all wee ones my boy was a great pleasure, and seeing him growing up and all. If it wasn't a happy time it was a contented one, oh aye.

When I'd sufficient money put by I bought a little house of my own up at the top of Mercer Street, so I could still be near my family. Two rooms upstairs you know, and two down: and things went on nicely until the time of the troubles. My home was at the Shankill end of Mercer Street and I was a Catholic you see: and soon it was burned. Fire started three or four houses away: then another over there, and another one nearby, then another one on the opposite side. People running everywhere with bags and boxes and their personal possessions that were precious. In my case it was my wee boy. I tried to take him to my mother's house you know, but it was a great barrier of fire all across the street, so the only place I could go to take shelter was the church hall. So I ran in there with him in my arms, and oh, there must have been another two hundred people there already: and on and on they went on coming in through the night. Those who were setting alight places, they knew what they were doing you know, whose houses they were setting on fire: but flames don't know such things, so Catholics as well as Protestants were burned out of their homes. I'll always remember that night in the church hall, 500 people or more we were, we thought we were all going to be killed. Why should people who'd lived together for years suddenly set on one another like that? I'll never understand what it was about you know.

I'm a Catholic woman so I blame the Protestants of course: but if you talk to a Protestant woman she'd blame the Catholics for it she would. Neither of us would ever be able to tell you really though why it seemed the world was falling in on top of us: people chased out of their homes, houses burned down, wreck and ruin everywhere. But for why, what about? Didn't we all worship the same Lord, wasn't our only difference we did it in different ways? I've never understood it you know.

I don't know anything I've said could be of great importance to you dear, is it?

Deanna Joyce,

teamaker

A slender young woman in jeans and a thick roll–neck wool pullover, she sat on the edge of a formica worktop in the community centre kitchen and lit a cigarette. She swung her legs backwards and forwards while she talked, like a child on a swing.

– Oh great, a few minutes relief eh? Now and again all the noise drives you mad it does. I mean I love being here at the centre and everything, I wouldn't miss it. But all that racket, eh? Never think ten wee little ones could make that much noise would you? Oh well, my three contribute their share or more, I don't suppose it's for me to be complaining is it?

Well sure and I don't know at all what could I say to you about myself that might be interesting: I mean I'm only twenty-two still, I've not had my life yet have I? When I get to be as old as Norah, I expect something might've happened to me that someone might want to hear about. Who knows I might write a book myself one day eh? There wouldn't be much to put in it so far though, not a thing: two or three pages at the beginning and then the rest of it blank, eh? Go on then, ask me some questions, that'll help me know what to say.

What do I do here? Well nothing really you know, I come along every day from ten in the morning till three in the afternoon and make the tea and perhaps some sandwiches. I live just around the corner you see, this place is almost like home to me so it is. I know everybody who comes here and everybody knows me: it's a place that sort of gets hold of you somehow. I'm just a helper you know, who likes coming. Somewhere for me to bring my own three little monsters to too: when you're on your own all day with wee small kids from morning to night, you never hear anything else but their noise and their prattle do you? You start to wonder if you could ever talk to a grown-up. That's why Saturdays and Sundays are the two days I don't like: because here's closed, you know? I don't know why though: there's lots of people outside in the hall there, they've got nothing else to do when they don't come here. Specially some of the younger mums like me, they always find Saturdays and Sundays the hardest too.

I don't have a husband, not even a boyfriend at the moment. If I did I'd at least have someone to talk to eh? But I haven't been lucky, not so far. The first time I was married I was seventeen: that wasn't for love, it was because my wee little one was coming along. It'd have been better if we hadn't married, you know? I mean I think he thought he was doing the proper thing and I think I thought he was too. But the proper thing isn't always the right thing is it? I think when they grow up if either of my two girls got to that situation, I'd tell them not to make the silly mistake that I have. That's what my mother should have told me: instead she said the opposite, the only proper thing was for us to get married. Not the right thing, the proper thing. So there you are now, that's a different generation isn't it, you know? We lived in a little village in County Fermanagh, she said me and Danny ought to go and start a new life here in Belfast. So to be sure and that's what we did didn't we, had a whole new life and it carried on nearly six months? But he was, he was a nice boy you know? I wouldn't like to have said anything might give you the idea that he wasn't. We were both young weren't we? I don't know where he is now even, still that's the way things are isn't it often eh, you know?

What would I like to have done if I hadn't had kids so young and been married? All right then, I'll tell you. The big ambition of my life when I was a girl at school was I wanted to be a typist. You know, in an office, like one of those you see on the TV: a whole lot of girls in rows, and those earphone things over their heads. Audio-typists, is that what they're called? I wanted to be someone smart and efficient and business-like. Whenever I see something like that, I think well I had my chance and I missed it didn't I? They did teach us typing at school: it was the only thing that I enjoyed or liked or was any good at, I thought everything else was boring. I thought that was the thing I was going to do all day long as soon as I left school and got myself a job. I was silly, wasn't I, because what did I do? Got myself expelled for smoking in the lavatories. Smoking in the lavatories was a very serious crime at the convent school, it meant you were severely punished if you were caught: you had to stand on the platform at assembly with other girls who'd done the same thing, and everyone was told to look at you and see how sinful you were. It happened to me the first time I was caught, and then a second time: and I was told if it happened a third time, it would be very serious indeed.

So when I was caught again I didn't wait to see what was going to happen, I ran away from County Fermanagh and went to Donegal. My auntie had a holiday caravan there which she kept on its site all through the winter. I went with my friend Moira who was another one who'd been caught, and we broke in. We set ourselves up as little housewives there you know didn't we? We thought we were oh so brave: like you see in a fillum, two daring young girls hiding from the Law. We'd only been there two nights at the most, then the police came. They said we'd had boys in, which we hadn't: and they said we'd been stealing from shops in the nearby town which we hadn't either. They said we'd done a lot of other things too, like smoking drugs and trying to break into a farmer's house. We'd not done any of them, I swear: just two frightened girls we were, hiding, we'd not have done anything at all to bring any attention to ourselves. Nobody wanted to hear about that though, they took us back to the school and the both of us were expelled. My mother was very angry about it, she said I was wild and my head full of crazy ideas. But I'll tell you what the truth was: my head wasn't full of any ideas at all, I was just a plain daft girl wasn't I?

Well I always say you can't live in the past though can you? Sometimes I listen to some of the older ones we have come in: they sit and talk about how things were better in their day. They talk and they talk, you'd think they'd forgotten the present time altogether wouldn't you? The good old days they say, eh? I'm not a person like that, I get on with living in the present. When I get to be as old as they are I hope I don't talk in the way they do. These are good times for me, I'm a happy sort of person.

I like coming in here and making tea and cutting sandwiches, I like talking to people, I like cleaning up this kitchen and polishing it, I like the two little rooms I have for my home in my sister's house just around the corner. I like my three little wee ones, and there's nothing else I want. I'm paid a bit of money for working here, and I'm paid a bit of money sometimes for looking after people's kids for them. When you add it all up together, it's just about enough. I'd like to have a holiday, go to Spain and lie in the sun by a swimming-pool: I'd like that, I really would. Perhaps one day, eh?

Last year I went with my sister and her two to Blackpool for a week, that's the nearest I've got to it so far. It was really brilliant, we had a smashing time. I might be lucky again, go there this year too you know? I'd like to live in England a while, work in a hotel or something like that. This isn't a good place to be in really with kids, not with all the bombs and things. Don't ask me what it's all about, I've no idea, I don't pay no attention to it. But it's not a good thing at all is it, eh? Ah well, I'd better be doing some more of these sandwiches.

Billy McFadden,

bus driver

A plump bald-headed man in his forties with brown eyes and an occasional laugh, he sat smoking and drinking tea from a tin mug in the canteen at the rear of the bus depot.

– I've always wanted to be a driver on the buses, that I have, ever since when I can remember. I don't know why, even when I was a youngster at school that was my one big ambition it was. My father could never understand it: he always used to tell me the thing to do was go to college and study, get what he called a proper job. People have these ideas don't they about what they think's proper and what's not? I could never fathom the reason but to him there was something wasn't quite right about driving a bus, like it put you lower down the social scale. He himself, he worked in the docks: poor work, and other times he didn't work at all. I remember my childhood as moving from this house to that one, and always insecurity about work and money.

As soon as I left school I applied here, and I began work as a trainee in the engineering department. You got to know the inside of buses the way you'd never learn from a book. I did nine years of that, then I transferred on to being a driver. That'd be when I was twenty-three or so, I did my PSV licence training and then I went on from there. Between times they put me on other courses: they're keen for you to develop into management, move yourself up on the promotional ladder. But I liked the driving best: I still do, so that's where I've stayed. I've no reason for wanting to go on any higher up.

What I like with driving is most ways you're your own boss. You go out with your vehicle, and it's up to you to keep to your timing: so long as you do that nobody worries you. You sit there in your cab looking out of the window, and the scenery's constantly changing, no two of your runs are ever the same. The traffic's always different, the people who get on and off are always different, you're never bored and you never know what's round the next corner. You can drive through one part of the city and it's all calm and pleasant, people in the street going about their business: then you come back the same route the other way half an hour later, and you'll find there's a big hold-up, police and Army everywhere, the whole place unrecognisable. I like that: variety, that's the thing about it.

The only problem's sometimes unsocial hours. Early turns, mornings when you've got to get up at half-past three in winter so that you can be at the depot on time to start your shift. Or late at night when you don't get home till after midnight and you're dependent on someone taking you home in their car. But those things go with the job don't they? I didn't like it so much when my kids were young, I went three or four days sometimes without seeing them: away before they were up in the morning and not back till long after they'd gone to bed. But I'm not complaining, I wouldn't ever have done anything else.

Best of all though are the people you meet. You get some can be a bit difficult, asking you why there hasn't been a bus along and they've been waiting half an hour. You know the answer no better than they do. But mostly they're friendly and ready to have a laugh. All the buses are one-man operated, you pay the driver as you get on, so it brings you in touch with people, you've more chance of a chat. You can get ones who are a bit too conscious of it though sometimes. I had a young woman last week, when she got on she said 'One to the city centre.' I said 'Single?' She gave me a look and pulled herself up like this, and she said very sharpish 'No, I'm not, I'm married.' I said 'Oh come on love, I mean do you want a single or a return?' So of course she laughed and apologised, she said 'I'm sorry, I thought you were trying to chat me up.'

Once in a while you do have a bit of real excitement, specially if your route's in what we call 'Cowboy Land'. Those are well-known trouble spots, when there's a bit of tension it's not uncommon for people there to go for the buses as some form of protest. Why the buses I don't know, maybe we're seen as the possessions of those who rule: you'd have to ask them. I've had my bus hijacked twice and set on fire. I've never myself felt personally threatened though: they're usually very concerned to make it clear to you it's your bus they're after, not you. A year or so back now I was up towards Turf Lodge around 10.30 one night, and there was a young lad about twelve, waiting at a request stop with his hand up. Soon as I pulled in, he stepped back and out of a shop doorway came three men in balaclavas carrying pickaxe handles in their hands. They ordered everybody off the bus, and in that kind of situation you don't argue. There was just me and two passengers, so out we got with me carrying my money box with the fares in it. I'd gone only a few steps along the pavement when two big young lads appeared from nowhere and started jostling me, telling me to give them my box. I'm no hero and I did. But when the three in balaclava helmets saw what had happened, they went for the lads and told them to give me the money back. One of them actually apologised to me, he told me they weren't thieves, they didn't hold with that sort of behaviour. They gave me the box back, then they threw petrol all round inside the empty bus and set it on fire.

That was a bit of an uneasy incident I suppose I'd say. But then there was another one six months ago where I couldn't help but laugh. Same sort of thing to start with, stopped my bus late at night and made me get out: and that time I hadn't any passengers, there was only me. Again it was three or four chaps in balaclavas, and then the usual business throwing the petrol around inside the bus. But then they were searching through their pockets, and eventually the leader of them said to me 'Have you got a match or a cigarette lighter or something, none of us smoke?' I said 'No I'm sorry, I don't smoke either.' So they hung about and the first person who came along was an old man, and they asked him and he gave them one so they could set the bus on fire. Afterwards when I got back to the depot and was making out my report about what had happened, I left that out because I thought no one'd believe it.

Buses are, you know, they've always been my life. In fact if I'd not been a bus driver I'd never have met my wife. She used to be a regular passenger on one of the routes I was working at the time, fifteen years ago. You know how it is, you get to know somebody you're used to seeing and you get talking: then you find after a bit if they're not at the stop when you expect them to be, you start to wonder what's happened to them. She told me later she'd been the same: she told me more than once she'd let a bus go by if I wasn't the driver of it. So it was buses brought us together, there's no arguing about that: now sometimes she says it's buses are going to drive us apart, because I'll never refuse the offer of an extra turn. That's true and it's not just for the money, I like to have a professional approach to my job. If you're a bus driver, it's the same as being a policeman or a servant of the public of any kind: you put their interests first, and if a driver hasn't turned up and you're around, you step in and help out. I'm married to the job she says: but always with a smile. It's brought us together and it's kept us together and allowed us to have a decent standard of living and bring up our two kids, and they're both doing well at school. I don't know if you've heard of it but we send them to Lagan College: we don't want our kids growing up in a society forever at war with itself on religious matters. We hope they'll grow up tolerant about other people's ideas and respect them so in the future everyone gets on with one another, that's our big hope.

It's been my pleasure. If you're in the city and you see me driving by, give me a wave: and I'll look out for you. All the very best to you now.

Gerry Peel,

delinquent

The magistrate said it was a bad case. This sixteen-year old boy had been given probation, but he'd not taken advantage of the leniency of the Court: and here he was again, in front of the Bench after only two months, on a further charge. It was against his better judgement, he said, but he would continue the supervision order. But this was definitely the youth's last chance, and he hoped he realised it.

Gerry nodded his head emphatically that he did. Small, with wispy fair hair and hazel eyes, he wore a threadbare black bomber jacket, tattered jeans, and an old pair of high-top trainers.

– I was dead lucky there eh, I thought the old bloke was going to send me away you know. I think he recognised me from when I was in front of him before: they had that report, I mean that social-background report thing that was made for them, I think that's what probably done it to make him give me another chance. She's all right that Eileen, if you've got to have a probation officer over you she's as good as you'll get. Some of the others, from what I've heard I wouldn't like them to be in charge of me I wouldn't, that's for sure. Like now I mean, letting us sit and have a chat in her office, there's not a lot of them would do that.

She told me once she thought I had a future. She said if I could just get myself settled down and grow up, I'd be OK. She used to know my brother: she said she'd far more hope for me than she had for him. He went over the water with his girl to Liverpool, and it was only six weeks and he was in trouble there again. The last I heard of him was he was in HMP Walton, that's in Liverpool isn't it? Me, I wouldn't be doing anything stupid like that for sure I wouldn't, I'm

staying here in Belfast. I don't like living in a hostel place with all
young kids, but it's better than a prison in Liverpool, you can't argue
with that.

Eileen says she doesn't think I'm the criminal type. She's a good
judge of character, I think: I don't think I'm a criminal type either. I
mean there's a lot worse things I could be doing isn't there than a bit
of thieving from toy shops? It's not as though I want things for
myself: there's this lad I know sells them on for me. I mean you've
got to earn yourself a living haven't you? Eileen's told me if she can
get me on to one of those training courses, I'll have to stop thieving.
I've told her if she does I will. It's a sort of an agreement. The only
thing is the money's something terrible it is, I mean I'd have to give
up smokes to start. Still, I'd have to do that if I went away wouldn't
I, so it's the same difference isn't it?

I don't think I've got a father, or a mother. I don't really know
much about it: all I can remember of my life has been children's
homes, places like that. They're not so bad once you get used to
them: there's good ones and bad ones, you take your chance. Some
of them I've heard about, I've not been in them myself but they're
pretty terrible from all I hear. The best one I was in was one in
County Antrim: there was only six of us, it was in charge of a
minister and his wife, Mr and Mrs McIntyre they were called. They
were Presbyterians but nice people, you know what I mean? You can
get funny people running places like that, you've read about them in
the newspapers. I've had nothing of that sort if you know what I
mean, I've been lucky.

There was one man used to come there, I'm not saying anything
against him you know, but he was one of those you get sometimes in
those places, takes an interest in young boys. Don't get me wrong,
I'm only saying he was perhaps a lonely man or something. We all
used to wonder hadn't he got a home of his own, why did he come
every Tuesday evening and sit there talking to us, telling us jokes and
asking us to call him 'Uncle Sid'? He was a policeman: a funny sort
of man, he'd ask you whether you'd been saved? If you said no, then
he'd bring you religious pamphlets to read and tell you to pass them
on among the others.

I always think all the police are a funny lot you know. I've not ever
met one wasn't what you'd call peculiar: they seem to look at you in

a way that makes you feel they're looking through you, if you've done something wrong you'd better tell them about it. One I know, if I see him on the street sometimes he always gives me a big smile and stops and has a chat. He told me a funny thing once: he said if I ever told him anything that was of help to the police, he'd write it down on my file at the station, he said it'd go well for me the next time I was in trouble. Somebody says something like that to you, you feel it's almost worthwhile making something up for them, don't you?

I suppose he was meaning something to do with the paramilitaries I should think. That's all they seem to be interested in these days. Wherever you go there's all these little notices isn't there, have you seen them? It's a man in a balaclava, and underneath it says if you see something suspicious you should ring this confidential phone number that they give. I tried it once to see what happened: the first thing the man who answered the phone said to me was what was my name and where was I telephoning from? I can't see that's much help if they really want genuine information, I mean who's going to stick their neck out like that?

For myself, I'd say people like the paramilitaries make things more difficult for you. I'm not one for all this religious business, I'm just what you'd call your ordinary common or garden small-time thief. I don't want to be a millionaire or anything, I wouldn't go in for planning bank robberies or anything stupid like that: but if I see something worth having I'll have it, that's the way I'd put it. You can earn a good honest decent living if you're sensible, just taking things that come your way. I mean this morning in this Court it was toys. I don't know if that old magistrate feller thought I haven't grown up or what, but you'd have thought he'd been able to see it was obvious I wasn't into it for myself. I mean Action Man, Batman, I'm a bit old for all that aren't I? And what would I be wanting with a carton of Barbie dolls? Only he didn't seem to think that far did he? Obvious you're supplying the market stalls isn't it?

It's the same with some of the police sometimes too. They won't have it you're not supplying goods for sale so you can make a living: they're always trying to turn it round to make out you're connected with the UFF. One of them at Burton Street RUC station, he said to me these days nobody went thieving just to make a living, there was always a political background to it. I said to him I'd not got no idea what he was talking about, and that was true it was. Funny some people are though, he just shook his head and said he didn't believe me.

You can get into very serious trouble if they try and fix you up with something. What they do is kind of blackmail you: they tell you they'll overlook it this time, but you'd better find out something good for them by the end of next week, like who's in charge of the people you're working for. All the time they've got this idea the whole of crime goes back to the racketeers in the paramilitaries. For all I know they may be right, only I don't want to know, do I? I mean I'm trying to keep myself to myself and make my own way in the world aren't I?

Brenda Ferguson,

refugee

She sat on the hard red plastic typist's chair in the corner of the barely furnished front room, clasping and unclasping her hands between her knees. A thin white-faced woman in a threadbare cotton T-shirt and jeans.

– I mean you won't say where we are or anything as well as not my name will you? Some of the others said it wasn't safe to talk to anyone in case they recognised you afterwards, or if they told someone. I'm sorry, I know this sounds a jumble: but I'm nervous about it, you've got to think of the others who are here too, they don't like people knowing where it is.

I don't know where to start really. I'm thirty-two and I don't live here in this house. I was born in Belfast, I'll just say the east part of Belfast shall I so that it wouldn't identify it? I went to school there, I was supposed to be the clever one in the family: I had two sisters older than me but my daddy always said I was the one who was going to be a big success. He was proud of my singing, he used to take me to clubs where they had kids' competitions: I never won big prizes, but he was always talking as though I was going to be a star. I never had any ideas myself of doing that, I was a quiet type: if I ever thought about where I was going I suppose I had in my head the idea I might like to be a teacher of some sort. I used to think the teachers at our school were wonderful: they were all very nice and they seemed to know such a lot about all sorts of things. I thought they were very clever and I'd like to be like they were.

When I was sixteen my mammy went off with another man and it really broke my daddy up, it did. He took to the drink. I stayed home to look after him and my sisters, so what with that and every other thing, it turned out it was the end of my education. I was always thinking things would get better, I'd be able to go to college or something but it never turned out that way. A woman who was a friend of my daddy's moved into our house and I didn't like her very much. I don't think she was very keen either on having three young girls about the place: she was always complaining we were untidy, we stayed out too late, all we thought about was going to discos. It was no happy home life I had, I think that was why I married when I'd just gone eighteen.

I'd sooner not give the name to my husband, not even a made-up one. He was older than I was by about ten years. He didn't have a job or anything. Sometimes I used to wonder had he been married before: I don't know why I thought that, he never talked in a way that made me think about it, it was just his attitude somehow. I mean he always had the idea it was a woman's place to do everything for him just as he wanted, cook his meals, have them on the table ready when he came home from the snooker hall. I thought I was lucky with him though because he didn't drink. A lot of girls find themselves husbands who spend all their time in the clubs and the pubs, but he didn't. Now I think of it, that was something used to frighten me about him.

I'm going on too fast. We had three children, a boy more or less straight after we were married, then a girl, then another girl. The eldest boy, he's at a special school now because he was in a lot of trouble: and one girl's living with my sister, and the youngest somewhere else. I'd rather not say where.

I was too young to know any better when we got married. Everybody I knew round where we lived, none of the girls had boyfriends or husbands in a steady job. They were all unemployed, so there didn't seem anything unusual about my husband other than he didn't drink. Nearly all the others drank a lot but he never touched it.

Talking about him's like bringing him back to me again. I know it sounds like I'm mad but I've got to the state I feel if I can put him out of my mind it's a safeguard thing and he won't come back.

He first started hitting me on my birthday. The reason I remember it is when I came twenty-one I thought we might have a special meal. We lived with his brother and his wife, we'd two rooms in their house: she was very nice, I liked her. When she knew I was going to be twenty-one she said we'd cook something or get a Chinese take-away because we all liked that. On the morning of my birthday, after my husband had gone to sign on she told me he'd said there was nothing to celebrate, all he wanted was his meal should be ready when he came back. So I had it on the table: I thought he might perhaps bring me a present but he didn't. He just came in, it was seven o'clock in the evening and I'd put the kids to bed. He'd hardly come in the door when we started having an argument. I can't even remember what it was about. He started shouting and swearing at me and I said I was sorry for whatever it was I'd done. So then he just raised his hand like that and hit me across the face. He nearly knocked me off my feet with it. He said 'There you are, that's your birthday present, you're old enough for me to hit you now.' I've never known properly what he meant by that.

I've never known from one minute to the next afterwards what he was going to start knocking me about for. When we quarrelled he'd say 'I've had enough', and I always knew what that meant, that he was going to hit me then. Other times when he came in I'd think if I didn't say anything we couldn't quarrel, so whatever he started on about I'd stay silent. He'd hit me then and say it was because I wasn't speaking to him.

The one thing I'll say about my husband is he never laid a finger on the children and he never hit me in front of them. But sometimes he'd tell me I should get them to bed: I always knew that was leading up to, he was going to start beating me. Sometimes he hit me with a stick he'd got from somewhere. I never screamed or anything because of the children. Sometimes there'd be periods of a couple of months when he never did anything: I used to start to think if there was something wrong with him he'd got over it and everything'd be all right. I remember one night I tried to talk to him, I asked him why he hit me. He'd not done it for three months, I thought that would be a good time to try to have a discussion about it. He said he only hit me when I deserved it, and if I didn't want him to do it I should try to be a better wife. I never knew what he meant by that, I always let him do what he liked with me and I always tried to keep a neat and clean home for him. I'm sorry, it just makes me cry to talk about it.

Just before last Christmas my sister-in-law said to me she was going to take me to town shopping. When we were there in the afternoon she said she was going to take me somewhere to meet someone. She wouldn't say what it was about, and we went to this sort of unoccupied shop: it was what they call an advice centre just for women. She came inside with me and a dark-haired woman said to me to sit down and my sister-in-law went off. The woman locked the door and she told me my sister-in-law had spoken to her about me and the problems with my husband. I wasn't sure who she was, I was very frightened at first: but she made me a cup of tea and said if I felt I could tell her about myself she might be able to help me. I was so scared I couldn't talk at all to begin with: she said if I didn't want to say anything it was all right, I should just drink the cup of tea and that would be all.

The outcome of it all was she said she could get me a place here to stay for a while. It's called a refuge for battered wives and nobody's supposed to know where it is or who's here. I've been here three months now but I've no idea yet what's going to happen. Arrangements have been made for my kids temporarily. I heard my husband had been trying to find me, but I've moved on twice to different places so I don't think he'll be able to. I can't tell you much more, except to say I really think there's something wrong with my husband, only I don't want to go on living with him like I was.

I've talked to one or two other women here: some of them have had a much worse time than me. One told me about a woman who'd been here, her husband was a Protestant paramilitary: the organisation he belonged to promised her they'd look after her and they did. They gave her money and found her somewhere to live with the wife of one of the other members of the organisation. They said their organisation didn't want to get a bad name for having someone in it who maltreated his wife. I wish my husband had been involved in something like that: maybe then I wouldn't have ended up like I am now, not knowing where I'm going to go or what I'm going to do.

You will be careful won't you that you don't say anything about me that anybody could guess what my name was or where I was?

Anna Whitely,

waitress

After closing-time she brought two cups of tea to a corner table at the back of the little transport cafe where she worked. A small woman with short curly brown hair and green eyes, she spoke in a low harsh voice, intense and fierce and cold.

– You see them on the TV sometimes don't you? People who've lost someone who was very close to them, their husband or son or brother or sister? They say things like they don't feel any bitterness, they forgive whoever was responsible and hope there'll be no killing in retaliation. I just don't know how they do it: I don't feel like that at all, not me. I'm full of bitterness and full of hate: and the longer time goes on and nothing's done to bring the person responsible to trial, the only effect of it's to increase my hate every day and night. I hate the British Army, I hate the British Government and I hate everyone else who's doing nothing but covering it all up and hoping it'll go away. Well it won't, not while I've still got a breath left in my body it won't, I can tell you that.

The British Army, your British Army, they killed my husband: and not just that, they murdered him in cold blood. I don't want retaliation, I just want justice. Somewhere there's a soldier who did it and he's walking around free. He knows who he is, and so do a lot of other people: but so far no one will punish him for it or even bring him to trial. That's what the Director of Public Prosecutions goes on saying and saying: that no further steps are going to be taken.

People say to me 'Why don't you grieve Anna, why don't you cry when you talk about Joe's death?' They don't understand I don't because I can't. My mind's full of hatred and determination to do something about it, so there's no room for grief. When the soldier's brought to trial and punished for what he did, then I'll grieve, but not until. I will get justice one day, however long it takes: and that's the day I'll start to grieve, but only then.

– Joe wasn't anybody special, he was a nobody, or that's the way a lot of people would look at him. He wasn't a good man, he wasn't a saint: but then he wasn't a very bad man either. The worst thing anybody could say about him was he was a small-time criminal, and not very good at it. And the worst anybody could say about me is although we lived together for thirteen years, I was only what's called his common-law wife, our union hadn't been sanctified in a church. Two ordinary people I suppose we were, that's all. But ordinary people make up the world don't they? And ordinary people have rights just like anybody else, but they don't always get them. If you're special and you've got money it's easy to get justice: but if you don't have money and you're not important, then it's not. Only that doesn't mean you won't get it in the end: I believe you will, and that's what's keeping me going and always will.

Joe was an orphan. I knew him all my life. As long as I can remember there was always Joe. He was a boy who lived at the bottom of the street. I don't know exactly what his background was because he never talked about it very much. I knew he'd been brought up in a children's home somewhere outside Belfast: but since he never talked about it, I never asked him questions. One day when we met in the street he told me he shouldn't really be there. He should have been in the children's home but he'd run away from it because he didn't like it. Sometimes I've thought about him telling me it: I wondered why, because he didn't need to. Perhaps it was a test for me, like he wanted to find out whether he could trust me. He told me and he said he was going over to England on the night ferry that night, so he wouldn't get caught. I can remember it just like it was yesterday. I said 'I'd like to come with you. Can I?' He didn't seem at all surprised at me asking, he just nodded and said yes if I wanted to, as though it was the most ordinary thing in the world. So that was it and we went to Liverpool and then to Manchester. Both of us were sixteen. A lot of people would say wouldn't they we were young and foolish? But it wasn't like that. We had each other and that seemed to be all that mattered.

We travelled around, and we made out. Sometimes Joe got casual work and sometimes I did. It wouldn't be the sort of life a lot of people would think was what they wanted, but it suited us. We lived a free existence, free of everything and everybody else. At times you look back and you wonder how you could have been happy: but I've looked back often and I've never had that wondering. I was happy with Joe, he was all I wanted.

We stayed about two years in the north of England, content with ourselves but never really properly thinking about what we were doing, if you know what I mean. Joe wasn't a very reliable person when it came to work: he did a bit of thieving, but he was never into anything else, not serious crime of any sort. Until one day, I don't know properly how it came about, but he was mixed up with some other young men and they all got sent to Borstal for three years. It seemed like the end of the world: and it was the end of the world in a way for me. If I couldn't be with Joe there was no real life for me anywhere at all. So I came back here: I remember it was like the ending of a last chapter in a book. I thought everything was finished and when I went to see Joe in Borstal he felt the same. We knew we couldn't be together any more, so I'd have to try and begin again, and start a life of my own.

I tried not to think of him and not to think of us as a pair any more: and one of the ways I did it was to get married to the first man who asked me. I don't regret it, it wasn't foolish because it wasn't on the spur of the moment: it was a serious sensible attempt to start a new life. His name was Michael and he was a good man and a steady worker. We were both still young. I told him about Joe and he understood and said it was up to me whether I forgot about him and started again, or whether I wanted to wait. I said no I didn't want to wait, so we were married.

Well, that lasted for twelve years, and we had three children. I won't say I forgot about Joe because I didn't, but I forgot about the idea of spending the whole of my life with him. I decided instead to be as good a wife to Michael as I could. And I was. But then he was killed. I don't talk about this very often to anyone because I try not to think about it. He was shot, he was shot in the street: I don't know to this day who did it or why, because he wasn't political in any way, he was just an ordinary straightforward man. I've always thought what was done to him was a mistake by those who did it: I think they thought he was someone else. I hope I don't sound cold about it: I'm not, I liked him very much, he was a good husband to me and a good father to the children. If he hadn't died when he did and how he did, I know in my heart we'd still be together today, because by then I'd put Joe out of my mind, I really had.

After it happened I went to live for a while with my sister in west Belfast. If you're a person from a poor background and never had very much money, you take the troubles and sorrows and difficulties and unfairnesses of life as something that happens, that you put up with as part of everyday life. Besides I had my three girls to look after, so they were what I concentrated on.

Then I had a big surprise: only just a few months after Michael was killed I was walking home from doing the shopping one day, and I couldn't believe my eyes because there standing in front of me on the pavement was Joe. But also at the same time it wasn't something that I found surprising: in a way I almost expected it. Does that make sense? When we talked about it years later, he said he'd been looking for me, and he'd known one day we should come face to face. There was that kind of relationship between us that a lot of people wouldn't understand, because you can't explain it. It's like somebody's placed in your life, and no matter what you do or where you go you can't avoid coming together with them again. So there it was, we were brought together once more and it was normal and natural we should resume our partnership. We found a little house and Joe moved in.

I've already said it I know, but I'll say it again: Joe wasn't anybody special. He wasn't any different all those years later than he'd been from when I first knew him. He'd never married, he'd never changed his ways and grown up, and he'd never settled down to an ordinary straight way of life. Basically he was still thoughtless and foolish, and work was something I don't think he'd ever even contemplated. He'd done a lot of prison sentences, but what I'm saying is proved by them: they were all short, six months, three months, four months, every one of them short sentences like that. No big crimes and no big punishments, do you see what I mean? In all his life the longest time he'd ever been inside was nine months. I didn't have any fancy ideas about changing him or altering his ways, I knew that couldn't happen: only in the last three years of his life, that was the longest time he'd ever spent consecutively without going to prison. I'm not claiming I was reforming him or that he was reforming himself. I'm not claiming anything for Joe. I knew what he was like: but he was my man, and I accepted him just as he was.

And then there came that night. They came and told me he was dead because he'd been shot in the street by the British Army. It was about eight o'clock, and neighbours and friends, they all came to tell me what had happened to Joe. The RUC didn't come to tell me, and not the Army either. After all who was I and what was I? I was nothing but his common-law wife, wasn't I? He'd been shot trying to carry out the sort of event he'd taken part in before: attempted robbery of a shop. Two of his mates went inside, and he sat outside in the car waiting to drive them away when they came out. They came out running: and they ran straight into two passing soldiers in plain clothes, who straight away pulled out revolvers and shot them dead. Then one of them ran over to Joe and put his gun to his head and shot him dead. He was defenceless, he wasn't carrying a weapon of any kind and he wasn't trying to drive away: and yet that man, that soldier, he shot him dead. The autopsy report said the gun had been less than twenty-four inches away from his head when it was fired: that killed him, and then the soldier stepped back and put another five bullets into his body as well.

I sit here and tell you about it quite coldly as though I felt nothing about it, don't I? But I'm not cold about it inside: inside, hate's eating me up, it's festering inside me here all the time. My Joe was murdered in cold blood by you British. When someone's had someone close to them murdered, how can they not feel hatred? How can they say they'll forget it and go on with their everyday lives and not ask for revenge? There was an official enquiry into Joe's death by the Army: and what it resulted in eventually was a statement by the Director of Public Prosecutions. It said no further action was to be taken against the soldier responsible. That's all, no admission of guilt, not even one word of regret.

I'm only human, and I feel what anyone else who something like this happened to would feel. Today in Belfast there are men walking round with guns in their pockets who're licensed to kill. They're British. I don't mean it personally so I won't say it loud, but what I feel about the British I'll leave to your imagination. And I'll go on feeling it, I can tell you, until justice is done. When the man who murdered Joe is named and tried and punished for it, then I'll be satisfied: but not until. For as long as I live it's going to occupy my whole life waiting for that to happen: my hatred and anger, they'll never go away.

11 *The Army*

Jack Henry, bomb-disposal squad

Adrian Nevin, Major

Gary Parkin, Corporal

Heather Wood, Sergeant's wife

Colin Archer, Lieutenant, UDR

(Only after a long delay did the Army authorities agree to interviewing of (their) selected personnel: and only on condition that it was carried out in the presence of a 'minder' who tape-recorded the tape-recorded interviewing. An undertaking had to be given that they could censor any parts they wished to: and a further condition was that these conditions should not be mentioned.)

Jack Henry,

bomb-disposal squad

We talked in an afternoon, in a rest room in a Nissan hut: it had bare walls, but comfortable sofas and armchairs. The rain poured down unremittingly outside. Relaxed, he smiled as he chatted: his voice was quiet and firm and calm. On his olive-green sweater was a large embroidered cartoon-badge of Felix the Cat.

– I've been in the Army twelve years now. I'd always been interested in the idea of a career in the military, but when I first left school I toyed with the idea of working in a lab, because I liked chemistry. I'm not sure why, but eventually I chose the Army instead. I fancied myself driving a tank or something like that, but at the local recruiting office they suggested me being an ammunition technician, which is what I am now. It's somebody who deals with anything in the way of ammunition at all from bullets to guided missiles: the actual bomb-disposal side of things comes in as a sort of spin-off.

I've always been the sort of person who's basically curious, I like to know technically how things work and why things happen, and I get a lot of satisfaction when I've found out. My son takes after me, funnily enough. So far we've just the one child, a boy of three: he's curious and enquiring-minded too. My wife's an accountant. At the moment she's being a housewife and mother in Germany where I'm presently stationed, and I'm over here on my third tour, six months unaccompanied. I've just finished one month of it. The first tour I was Number Two in a disposal team, on the next I worked at the depot, and now I'm in a team again, this time as the Number One.

I like the work and I find it personally very rewarding, which is probably because of my basic curiosity I was saying about. Every time you're called out you go into an unknown situation, and until you get there you've not the faintest idea what you're going to find or how you're going to deal with it. If what you do results in the end in the safety of yourself and your team and everyone else in the area including the civilian population, well then obviously that's very satisfying.

I don't think I've ever yet been scared, no. Your whole training is aimed at teaching you to think clearly and take quick decisions about the correct way to deal with whatever the situation is. You have to make a very rapid appreciation of it: so when your mind's working like that almost automatically, as it's trained to do, you don't really have time to think about being scared. The main thing is you learn by your mistakes, and you don't make them twice. On your training course they put all the mistakes there for you to make, and when you do you learn from them and they stick in your mind. An example for instance would be putting two devices near to each other and encouraging you to feel the one you've dealt with has made everything safe. That's the kind of learning experience no amount of theory'll ever get over to you.

But you still do sometimes get a bit slack, you can't help it, it's human nature I suppose. For instance not long ago there was an explosion in a disused flat in west Belfast that I went to with the team, and afterwards I felt if I'd been in the same sort of situation again I might have approached it in a better way. I went delving into the area where the explosion had been and I rather quickly pulled out some bits of a device: reflecting afterwards about it I felt that wasn't quite the way I should have gone about it, because I didn't absolutely and exactly know what it was I was pulling out. There wasn't anything else there, but there could have been: or perhaps the device might not have fully gone off before I touched the bits. Anyway I was lucky and I'm still here. All the same it's still on my mind: like everyone else in the job I don't want to end up just another number on a sheet of statistics.

As I say though, I do like the job, very much indeed. It's never routine and you never know what each day's going to bring. You might be called out first thing, and again later, twice or three times in one day, in the evening, or at night: or you might simply spend a whole twenty-four hours sitting around drinking coffee and dozing. And there's always that sort of excitement about not knowing what you're going to find. A call-out might be a hoax, about thirty per cent of them are: but you mustn't make your mind up about it first, it could be dangerous if you start having gut feelings about it. Until it's absolutely and definitely proved to be one, your presumption has always to be that it's real. It's only when you've actually looked at the situation itself that you can say with any degree of certainty if it's a hoax or not.

We don't get a lot of time off: we're on a shift system with the other teams, but if you are not on an immediate response team you'll be on the back-up, which means you have to be ready within thirty minutes. As you can get two or more calls in quick succession though, you can't always afford even that amount of time before you go. At the moment we're getting I'd say about eight or ten calls a week, but the figure doesn't mean much: you can have two days when nothing happens, then two days when you get five calls on each one.

When I've time, most of my relaxation is done in one of two ways. I'm not a great one for reading or the TV, but I like model-making, out of plastic kits. At the moment I've just finished and I'm now painting a set of soldiers in a bomb disposal team. The other and more important way I relax though is I write to my wife and child every day without fail: about what we've been doing, how things are going, anything and everything that's in my mind. It passes the time, and it helps me feel close to her and our boy.

So, that's about it really, that's my story. The badge of Felix the Cat? Oh, we all wear these because he's supposed to have nine lives, isn't he? Me? Well I'd say I think so far I've only used up one.

Adrian Nevin,

Major

We talked in the evening in front of the fire in the warm comfortable sitting-room of his house. A sturdily-built man, fair-haired and blue-eyed, from time to time he touched his finger-tips together under his chin while he paused and thought.

– Well, I've been in the Army for eighteen years, and this is my one two three four five, good Lord, sixth tour of duty in Northern Ireland. So far I've been here on this occasion for almost two years. My wife's here with me, we live in this rather nice estate of houses inside the perimeter of an army base, and we have our two children with us, they're both boys, one four and the other one two. I actually came to Northern Ireland right at the beginning, immediately I was commissioned: I joined my battalion where they were then stationed, in the south of the Province near the border. Being there that first time was an experience which to be perfectly honest I can't recall in any great detail.

I've been of course in several other parts of the world during my service, and I must say I've found wherever I was and whatever I was doing, it was always something that was challenging and rewarding. I don't come from an Army background, as a matter of fact my original ambition when I was at school was to be a vet, but my academic qualifications weren't good enough. It was the careers adviser at the public school where I was who suggested I considered joining the Army and going for a commission. In a way being a public school boarder prepares you I think quite well for army life, it gives you certain advantages to begin with, which you can build on. At the moment we don't have to make a decision about it yet, but my wife Jenny and I have already discussed quite a lot whether we feel it'd be best for our own children to go to boarding-schools. That's providing we can afford it of course: the fees now are absolutely horrendous. But if you have the sort of life we do, where you have to be prepared for regular moving and family separation, then it's one way of giving them at least a degree of continuity and security. My wife was at boarding-school herself, so I think we're both well aware of the advantages and disadvantages. Mind you, by the time the boys get to that sort of age, goodness know where we'll be.

We've been extraordinarily lucky so far: I don't think we've ever been separated longer than a couple of months or so since we got married eight years ago. This education business is a problem which faces all soldiers: whatever solution they choose for their children, no one I've ever met arrives at a decision about it without a great deal of careful thought, because of course it's important for the family as a whole, and particularly for the children's future.

A difficulty which often does arise is that in many instances you can never be certain of your own future. Army life nowadays is not just endless routine without disruption, and a pension at the end of it. I've spent a good part of my time in Germany, and was able to have my family with me there: then on more than one occasion when I've been here, they've been able to join me because we could to a certain extent foresee a period of stability. But this doesn't at all mean things will remain like that for ever. As different situations arise throughout the world, our role requires different sorts of presence: and I don't know what particular kind of job I'll be doing. As a soldier I go where I'm needed and as a result of the demands of whatever the particular situation is.

What I'm currently doing here could roughly be described as administration: but not long ago I was on operations on the border. That's something I've done more than once, sometimes for almost as long as a year. It's the sort of work which is very different from anything else, and I can't think of anywhere at the moment where you'd experience anything like it. In the Gulf War for example you had a situation where armies were in conflict facing each other, which isn't in any way similar to the situation here. In the border area the only thing predictable was the total unpredictability of the situation. It was very taxing and very stretching, and required a good deal of mental flexibility. You could never afford to take anything for granted about what the enemy was going to do next, or how. It was harder for soldiers' wives too: they couldn't be with them, and couldn't be told much about exactly where we were or what we were doing. My wife's told me all the wives were very supportive to one another, but it must have been very difficult for them.

It wasn't possible then, but it has been before and afterwards, for us to have quite a nice life here. Whenever we go home to the mainland for a break, people are always asking us what it's like to be serving over here: and well, one has to say that for quite long periods life is absolutely normal. Occasionally I'm able to go out for a day's shooting, or we go to the races or something of that sort, and we've made a large circle of friends. Obviously one keeps a low profile and doesn't go out of one's way to look for trouble: you don't go sight-seeing round some of the areas of Belfast where sections of the population are not entirely friendly to the Army, for example. And soldiers off duty don't go to any places where they'll be conspicuous by their appearance and the way they talk, with of course an English accent. Terrorists are on the lookout always for off-duty soldiers or off-duty policemen: so it makes sense to confine one's travels to areas where there isn't too much likelihood of being in danger. You can't ever forget the possibility of it, that's ever-present.

I must say though that the kindness and generosity of local people constantly amazes me. When people say as they often do on meeting you 'You must come and have lunch with us' or 'Do come round and have a drink', they really mean it. In England it's said without any great conviction, but here it's not unusual for an invitation to be followed by a telephone call a couple of days later to fix a date. This is something we'll miss very much when we go back: we'll be leaving so many friends. But on the other side of the coin, one undoubtedly feels more relaxed in England: you can mix with people in shops or on special occasions without bothering very much about whether they're wondering whether you're in the Army or not, and possibly passing it on if they know you are. It's nice occasionally to have a break from that feeling.

Gary Parkin,

Corporal

A round-faced young man with brown eyes and cropped hair, he talked rapidly and enthusiastically about Army life in a flat-vowelled northern-accented voice.

– It's really great, the Army, but it were a bit of a joke really, how I come to be in it in the first place. I were down the town one day with me sister where we lived, and there were an Army Careers Office in the High Street: and as we was passing it she said to me 'I bet you daren't join the Army.' And I said 'I bet I dare', so she said 'All right then, go on' so I said 'All right I will' and I went straight in and got the application forms and filled them in and that were it. You do your tests and have your interviews in the next few weeks, and then a few months later there I was at the depot on my basic training.

At the time I first applied I was coming up to nineteen, and I'd got a job of sorts but it weren't very much of a one. I was driving a tractor for a local market gardening firm, and I couldn't see how it was going to get me anywhere: the wages was bad, there wasn't anything in it that really interested me, and it didn't feel as though it was the sort that was going to last long anyhow. So that was really about all there was to it as to how I came to join up. And now here I am five years afterwards, married with two kids, and I don't regret it one bit and I never have. It's an interesting life, full of variety, and as far as I can see I'll make it my future, well certainly for the next few years at least.

Coming here to Belfast is my first posting, I've been here two months, and it's the longest so far my wife and I've been separated since I joined. Before we got married I asked her what she thought about the idea of being the wife of a soldier: we talked it over, what it would mean, me going away and that, and she said she thought probably it was something she could get used to. In a lot of ways the advantages to it outweigh the disadvantages. I've got steady money coming in all the time, and it's quite good money: we've got housing that the Army provides for us, and all right so even if I do have to be away from time to time, that's not the worst thing could happen to someone is it? During my training and the rest of it I was away on courses, or on exercises sometimes for a few weeks: not as long as this has been, but you learn to adjust to it. At the moment the wife's back at her mother's which helps her feel not so lonely as she might on her own. I phone her up twice a week, and as far as I can make out she's doing OK. I don't think separation's going to be a big problem to us: it's part of what you accept as Army life when you join, and it's the same for everybody isn't it?

Of course it was a bit of a shock and she wasn't too keen at all when I told her my first posting was to be Northern Ireland. Nor was I you know, if I'm going to be honest about it. Beforehand you imagine it's going to be incidents all the time, but you get a different idea of what it's really like when you come here. It's not really like you thought, on the whole it's mostly like what you might call ordinary life. It's partly because your training for it is how to deal with incidents and situations you might be in, so of course you think that's how it's all going to be when you get here. But after you've experienced what it's really like for about three weeks or so, you calm down and take things as they come. I didn't let on to the wife about it, but at first I was a bit worried myself and got a few butterflies: but I think she's beginning to realise by now from what I'm writing in my letters to her that it's not too bad. Once you've got here you're kept busy, you've had your training which has put a lot of confidence into you, you talk to other blokes you meet who've been here a while, and so like I say you get the whole thing into perspective.

There's some who find it very exciting just to be here, but I'm not one of them. They say it's 'proper soldiering', by which I suppose they mean there's a certain danger to it. But I don't see it that way. To me it's my job to be here so I'll do it to the best of my ability. After you've been out on vehicle patrol or foot patrol in the streets a few times, you think nothing of it. Most of the people you meet are pleasant and friendly, they smile at you and say 'Good morning'. That makes you realise you're not in an enemy country where people are out to get you all the time: most times and on the whole you're amongst friends.

Of course you will get the odd person or two who's going to be difficult and not friendly, but you have to learn from experience and watching how other soldiers do it, what's the best way to deal with that. You soon pick it up. If you always start by being polite to people and not aggressive, that'll get you a long way. When you're doing a 'P Check', which is a personal check when you ask people their name and address and date of birth and so on, they're obliged to give you them under the Emergency Powers Act. If someone decides they're not going to co-operate you call over the nearest RUC man to deal with it. But on the whole most people are reasonable about it, and I've never had any serious trouble.

One of the chief nuisances we have sometimes is little kids: only knee-high you know, a lot of them, and their parents put them up to throwing bricks at soldiers. I don't understand the mentality of people like that, I've even heard some of them will give their kids a quid to do it. But you do meet kids who're friendly and like to talk with you too: and so long as they don't touch your weapon, you can let them have a look at it, give them a squint down the sights and the rest of it, so they come to realise the soldiers are their friends.

I'd say on the whole that as long as you always keep up your concentration one hundred per cent when you're out, and remember every minute of the time your life depends on you doing it, then you'll be OK. To me the best part's going out on street patrol now, specially if I'm doing what we call top cover: that's when you're in a vehicle standing up by the side of your mate with your heads out of the roof of it, him looking one side and you the other. It's really interesting and so long as you keep up your concentration, that's the most important part. Mind you, there's some lads who if they see a pretty girl walking along, they do spend a bit too much time with their eyes in one direction, looking at her legs instead of keeping lookout everywhere all round. Not me though, I'd never do such a thing as that of course, ever.

What's drummed into you in your training, and the thing you have to keep in your mind all the time is the unusualness of this situation here. As a fighting soldier you'd normally expect to be face to face with your enemy and try to kill him before he kills you. But here though it's not like that. The enemy doesn't wear a uniform, he doesn't move in battle formations, and you've no way of ever telling who he is, or where he is. Even when you're talking with kids, you've still got to keep in your mind that somebody might have his eyes on you at that very moment and be waiting for his chance to shoot you or one of your mates if you drop your guard. There's nowhere else in the British Isles that's as dangerous like that as it is in Belfast.

I don't regret the day my sister made me that bet. I think it were a good thing she said it and I took her up on it. I've felt much more grown-up ever since, I've got a better idea what I want out of life and how to get it. Security, professionalism, and a feeling of job satisfaction and pride in yourself: those are the things that matter. How long I'll stay in I don't know, but I should think it'll be a good length of time. I'll never get anything like as good a job outside the Army, things being like they are now, will I?

Heather Wood,

Sergeant's wife

Her small neat semi-detached house was no different from any of the others in the long quiet side road in the council estate. She was tall and dark-haired, and wore a red roll-necked sweater and jeans.

– I'm an east Belfast woman, and Bill and I've been married eleven years. He's from south London: as a child he was brought up in different children's homes in England until he was old enough to join the Army. He signed on for twenty-two years: so far he's reached the rank of Sergeant, but he hopes to become a Warrant Officer and possibly even progress beyond that to a commission. He's always said he feels that because of his childhood upbringing, he fits in best with an institutionalised life: and I think he's right, the Army does seem to suit him very well.

Myself, I come from a large Protestant family, who've all welcomed him in as one of themselves. It's happened to such an extent now, I think that although he's a born and bred Londoner, he prefers living here in Northern Ireland. He always says he does, anyway: and he gets on very well with everybody, he likes them and they like him, and they always have ever since we were married. We've two children, one eight and the other one six, and this nice house we have belongs to the Army: it's modern and a good size, and it has a garden and three bedrooms. A lot of soldiers and their families prefer to live inside the base camp they're stationed at, but we don't. This isn't an area where there's any trouble, so it's more or less as though we were living on an ordinary housing estate anywhere else in the British Isles. The only restrictions are certain pubs are out of bounds, but that's no great burden for Bill: and of course we have to take the usual security precautions about where we leave the car and things like that, but otherwise life's perfectly straightforward.

One way in which we've been very lucky is that since we were married, we've hardly ever had to be separated. Bill's had to go off sometimes for a few weeks on a training course or something of that sort, but on the whole we've always managed to be together on long postings. Before we came here we were in Cyprus for two years: that was wonderful, except it meant we couldn't see much of the family. But so far he's never ever had to go on an unaccompanied tour: it's unusual, but it's certainly not something we'd ever complain about.

Being an Army wife suits me: I come from a forces background myself. I was in the Territorial Army when Bill and I met, I've a brother in the police, another member of the family was in the UDR, and so it's the sort of life I understand and am familiar with. I'm involved with a lot of the activities there are for other soldiers' wives, like social clubs and so on: and at the moment I'm President of the wives' club. I always think life's what you make it: when I married Bill I'd a good idea what would be involved, and far from accepting it with resignation, I really enjoy it. It's nice being near my family as we are now, but I wouldn't mind at all if our next posting took us away again to Germany or somewhere like that. They say if you marry a soldier, you marry the Army: and so you do, that's quite right, and it's all right with me.

The big problem which might have arisen is the common one, what to do about the children's education. It's something which fortunately hasn't presented us with difficulties up to now, we haven't had to consider boarding-school for instance, because we could have them with us. In Cyprus they went to an Army school, here they go to a local school, which is a good one with high standards, and they're making good progress and like it. When they reach eleven, they'll move on to secondary education: we hope it'll be possible for them to go either to an Army school where we are, or we might find a way for them to continue their schooling here. It's something we don't yet have to make a decision about, so we've not talked very much about it or the idea of boarding-school. I don't think we'll be too keen on that though when it comes to it, unless the children themselves want to. I'd certainly miss them if we were parted, and so would Bill, but maybe our luck will continue.

Even though they're surrounded by all my relatives and I'm a Northern Irish woman, I think our children are both more English than Irish. One of my relatives once commented they imitated their dad in the way that they spoke, but to me things like what accent you have doesn't matter. They get their legs pulled a bit at school because they definitely do speak more like Londoners than Belfast boys, which can sometimes sound very funny. The elder one, John, he came home one day from school a few weeks ago and told us his class teacher had asked him to think of three words that began with 'F'. He put his hand up straight away and said 'free, four and five, miss.' We got the impression the teacher tried not to laugh but wasn't successful, nor were the rest of the class. One thing we do have to do though of course is tell them not to talk too much at school about what their daddy's job is: we say if anyone asks them they should tell them he works in an office. We tell them why: and while on the one hand we don't want them to be frightened, on the other it's only sensible and I think they see that.

Another problem as far as children are concerned, and all Army wives have it, is over matters of discipline. Sometimes daddy's here and sometimes he's away, so there can be a bit of confusion in your children's minds about which one of you is Boss and which one is Big Boss. Bill and I sorted this one out long ago. We're both fairly strong on discipline, regular bedtimes, doing what they're told and so on: though we draw the line at smacking because we don't believe in it. What we decided very early on was that as I was the one who was here all the time, I'd be the one who made the rules and enforced the discipline. So Bill leaves that side of things entirely to me, and it does seem to work out pretty well.

Whenever he's been away, on a training course or something, I've always felt I could cope with the situation, because I always knew I could. When our youngest was born Bill only came back just a week before the birth: it was something I was naturally very pleased about, but I could still have handled it if I'd had to on my own. I'm hoping when the children are older to get a job again: I used to do secretarial work, and in my spare time now I'm studying how to work word processors and things of that sort. My aim is to get a part-time job at first, and then go on to full-time when I can. It'll help financially, but also I know I do want to work again and not just stay a housewife.

Colin Archer,

Lieutenant, UDR

He sat with his long legs stretched out in front of him as he talked: an amiable softly-spoken young man with a direct look and a self-confident manner.

– I'm twenty-three and I've lived in east Belfast all my life. So far I've been in the Ulster Defence Regiment for five years: twelve months as a private, a year at Sandhurst, and now for the last three years I've been a commissioned officer. Like everyone in the Ulster Defence Regiment, I serve only in Northern Ireland: for two years I was in Ballymena and then one in County Antrim, with a couple of brief periods abroad on exercise or attachment in Gibraltar and Cyprus. The UDR's locally recruited and has only been used locally so far: but when we merge with the Royal Irish Rangers in the near future, we'll then have an overseas battalion as well. Altogether the UDR has a strength of about 7,500 men: slightly more than half are full-time, and the rest part-time.

I joined straight from school when I was eighteen. My family'd no previous connections with the Army and I didn't know anyone else who was in it: but I'd already had an interest in it at school, where I was a cadet in the TA. I'd got eleven O levels there, and my principal ambition was to be a marine biologist when I left because the two things I was most interested in were biology and the sea. But when I did my A levels they weren't good enough to get me the offer of a university place. I hadn't thought much about what to do instead, and then I saw an advert in the local evening paper inviting people to join the UDR and take a three-year contract commission. My mother was keen on the idea and to a certain extent she pushed me towards it.

Because I'd spent all my childhood and adolescence in a very troubled area of east Belfast, I often felt I wanted to do something to help settle the troubles and bring Northern Ireland peace. Fundamentally Ulster's a beautiful country and a peaceful one: but I also remember as a child somebody being shot by terrorists in our road, and someone else having their house blown up only two streets away. Things like that leave their mark, and I felt it would be worthwhile trying to do something practical and constructive, and stop things like that happening. We've got to create the conditions in which peace is permanent, that's the pre-requisite before there can be further development.

The UDR's like any other part of the Army, and my present job in it's almost like an ordinary job in civilian life. At present I'm concerned with administration and office work for most of my time. I enjoy it, it's interesting, it carries a lot of responsibility and calls for a lot of commitment, and all those things suit me. Especially the responsibility: I've come from a working–class background, and I feel within my limitations I've got on and done as well or better than a lot of other people of my age. I feel what I'm doing is really worthwhile and I intend to stay with it. My fiance and I are planning to get married next year, and after that I don't know what direction I'll go in, but we'll wait and see.

Before doing this admin job, I had a good bit of experience of patrol work in the streets, search operations and that kind of thing, and I enjoyed that very much. The principal areas I've worked in so far have been in County Antrim and east Belfast, where the largest majority of the population is sympathetic and help us. Being a Northern Irish person myself, it does have advantages in face-to-face dealings with people, especially when you're doing identity checks and things of that sort. There's more rapport between ordinary people and a soldier who doesn't have an English accent: they understand we're one of them and why it's necessary for us to be there doing what we do. You will get an occasional difficult person, but I've not met many. I wouldn't say it was any worse in that respect than if I was working in any other job anywhere else. Sometimes someone at a road checkpoint will turn his car stereo full blast, wind up the windows, and sit there pretending he can neither see nor hear us: but that sort of thing doesn't happen often.

You have to face there's a slight element of danger in the job, as there is in any soldier's life: but it's something you accept. You take things as they come: after all if you were to spend your life worrying about what was round the next corner, you'd not be able to work properly whatever you were doing. We're professionals trained how to handle situations, and more importantly we learn how not to get into situations in the first place. Checking your car to make sure it isn't booby-trapped with a bomb is second nature, and so is taking security precautions at your own home. I suppose the main difference between being a soldier in the UDR and being in an ordinary civilian job is you become careful automatically in conversation. If you meet somebody you don't know, obviously you're going to find out a little about them, who they are and what they do, before you reveal to them very much about your occupation. It means you go about your life in a sensible way.

My future's fairly uncertain. After our merger with the Royal Irish Rangers there'll be opportunities for signing-on for a longer term, and I'll definitely consider that. But I've no great desire to go to foreign parts: that wasn't what I joined for. My home and heart are here, and I feel more at ease in Ulster than anywhere else. It's where I'm used to, and I have a strong sense of belonging here. I like Scotland, Wales and parts of the north of England when I go over there, but I feel rather out of place in the southern parts of the mainland. I'm provincial in every sense. I remember an occasion when I'd been at Sandhurst, and it just happened that the weather had been absolutely glorious for weeks and weeks. And when I came home, exactly as our plane flew into Aldergrove and touched down, the skies turned black and the rain started absolutely pouring down. But I had an enormous sense of relief at being back, all I felt was it was wonderful to be home.

12 *The RUC*

Ray Thomas, Chief Superintendent

Max Harvey

Irene Marshall, RUC man's wife

(I received neither encouragement nor help from the RUC and they would not accept assurances, nor stipulate conditions, under which permission for interviewing would be granted.
Superintendent Ray Thomas eventually however agreed to a conversation being recorded with him as an individual, within strictly pre-determined limits and on condition he could edit the transcript.)

Ray Thomas,

Chief Superintendent

We drank mugs of coffee and ate biscuits in his office at Castlereagh. He wore a light grey suit, a white shirt and a dark blue tie, and spoke quietly and without any cautious hesitations. Afterwards, he asked for and was given the tape of the interview so he could make a copy of it.

– I've just completed twenty-six years in the Force myself, the last sixteen of them in and around Belfast. I joined when I was eighteen and in those days the size of the RUC was in the region of 2,250 men. It's now well over 8,000 plus another 4,500 in the Reserve, so that gives you an idea of the way its size has increased. As a matter of fact it's now the second largest police force in the UK after the Metropolitan Police. I'd no family connections with it, it just appealed to me when I left school. My first years were spent at a small two-man station in a quiet country village in the north-west of the Province. That was the time of the very beginning of the troubles: I never expected any more than anyone else did that now, such a long time afterwards, the position would still be what it is.

I've spent over half my time in the field, or more correctly I should say on the streets. My progress up to my present rank has been fairly steady and in some ways it's been uneventful. One of the consequences of promotion is you inevitably become more of a manager: but you never lose the basic feeling, or at least I've never done, that work in the field is still what you feel the job is principally about and in some ways you'd prefer to be still doing it. The backbone of the Force is the Constable and the local Sergeant: and however far on you get into management, you miss the daily involvement you had in the past. The continuous change and challenge of it gave you much more a sense of being part of the community than you have when you're sitting behind a desk.

The general idea of police work being mostly concerned with catching criminals, which is a popular one put over on the TV, isn't what it's really like at all. A very small percentage of what a policeman does is connected with straightforward crime. The Force is an all-encompassing public service, available to the community twenty-four hours a day, seven days a week, fifty-two weeks a year. The public know they can rely on their help for almost anything. If someone locks himself out of his car for instance, the first people he calls on for assistance are the police. Or if there's a cat stuck up a tree, the police are the ones called to do something about it. The Force can't and doesn't ever work on the principle of 'It's not our responsibility'. If assistance is requested for anything by a member of the public, we try to provide it: and the man in uniform's usually the person the public waits for to give a guide and do something about the situation.

Mind you, sometimes you get it right but sometimes you don't. I remember once when I was a young constable having pointed out to me by several concerned passers-by that there was a baby in the back of a parked car: it had all its windows shut, it was a very hot day, and it was obvious the child was suffering. I happened to be passing and there I was, and people expected me to do something about the situation. So I smashed the quarterlight of one of the car's windows with my baton, unfastened the door, and lifted the child out into the fresh air. That satisfied the people who were watching: but it didn't at all please the mother herself when she arrived just afterwards. She was very irate about what she called my unnecessary interference, and told me so in no uncertain terms. So that's an example of how you take a decision and follow a course of action and please some people but not necessarily everyone.

Now I come to start thinking about things like that it reminds me of another experience which still makes me blush to this day when I remember it. I was on street patrol one night, and part of the method of it is to stop now and again in a shop doorway, and just stand quietly there. I was doing that on this occasion, when I heard the sound of running feet, and I stepped out of the door right in the path of a sprinting young man. He didn't see me, knocked me over, tripped himself, and we both fell to the ground. Seeing by my uniform what I was, he yelled at me 'Help me, help me, they're going to kill me!' I could hear more running feet approaching, so I stood up and braced myself to face whoever it was who was after him. He left me to it: he got up and ran on down the street and disappeared. Next thing that happened, round the corner came two policemen running after him trying to catch him because he'd committed a burglary. I don't need to tell you they weren't at all appreciative of me for what I'd just done.

Ah well, we're all the same. Get us talking about things that have happened when we were in the field and you'll be hard put to stop us. But none of us you see have the chance of a similar fund of occurrences when we're behind a desk, and that's part of what you most miss.

I've served part of my time in areas of Belfast where there've been troubles of one sort and another over the years. Only I can't talk about things like that in much detail. I'm sure you'll understand. It's an extremely difficult and tense time for the RUC at present: we've had some unfortunate experiences with people from the media, both television and the press. We've felt quite often we've been misrepresented, so it's made us rather reticent. So I'd much prefer it if we could talk only in general terms.

– Working as a policeman in Northern Ireland is in many ways quite different in kind from being a member of the police on the mainland. As far as what might be termed ordinary crime is concerned – robbery, burglary, housebreaking and so on – Northern Ireland is in fact the most law-abiding part of the United Kingdom. All the figures show not only that crime is at a lower level here than anywhere else, but that our clear-up rates are as good or in some cases better than those of other UK police forces.

It's our misfortune that despite that, in the present situation we find ourselves facing a problem which is unique to us. It's that here, simply as a policeman, you're a target for certain elements in the community. On duty or off duty, at work or in your home, to them you're always a target: and you have to work all day and every day, including those called days off or holidays, with this knowledge in your mind. So inevitably that causes a much higher stress-level in the job than most policemen anywhere else have to bear. We've an Occupational Health Unit to help members of our force deal with it: it's the first of its kind in the United Kingdom, and referral to it and the work it does is totally confidential between the Unit and the individual. A wide range of counselling services is available from it, and it doesn't affect an individual's career prospects if he or she seeks help from it. What I'm sure everyone would agree is an enlightened attitude prevails: to give only one example, alcoholism is recognised for what it is, an illness, rather than a character weakness. What the Unit offers is far in advance of the kind of help policemen in many other forces can get. Help with depression's another example, or with marital problems: everything possible is there for the asking. I don't know that the RUC has a higher incidence of problems of this kind than any other force, or for that matter whether they're even more predominant than in other occupations, because I think studies of that kind haven't been made. But if and when they were, as usual anything of that sort involving the police would receive more than its fair share of publicity.

One thing that many of us feel doesn't attract its fair share of attention is the rewards and satisfactions aspect of the job. Because it's in many ways unusually dangerous, the challenge it presents is very great, which is why there's such a high degree of comradeship between us. When you're in a constant crisis situation, you have the feeling it's only other people who are similarly engaged in it who really understand exactly what it's like to have your whole life affected by it. Imagine: you can't go home at the end of your on-duty period and say 'Now I can relax, I'm not a policeman again until tomorrow morning.' In Northern Ireland that situation just doesn't exist. Even when you go on holiday, say for example you and your family go to a campsite, not just on the mainland but in Europe anywhere: you can never know for sure who exactly your immediate neighbours in the next tent are. So you become very cautious about talking to people, especially when they start asking you where you come from and what you do. You daren't say too much about yourself to anyone. And this affects your children as well: right from the beginning of their lives, you have to bring them up to take care what they say about their father's occupation, where he lives and so on. You have to find a way of telling them this is a safety precaution. And to strike a balance between that and making them feel they're in some way different from other children and there's a perpetually threatening situation all round them, well it isn't always very easy.

I think it's generally true that as a policeman you have to learn to live with the fact that while some people regard you in an almost entirely bad light, others look on you with admiration. I think in the main you're seen as necessary for the preservation of an orderly and law-abiding society. But the dilemma of the Force's position is one most of its members are aware of: people don't like our presence to intrude on their everyday lives, but all the same there are occasions when they're profoundly grateful we're there. Some people are not prepared to give up any part of what they consider to be their individual rights for the good of society as a whole. But I inwardly and honestly believe most people think on balance that the Royal Ulster Constabulary don't do too badly: most of them too quite often ask themselves where they'd be without us.

Max Harvey

The agreement was simple and straightforward. A completely false and misleading name, no description of appearance or manner, and no indication of where the conversation took place.

– If it was known I'd talked to anyone it'd be as much as my life's worth: my life in the police anyway, it'd be the end of that. It might even be truer about other aspects of it too, including yours: certain people would go to considerable lengths to find out my identification from you. I'll say no more than that about it.

I've been a policeman for let's put it at quite a number of years. I've never had any other job, and I joined at the age of eighteen or thereabouts when I left school. I won't mention my rank or anything, but let's say I'm about in mid-career. I'm married with two children, and although I work in Belfast I don't live actually in the city, I live to the north of it.

What I'd like to say about myself first of all is that I'm not a fanatic. Some people have the idea the RUC's an entirely Protestant organisation, but in fact it's not: in the region of ten per cent of its members are Catholics. You don't see many of those who are on the streets. They wouldn't like to be identifiable within their own community because it'd be dangerous for them, so they're mainly doing office work. My own background's Protestant but that doesn't mean much: I'm not a religiously inclined person and anyway I was brought up in a perfectly ordinary family that didn't encourage religious prejudice. My father was a very strict man, especially about fanaticism. In his view it was people's own affair what they were, Protestant or Catholic: and so long as they weren't bigoted with it, it had nothing to do with anyone else. One of my earliest childhood memories is of coming back from school one day and saying something when we were all sitting round the table having tea. There was a boy down the street I didn't like, and I made a remark to the effect he was a no-good Fenian Catholic. The room went completely silent, and my father looked at me across the table and said very solemnly: 'If I ever hear you say anything like that in this house again, son, I'll give you a leathering you'll never forget.' He felt very strongly prejudice should be stamped on whenever it appeared.

He was the biggest influence in my life, and I've always remembered him as a good man who looked after his family and did the best he could for all of us. My sister was the oldest, then me, then my younger brother: and I think if you asked any of us what sort of early life we had, we'd all three say that though we never had a lot of money we had a good upbringing in a loving family atmosphere. The worst thing that happened for us was he became seriously ill in his mid-forties and couldn't work for something like two years. My mother went out doing cleaning and as a general household help. As soon as she was old enough to leave school, my sister took a job as a shop assistant in one of the city stores to help bring extra money in: and so I never had any ideas of going to university or anything of that sort, I only thought of leaving school and getting a job.

Eventually in the end the people my father worked for had to say to him they couldn't hold his job open for him any longer. That did a lot to his self-confidence: he didn't say much but I know he was very worried about the situation. He tried for several jobs and didn't get them, and then one day he went after some light work as a storeman in a factory. He was very hopeful he was going to get it, but in the end he didn't: there was a choice between him and another man who got it because he was a Catholic, though the company itself was owned by Protestants. They had to employ a certain quota of Catholics and so they discriminated against my father for that reason. It was no big job, only poorly paid manual work, but for years afterwards my mother always talked about it with great bitterness. She said if he'd been given the job and got a bit of confidence back, it might have made a difference, because he died not long afterwards. You never know how much truth there is in things like that.

After he died it made me more determined than ever to leave school and work, so in a few months afterwards I did. I tried to get a job, but not having much in the way of qualifications, I didn't get very far. For a year or more I spent a lot of time hanging about in the streets with other boys of the same age. I had an uncle who was my mother's brother, and he was in the police: I think he influenced her to suggest I applied to join. I didn't have ideas about upholding law and order or anything of that sort: the only thing was it offered security as long as you behaved yourself and did as you were told. I've met quite a lot of people who joined because they were concerned about the situation in Northern Ireland, but I wasn't one of them. I'd not directly experienced anything much of the actual troubles, they were things that went on in the streets of Belfast you read about in the newspapers. In the place where we were living, it seemed it was all happening a long way away.

I think I'd better not say much more about my background or how my career's developed: and I can't talk in much detail about individual experiences I've had, because somebody might put two and two together and recognise me. I've had no experience of police work anywhere else so I can't make comparisons between what it's like here and other places. But obviously it's difficult because our number one concern is security. There's a war going on, and the mere fact we wear body armour and carry weapons makes us different from other policemen in the UK. Your attitude tends to be that that comes with the job: you get used to it, and you don't think there's anything strange about it. There's also the aspect that you're in constant danger and there's a lot of stress in the job. I leave my car outside my garage at home sometimes: and now and again I start up and drive away, and suddenly I think 'Christ, I forgot to look underneath before I switched on the ignition.' You have to live with it that sometimes you'll do that. And if you haven't got the right temperament you ask to be transferred to clerical or other work. But if you have got the right temperament, part of it is that you don't spend too much time dwelling on such things.

Now and again you get surprises. In certain areas you know the police are, well, let's say not exactly popular. You tend to think twice before you speak to somebody: once about exactly what you're going to say, and secondly about how you're going to say it. If you adopt a rough rude approach, you'll get an aggressive response every time. Now and again people'll be reasonable and polite when you speak to them: and that's the surprise, rather than the strength of the anger in them when they reply to you. That's the way life is here, and it's no use pretending it isn't. There are parts of Belfast I could take you to, I'd guarantee you couldn't walk with me from one end of a street to the other without having something thrown at us. There've been occasions when something's come flying through the air like a tomato or a piece of wood: and it might even be in part of the city centre, say in one of the pedestrian precincts. You can't help thinking sometimes it might have been a bullet, and you'd not had the faintest chance of even knowing it was on its way. The vast majority of people don't wish you any harm: but there's always that one individual whose mission in life is to try and kill you. Some people I work with, that sort of thing gets to them: and the result is they hate everyone, everyone civilian I mean. They hit back before they've been hit is the only way I can put it. They start taking exception just to the expression on someone's face, and wade into them straight away.

I don't like arresting people on the street, particularly youths: I never think that sort of thing does the image of the police any good. A lot of young lads are rowdy, I was rowdy and cheeky a bit myself when I was their age. You can sometimes come down heavy when it isn't really necessary, it's all noise but not seriously threatening to anybody: when you do, afterwards you should think you've not achieved anything except reinforcing the idea in their minds the police behave like that just because they like doing it. But there's another side to it too: you're provided with fairly high-level information about people who you should be suspicious of whenever you see them. That's tricky when you know somebody's responsible for something but there he is, still walking the streets, because nobody can get sufficient evidence to put him inside. And it makes you sick the number of acquittals there are in the Courts of people you know are menaces, and if there was any justice they should be behind bars. But they get themselves clever lawyers who get them off on technicalities. It's not easy to keep cool when a person like that looks at you in the street in a provocative way. He's telling you he knows that you know what he's done, and he knows that you know there's not a thing you can do about it.

The most important thing of all if you're a policeman is that you support your own mates, always: and you always know that if you do, they'll support you. Perhaps I shouldn't go this far: but I don't suppose it's much of a surprise to anyone to hear it said. There are times you'll say black is white, or you heard something that you didn't, or you didn't hear something that you did. You're doing it because in your view you consider it's for the greater good not just of the police, but for society in general. I'd better not be more specific than that. But one of the reasons why the Chief Constable of the RUC, Hugh Annersley, is looked on with such regard by most of us is that he won't let even the slightest criticism of any of his men's behaviour by the press go unanswered, he'll send off a letter refuting the charges straight away. You have to smile sometimes at how far he goes, to be honest: but I admire him for it, and I think most of us do.

I realise I'm taking a risk in even talking to you at all, and I hope you won't let me down. A lot of people wouldn't thank me for it if they knew who I was, but as far as I know I haven't said anything that isn't true. If there's any chance of someone knowing I've met you, I can tell you now I'll say I never said any such thing as you claim, it was someone else. OK?

Irene Marshall,

RUC man's wife

She brought cups of tea and a rich chocolate cake into her sitting-room, and put them down on the mahogany coffee table. A friendly and precisely-spoken woman with long dark hair, she wore a brown velvet skirt and an ice-blue blouse.

– My husband's not too keen on the idea of me talking to you. But I make up my own mind usually and I've decided that as far as I can see on balance there'll be no harm in it.

I'll give you a bit of background about myself first shall I? I'm the wife of an RUC sergeant, we've two grown-up children, we've been married for twenty-four years and I've lived here in this house in north Belfast for most of my life. I married when I was twenty-four, and I'm now almost forty-nine. Will that do?

I left school when I was sixteen: I wouldn't say I was particularly academically-minded, and I'd no special ambitions about what I wanted to do. Always in my recollections my father and mother were both quite elderly: my father worked for the Army in a clerical job, and so while I couldn't say I come from a military background, there was nothing unusual about the Services to me in any way. In addition I'd two brothers, one in the navy and the other in the UDR. As a result of all that we usually mixed with people who were in one way or another connected with the armed forces or the police. It was at the wedding of a friend of mine to someone who was in the RUC that I met my husband, who I'll call Leslie. We had a fairly steady and conventional kind of friendship at first: he lived on his own with another policeman because he was married but separated from his wife. He had two small children, he was devoted to them, and it's remained like that ever since. I'm glad to say that I've always got on well with them, and we're still on good terms even now they're grown-up.

Among the jobs I had both before and after I was married, the one I liked far best was working in the kitchen of a big hotel in the city. I was one of several young women assistants to the chef: I enjoyed it thoroughly because I've always liked cooking and I still do. Leslie was my first serious boyfriend, and although I didn't talk much about him being in the police, I felt both then and later when we were engaged, and after we were married as well, that I couldn't possibly work every day with people and not tell them what he did. Naturally you're always unsure about it, because you don't know who the information might be passed on to. All the same I think a point is always reached when you have to decide whether you're going to make up some sort of fiction about yourself or tell the truth. I've known people who've done that and gone to great lengths to conceal what their husband's job is when he's in the RUC. But it gets too complicated altogether to do that for ever: you have to have a relationship of trust with people you work with, you can't be on your guard day in and day out, and anyway it's too easy to make a slip. What I don't do though of course is tell people where we live, not unless I'm absolutely certain the information won't go any further.

A few years ago I had a job with a firm of business conference caterers, and several of the girls who worked for me came from west Belfast. As you know that's considered to be a hotbed of Republicans and members of the IRA: I've never been in that part of the city myself so I don't know whether it is or not. But on one occasion one of the girls I mentioned asked me one day if we could have a confidential chat. So when work was finished for the day we went to a cafe for a cup of tea, and she told me she was very worried about her fifteen-year old son. She said she was fairly sure he was getting mixed-up in activities that were against the law and dangerous as well. And she said there was one particular friend of her son's, older than him, who she'd reason to believe had arms and explosives in his house. She said she knew my husband was in the RUC, and asked me would it be possible, without anyone knowing where the information had come from, for a police raid to be made on this particular house? She said at least if nothing was found, it might act as a warning to her son about the sort of things he was getting mixed up with.

The girl was someone who'd worked for me for a year, I liked her, and I'd no reason to believe she wasn't trustworthy. When I came home and told Leslie about it though, he said there was absolutely no question of anyone in the RUC following it up. It might be a genuine tip-off he said, but on the other hand it might be to test me, to see if I'd pass on what I'd been told. If the police turned up at the address the woman had said she'd give me, it'd confirm I wasn't the sort of person who could be trusted. He also said it could even lead to me being in personal danger as a known informer. So nothing was ever done, and what the outcome was as far as the girl's son was concerned I don't know. Leslie said it could even have been a sort of double bluff: where explosives and weapons were in the house, but the people they belonged to were trying to make the police believe it was a trap.

The conversation the young woman had with me is an example of the sort of difficult situation you often easily find yourself in. Somebody else could have tipped-off the police and the arms be found: and if that happened I'd have appeared to the girl to be the one responsible. It's like that all the time: you have to try to think not of one outcome, but three or four or five or as many as you can, and try to weigh them up in your mind and consider what's the best thing to do. I'd summarise it all by saying that as the wife of a policeman, I usually conclude Leslie's advice that the best thing to do is nothing is right. Which now I come to think of it I'm not doing in your case, am I? Oh well.

I don't want to give you a false impression of the sort of life we have to lead. Don't think we live every single day on a knife-edge, because we really don't. As far as our personal relationship is concerned, we're very happy together and we love each other very much. We like the same kind of things, whether they're paintings or books or music: we go to the theatre or the cinema often, and we go out in the car on our own or with one of the children when Leslie has a day off. As much for their sakes as for our own we've always tried to lead as normal a family life as possible. Before he goes off to work in the morning Leslie always automatically inspects underneath the car. I don't stand and watch him do it, but I know it's being done.

Inside me there's always that slight feeling of apprehension as I hear the car start up and drive away down the lane. But I know he's a professional, and I know he always checks without fail. And once I can no longer hear his car, quite illogically I feel relief: and I have the same sort of feeling in the evening when I hear his car coming back again too. We have an arrangement that he phones me every day from work for a chat so I'll know he's all right. When it gets to about four o'clock if I haven't heard I start to get a bit edgy: he knows that of course, so he usually phones round the middle of the day.

I'm sure I'm no different from anyone else whose husband's in the RUC: I've been to his funeral a hundred times. We've lost several good friends who've been killed on duty over the years: you always have to live with the possibility of that happening. My closest friend's the wife of a policeman, and one day last year at the funeral of a colleague of Leslie's, she and I were standing outside the church together after the funeral service. We were crying, naturally: and suddenly she said to me 'I suppose we're both thinking the same thing Irene, aren't we? In our hearts we're saying "Thank God it wasn't my husband"?' There can't be any pretending about it can there? She was right. I'm sorry: excuse me.

You see I don't understand, and I never will understand, why there are people in this city today who want to kill my husband. And they'd regard it as an achievement to be proud of if they did. Years ago I read a book by Howard Spring, I think it was called *My Son, My Son.* There's an incident in it where a father says about his son who's been killed in a riot in Cork: 'God damn Ireland and God damn any man who thinks his aspirations are worth a young man's blood.' That's stayed with me, it's exactly what my own feelings are. My husband chose as his job to enforce the law and to keep the peace: he doesn't go out each day to kill people, he goes out to do what he can to stop people killing each other. He doesn't give any thought at all to whether they're Catholics or Protestants. I'm proud of him and I think he's a hero. He puts on his uniform and walks the streets wearing it: and he knows that that clearly identifies him in the eyes of some people as a target. But he wears the uniform because it symbolises what he believes in, whereas the terrorist doesn't make himself obvious and his success is in not being identified. Which of those two is the brave one? Leslie's standing up for the right to be a

British citizen. He's not wanting to murder people because of his belief in being British, and he's in the police force of the majority of the Northern Irish population. He doesn't do it for honour or glory, but simply out of his sense of duty. He doesn't want to sweep all the Catholics into the sea or make them give up their homes or their jobs or their way of life: he just wants us, the majority, to be allowed to get on with our own lives in peace. That's what he's dedicated himself to, and it makes me furious when I read things in the newspapers or see them on television which give the impression the RUC spends its time harrying and harassing people, charging at them with batons and beating them up. The media's always giving the impression the RUC picks up youths off the street for no good reason, threatens them and intimidates them, and takes them to Castlereagh and tortures them. I think it's completely one-sided and very unfair. I know I shouldn't get so upset about it, but I'm sorry, I do. Perhaps that's why Leslie thinks I shouldn't have talked.

13 *Priests and clergy*

Brother David Jardine

Revd Valerie Morton

Father O'Mallie

Father Des

Brother David Jardine

He sat in an old chair in the sparsely-furnished front room of a house in a row scheduled for demolition. A heavily-built tall man with short cropped grey hair, in a check shirt and corduroy trousers.

– Yes Tony, gladly I'll try and explain who we are and what we're doing here. You're in the temporary headquarters of the Ministry of Healing in east Belfast, which exists because we believe an integral part of Jesus's ministry was to heal. In the Acts of the Apostles there are accounts of nine miracles which were worked in response to prayer and for the first three centuries of the Church's history, healing the sick was widely practised. Then that Ministry was lost from the Church for a long time, but I'm happy to say this century it's started to come back very strongly again.

As for myself, I'm fifty and was born in County Down. I went to grammar school, then to university, and took a degree in Spanish. If you'd asked me then what I wanted to do I'd probably have said teach. But I had an inkling God had something different in mind for me: and although I was reluctant about it at first, eventually the feeling became stronger and I went to see the university's Church of Ireland chaplain and told him I wanted to offer myself for the ministry. He was a member of the Society of St Francis, in Dorset, and I went there to join them. After that I did my theological training in Dublin, was ordained at twenty-four, and was then sent to work in a parish here in east Belfast. After that I went to England, and then again came back to Belfast, where I spent ten years as a Church of Ireland chaplain in Crumlin Road gaol.

Afterwards I wrote a small book about it: it was a necessary and enlightening experience for me, but the mass of rules and regulations needed for security can never give you the freedom to work in the way you wish, so in that respect our work here I feel is more rewarding and presents greater opportunities.

I think a clergyman's job has to be first and foremost to bring people to God, and here in the outside community we try to allow people to experience God's healing power. We hold three services every week and on Sundays we go to different places where we've been invited to talk and preach. Our ministry has the opportunity to work across denominational barriers, for example at our service in St Anne's Cathedral on Fridays. We work as a team: and there are thirty-three of us all together, six of us paid and the rest are volunteers.

As for healing itself, a good definition of it might be to describe it as Jesus Christ meeting you at your point of need. It's an endeavour through prayer, counselling, laying on of hands and anointing with oil, to bring to someone in need of wholeness the healing love of the living Christ: and it's neither purely physical nor purely spiritual, but a combination of the two. We believe very much in the power of prayer: when we pray we approach God as his children and think of him as the heavenly Father who responds to the requests of his children. That's a straightforward view of God, and it's how I see him, because I like to relate to him myself in an extremely personal way.

You know, Tony, I believe that in the situation in Northern Ireland today, there's only going to be a real healing of our society by the help of God. We believe God responds if we pray for sick persons, and we believe that if we pray for Northern Ireland he'll respond in the same way to that too. There are a million and a half people living here, and it needs many more to do so than have done already, to show God we're all very serious indeed about needing and wanting help. I believe that if enough people pray, most of our problems could be sorted out in a permanent way. But it's not just a question of prayer of course: it's also one of showing Christian love in our attitudes to one another. Unfortunately all of us still carry with us very many prejudices and hurts. I can't help thinking there are a number of ways in which we've all failed to show Christian love, and I think that's at the heart of the matter. People say they hold particular points of principle, so that's why they can't worship with the Roman Catholics or whoever it happens to be: but my view of it is that that displays lack of Christian love, and we should be quicker to acknowledge readiness to change our attitudes. For instance recently the President of the Irish Republic, Mary Robinson, made a visit to Belfast. And when she did, the Lord Mayor refused to meet her. Well you know, frankly I think that's absolutely awful: I wrote a letter to him and said I was extremely disappointed about it. I tried not to be too critical because I don't think that gets you anywhere: but I said that to be friendly towards people whose politics and ideas are different from yours doesn't necessarily compromise any fundamental principle.

I've never forgotten, and I hope other people haven't, that when Mother Theresa founded a house here, after only a year she gave it up. She pulled out in fact at twenty-four hours' notice, and I was told when she went that she said: 'These people haven't suffered enough yet.' I think she was saying that people in Belfast can't yet show enough of the humility that's needed, they're not prepared to drop their pride and their prejudices, and come simply together. We desperately need God's help to heal Northern Ireland: only until we recognise it fully, not much progress is going to be made. The Churches here lack love for one another: and though some barriers have been broken down, the Churches are still part of the problem, rather than being active in making a practical solution to it. There's such a lack of humility and charity in the Church. I think we should try to come together in repentance, and maybe apologise to each other for what we've done in the past. Instead of trying to justify ourselves and our attitudes to one another, let's just try saying 'Sorry': and pray to God together to help us try and solve our differences.

To put it another way, in personal terms I'd definitely call myself an Irishman: yet to many people in the Protestant sector here to which I belong, that's something they wouldn't be happy to hear me say. What it means to me is that I was born in the island of Ireland, and that's what gives me my identity. But being brought up as an Ulster Protestant, that means being brought up to feel British: and that's not something I'm happy about. I feel that English people, which is what most of us mean by 'British', really do rather look down their noses at us, and I don't like being identified with them.

I'd agree with those who say the Republic of Ireland hasn't always been as warm to us in its political statements as it could have been, in fact on occasions it's been quite aggressive. But I return to my fundamental belief that there's great healing to be done in all ways and from all directions between Belfast, Dublin, and London.

I'd very much like to see more English people being less critical of us all, for misbehaving ourselves for the last twenty years or more. We have done it: but the thing I'd really like would be for you English to acknowledge it was your country which first created this problem by dividing our country when you brought in Partition in the early 1920s. That really did drive such a wedge between one part and another: and ever since, we've been so strongly and deeply divided we're almost like the damaged child of separated parents. We're scarred from birth, because we're brought up to regard ourselves as fundamentally different from each other. In those circumstances it's very hard for healing to take place, yet the Irish people themselves are the only ones who can heal the scar. And we can't leave it all to a few helpers and triers here and there, individuals working on their own in different ways and different places. Everyone has a part to play, and the churches more than anyone should give a lead. It's got to be done, and I personally think it can only be with the help of God. All the people of Ireland have all to acknowledge our differences and yet at the same time stress our sameness. We must do it instead of continually stressing our differences, and continually say to each other we're sorry for what we've done to each other in the past.

Personally I feel I've still a considerable distance to go myself as far as that's concerned, in reaching out the hand of genuine Christian love to Catholics. I'm sad to say it, but I know I've been touched by twenty-two years of violence here. It's created in me an atmosphere in which it's very hard for me to say in a truly Christian spirit 'Let us come together'. I've preached in a Roman Catholic church, but I know that I still have to ask God to bring about a more fundamental change in my heart, and make me more loving and forgiving towards people of a different faith.

These political talks, that seem to perpetually start and stop and start again and then stop once more: we must ask ourselves why is it that they've not yet succeeded. I think it's because God's saying 'I

want politicians to get together, I do: but there's a lot of spade work
to be done first. A lot more work's needed on relationships between
the communities: there's still much much more love and forgiveness
to be given: and it's only when that's been done that it'll be possible
for politicians really to come together, after a strong foundation's
been laid for their work.'

*

(David Jardine's *Belfast's Bleak House* is published by Marshalls
Paperbacks.)

Revd Valerie Morton

A smartly-dressed woman in a brown tweed jacket and skirt, she spoke easily and fluently, articulating and ordering her thoughts. We talked in an office at the school where she was one of the governors.

– I've worked in Belfast as a minister in the Presbyterian church for twelve years. Before that I was at times a teacher, and a church youth organiser in the Caribbean. When I was first ordained I was only the second woman Presbyterian minister: I'm not sure now how many others there've been since.

I'm the oldest of eleven children, and I went to school in a small village in Northern Ireland. My father was a labourer in the shipyards, and while I was growing up I always wanted to be either a teacher or a missionary though I don't really know why. The whole family went regularly to church, but I wouldn't say we were particularly religious apart from that, we didn't have prayers at home or that kind of thing. After my primary school I went to a co-educational high school in Belfast, and from there on to university where I took a general degree and teaching certificate. By then I'd joined a church missionary organisation, and I went to a Presbyterian college in Edinburgh for a year, with a view to going eventually to India as a missionary. The standard of teaching we had there was good: it was impressed on us again and again that whatever country we eventually went to, we were there as guests and should study and learn as much about that particular country as we could. It was made very clear to us that before we did any proselytising of any kind, we must study the religious beliefs of those we were talking to. It was even suggested we might possibly be the ones who were converted ourselves in India, for example to Hinduism or the Muslim faith.

But I never had any serious doubts about whether I should go to India or not: it seemed to me that this was the way in which I should demonstrate faith in God. So at the age of twenty-six my future looked quite clear to me. My luggage had been sent on ahead, my boat tickets were booked, and there was nothing else to do but look forward to it all happening. Then, slightly less than a month before I was due to sail, the Indian government brought in new regulations about missionaries, and I was refused a visa. It seemed like the end of the world. I came home to Ireland from Edinburgh hoping very deeply that when I arrived I wouldn't find the family in the house, all waiting to greet me on what was supposed to be my farewell visit before departing for Bombay. When I got there, to my relief I found my youngest brother was the only person at home, and so I was able to go upstairs and shut myself in a room for about two hours. I didn't want to weep, there was no point in doing something like that, but I wanted time to think out on my own which direction I was going in next, and be able to talk about it calmly with everyone.

Often in situations like that one door closes but another one opens almost at once. Within literally a few days I'd been offered a chance to go to Jamaica and work there as a Girls' Brigade organiser, so I immediately accepted it. And I think that was an experience from which I benefited very greatly indeed. I found everyone in Jamaica wonderfully friendly and accepting, there was a kind of light-heartedness about the way everyone conducted their life which I'd not experienced anything at all similar to ever before. I was a rather serious-natured young woman until I went there: what I gained from it most of all was a sense of the joyfulness of life itself, and I became very much more relaxed as a person altogether.

I stayed in the Caribbean for three years. When I came back, I was conscious that from early on in my stay I'd had what you might call a 'mosquito experience'. You know how you hear one buzzing around, and how it goes on but doesn't settle or bite, and yet it doesn't go away? However hard you try, you can't ignore the sound: and you know for certain that eventually it's going to land on you and bite you? Well, all the time I was in the Caribbean I'd had that feeling which wouldn't go away, that I wanted to be a minister. But the Presbyterian church didn't have women ministers at that stage, so I really didn't know what to do. I prayed, asking God for assistance and guidance: but it seemed like talking to a brick wall, because nothing came back at all. I went and talked to some friends, I think in the hope they'd tell me it was a foolish idea and I shouldn't pursue it. But on the contrary, they encouraged me to go ahead and try. So I applied: and to my very great surprise I was accepted as a candidate, together with one other woman.

By then I was thirty, and while I was waiting to start at the theological college in Edinburgh I taught in a large secondary school for boys in east Belfast. That too was another very good experience. All the pupils were ones who it was described in those days had 'failed' the 11-plus exam. The school's whole purpose was to try and help them discover other things they were good at rather than scholastic subjects, and get a sense of achievement out of those instead. For me it was very useful, because I felt by my own standards my three years' work in Jamaica had been a failure too: so in many ways I was like the pupils I was teaching, and I know I learnt as much from them as they did from me.

After that I got to college and was ordained, and then came to this parish, eleven years ago as I said. It's been my first and only parish, and after five years I met and married another minister of the Presbyterian church, a widower with grown-up children. He has a church of his own a little way away from here, and we both have slightly different congregations. Mine is very Protestant, and is in the middle of a mixed area of housing. One part of it comes from a housing-estate, and the other from houses in the private sector. We have 430 families on our register: and in this area, apart from us and the Church of Ireland there are two smaller denominational churches. There are no Roman Catholic churches anywhere in this part of Belfast at all.

The consequence is that much as we'd like to, there's an actual geographical difficulty about forming links. Those that do exist are between other groups that are not of the church, and I feel this is a great pity. The church is seen to be lagging behind in this important matter: and not only seen to be, but is. We're as ecumenical as we possibly can be with the Church of Ireland, sharing very many activities: I frequently preach in their church, and their minister comes to preach in ours. But this is a very long way indeed from what needs to be done in bringing Protestants and Catholics into contact. I know it can sometimes be counterproductive and lead to hardening of attitudes, but nevertheless it's an important thing for the future that it should happen.

I worry considerably about the local situation today, as well as in Northern Ireland generally. I don't know quite in which direction we can go here as Protestants when we've no Catholics near us at all. And I do have to admit there's little sense of common ground with them here in this area. It's very rigid in its Protestantism, and the ideas some of my parishioners express to me from time to time aren't ones that make me very hopeful for the future. People here tend to be very judgemental about the Catholics and they blame them for all the ills in society. In conversation when somebody makes what I think's a far too prejudiced remark about Catholics in general, I always say when I was at theological college I was closely involved with a group of Catholic nuns, and found myself very much at ease with them. And frequently this brings back a response from the person who's been criticising them that in actual fact they've never themselves met any Catholics. It's true, they haven't: and it's hard work to try to get them to be less judgemental when I can't offer them any kind of cross-community meetings.

Another thing which creates a lot of difficulty too is that the Protestant community's divided within itself. Many Catholics imagine all Protestants to be Loyalist, which means British. This isn't correct: personally for example when I have to state my nationality on a form that needs filling in, I put down British. But in fact, I really feel much more Irish than I ever do British. To say that though is not very acceptable to some Protestants: they say they are, and pride themselves on being, more British than the British. What they really mean though, I think, is that they're loyal only when the British do what they want. They tend to forget that many of the people who came from Scotland generations ago to settle here were actually escaping from Britain, and seeking opportunities which they couldn't get there.

The border's to me a false political division: I wish it didn't exist and in that sense I'm a nationalist with a small 'n'. I definitely feel more at home here than I ever do on the mainland, and I've more in common with Irish people in both the north and the south than I have with the English. I can't help thinking, and nor can many other people I know like me, that if they're honest they think of us as inferior people who're something of a nuisance. It's a very serious fault in our educational system that we're not taught at school to have any proper sense of our Irish identity. We're only taught British history, and that's mainly in terms of kings and queens, battles won, colonies gained and the rest of it. Northern Ireland's own history usually occupies no more than a couple of lines in our textbooks: something about Partition, something of a generalised nature about troubles between Protestants and Catholics, and very little else. No Northern Irish person is taught about either history or culture that's particular to this part of the British Isles. The Scots and the Welsh are now actively promoting their individual identities and difference from England and the English, but we're not.

Finally I'd like to make a point about religious division here. It seems to me the Catholics have a much greater sense of community amongst themselves than we Protestants do, and I think it's a great strength for them. In a parish Catholics have one church and perhaps one school, to which all the people go or send their children to. This gives them a feeling of closeness and everyone being together. But in the Protestant church, first there are a number of different denominations which create feelings of separateness, and secondly there's nothing like the same loyalty to a parish: it's more to the congregation and the area. If people move away, they'll often go back and attend the same church they went to before, because it's where their friends are. There's a marked sense of class distinction too in the Protestant church: one which doesn't exist to anything like the same extent among Catholics. There's no question about it, in this area and many others, we present a middle-class image even though we're on the edge of a public-sector housing-estate. It's the middle-class people who involve themselves in most of the running of the church, serving on different committees and so on. Some Protestants go to a particular church even it it's outside their immediate area, mainly because they feel comfortable there, it's in their class. I regret this very much and wish something could be done about it, and perhaps one day it'll be different. Meantime I'll do the best I can to change things, but one individual's contribution can only be very small.

Father O'Mallie

The ground-floor windows all round the presbytery at the side of his church were protected with thick wire mesh, and there was an electronically remote-controlled entry phone at its door. When I pressed the bell and said who I was into the speaker, the buzzer sounded the release of the lock, and I could go in.

A small bald-headed man with a warm handshake and a lively smile, he took me into the large high-ceilinged dining-room off the entrance hallway: we sat at the end of the long polished-wood table, and after we'd been talking for a while a pleasant middle-aged housekeeper in a white jumper and blue skirt brought in a tray with coffee and biscuits for us.

– Welcome to you, do you know this area at all now Tony? Well it's nowadays usually known as 'Short Strand', after the name of the street outside. This is its parish church, and we're a tiny Catholic enclave in the middle of a highly Protestant area. As you saw when you came, the presbytery has to have protective grilles at all its windows and an entry phone at the door. Things are not quite as bad as they were a few years ago though: then we had to have wire fencing all round the whole property including the church itself, and the gates kept locked day and night. During the last twenty years of the struggles this entire area has been devastated several times, and this is one of a number of Catholic churches in Belfast where more than once we've had British troops actually stationed here for our defence. Once there were eight or nine thousand Catholic people living in the district: but so many have left and gone away there's now no more than about three thousand here. I don't know whether they'll gradually come back, but I think not: most have settled now in west Belfast. The Catholic population's much larger there, they're in a majority, so understandably they feel safer.

I'm not exaggerating when I say of my parishioners there's scarcely one family among them which hasn't lost one member at least, as a result of sectarian fighting. A woman living just opposite us over there has been widowed twice: the last occasion was only twelve months ago, and she's still a comparatively young woman in her mid-forties and with four children. In the last few years there's been less destruction of property, but tit-for-tat killings go on. Last week there was yet one more incident, and somebody narrowly escaped with his life. So my security precautions are still necessary without any doubt, and I keep them in place on the police's advice. There's fear in the air all the time, especially following a recent incident such as last week's. People who still live here think with good reason they're vulnerable to retaliation and they are, even though what it's for had nothing to do with us. It's a very very unhappy situation and one I can't see changing or being changed for a long while yet. Every member of our small Catholic community here feels all the time mentally that he or she's living under siege.

I'd dearly like to be able to talk to you Tony with conviction about positive aspects of the situation here, particularly in Belfast. There are some, I'm not saying there aren't: but all the same I can't really see an end to it all, because there's such deep antagonism towards Catholics in Protestant hearts. People continue to say, and be quoted in the newspapers as saying, all the old entrenched slogans: 'No surrender', 'Not an inch', and so on. You've probably seen for yourself that huge banner hung round the dome of the City Hall, proclaiming 'Belfast Says No'. I'm not sure what it is they claim Belfast is saying 'No' to, nor are ordinary people in the street if you ask them. Sometimes I feel it's just to anything and everything of a constructive nature: and it does nothing else but make me sad.

To a lot of visitors like yourself, I know the situation must seem utterly incomprehensible. English people must feel that all the Irish are crazy, and are carrying on religious sectarianism, which is something quite barbaric: it's right out of keeping with our time that Protestants and Catholics can't live together in peace. I can understand English people must think that: they read in their papers or see on television explosions caused by the IRA, and shootings of innocent Catholics in retaliation by Protestant paramilitary gunmen. I don't know how, but I wish they could try to understand that the religious problem is only the tip of the iceberg, one small part of a huge conglomerate of problems. If they'd study, or at least read a little about what's been occurring here for almost the whole of this century, perhaps they'd better understand the complexity of the situation.

So much has been done in the past in Northern Ireland to Catholics, by the Unionists when they were in government, that it's hard to see how this can easily be forgiven by them, let alone forgotten. There are many Catholic people who've never in their whole lives known anything but discrimination being practised against them. All the big industries here – the shipyards, the aircraft and munitions people and the rest – they've always been dominated by Protestants. Whenever government grants were given to revive the economy, they were always given to companies to develop in Protestant areas. It's not much use saying now that things are getting better, and for instance that religious discrimination by employers has been made illegal. So it has, but there's still a long long way to go. It's only employers who engage more than fifteen people, or possibly twenty, I'm not sure of the exact figure now – but it's only by them that a return has to be declared of the number of Protestants and the number of Catholics they employ. So in the hundreds and thousands of small businesses and shops there are, this means discrimination continues on a day to day basis without any curbs. So you can say progress has been made towards ending it, but not that it's been eradicated or anything like it.

Let me say too though that there's no doubt at all in my mind that direct rule by Britain brings benefits to Catholics. In areas such as housing, central government now has control of allocations: and you'll hear Protestants saying bitterly now that Catholics are being given preferential treatment. There's some truth in it: and the reason is to make up the ground from the past when discrimination was blatant against them. But while people can be and are being rehoused, there's still little being done about the employment situation. We're suffering more badly here from the recession than anywhere else in the British Isles. And the effects will be very long-lasting: the Protestants in their own areas have high unemployment, and this does nothing at all to make the situation between the two communities any better. In many ways it's similar to that in certain cities in England where you hear ill-informed people complaining immigrants have taken their jobs. Here a Protestant is only too ready when he's unemployed to see employed Catholics everywhere, and vice versa. When you haven't a job and are unoccupied you've all the time in the world to dwell on the unfairness of the situation you're in, and ready to blame it on a scapegoat group. Also, it's far too easy if you're out of work and somebody comes along and asks you, to accept an offer to earn a few extra pounds for yourself by acting as a lookout, or a car driver who doesn't ask questions about what he's taking from here to there. Once you've become trapped in that net of activity, it's difficult to extricate yourself. Do you know what I mean?

The English have a great deal of responsibility about this: they've in many ways provided breeding grounds for the paramilitaries both by allowing discrimination to continue, and by taking no steps to lessen unemployment. To my mind these two things are the root causes of the divisions in our society, and the awful continuing consequences of them. It's not as simple as religious prejudice at all: it goes much deeper than that, and I think it should be recognised in Britain that you have a great responsibility for causing it and allowing it to go on. And you can't solve it merely by keeping an Army here, or piously hoping you can get us all round a table for talks. I think many of the Protestant and Catholic people here – and not just many but by far the majority of them – genuinely want to be allowed to live together in peace. Fanatics on both sides play on the differences, but the sameness in wanting peace is truly there.

But often neither side can understand the other at all. To give you an example from my own job, take the matter of burials of men who've been killed when they've been involved in IRA activities. This can lead to very strong reactions: people ask how it's possible for a priest of our Church like me to give Christian burial to such a man, when it's known without a shadow of doubt that he died on 'active service', as the IRA themselves are the first to claim. I wish they could see that what a priest is doing when he performs the funeral service is doing it as a mark of Christian recognition and affection for the man's family. We're not denying him what we feel is his right: and it doesn't in any way condone the action or actions of the particular individual himself. Very often such people are no longer themselves practising Catholics, but that doesn't alter the fact that their families still are. Sunday after Sunday the Catholic Church condemns paramilitary action and violent activity: only it's invariably to a congregation of Christian people who themselves wouldn't shoot a mouse. The IRA, and paramilitaries of other kinds, are not even there in the church to hear this condemnation. Being Catholic doesn't at all mean you're necessarily a military-minded Republican: being Catholic primarily means you're a Christian, and one who in most cases practises Christian virtues of tolerance and living in peace.

Father Des

A cold rainy morning, and in the turns of same-looking streets I couldn't find his house. 'I'm trying to find Number 22,' I said to the young woman pushing the pram.

'Father Des's?' She held her hand to her windswept hair. 'Ask at that top corner there, anyone'll take you to him.' As I started to walk away she called: 'Tell him love from my Danielle – he baptised her for me.'

A short broad-shouldered man with ginger hair, he turned his typing-chair back to front and sat astride it: he talked intently, emphasising things he felt strongly about by gently tapping with a clenched fist on his palm.

– I've been a priest without a parish for fifteen years now: I work in the education field a bit, but mostly do community and youth work. This was because I found myself too out of sympathy with several aspects of church policy. As a young man I'd been to university and Maynooth before I was ordained, and at twenty-four I was appointed a religious adviser to theological students: then later I worked as a priest at the Mater Hospital in the Crumlin Road for fourteen years. The time at college with students had been like living in a cocoon: and it was only when I came to Belfast that I began to see what things were really like, and the appalling poverty many Catholics lived in here. At the same time the experience I was having in the hospital showed me very clearly the lowly status the church accorded women. The nurses were terribly exploited, advantage was taken of their sense of vocation, and they'd nobody to speak up for them. It wasn't my job to do it: in my position at the hospital I was supposed to be primarily concerned with the welfare of the patients.

But I heard from them too how life was for women outside in the community: for instance women had no support from the church if they lived as many of them did with violent husbands. They were always told they just had to accept their situation. I remember one day one telling me about her husband's behaviour and how he had hit her when they quarrelled: and she said 'Well I suppose I deserved it.' That was the way the whole situation was summed up: and for me as a pacifist, I couldn't accept that anybody ever deserved to be hit under any circumstances whatsoever. Other things which I felt added to women's problems as well were the Church's rigorous opposition to divorce, and its refusal to agree with birth control. I realised women's lives in very many ways were being impoverished, both materially and spiritually.

There's no point in me going into it in much detail: but that's why I don't now have a parish, because I was increasingly unhappy with many things I saw, and in fundamental disagreement with my Church. I felt it wasn't using its resources to alleviate poverty, it wasn't really trying to bring about world peace, and I was in an untenable personal position. I belonged to a wealthy and powerful organisation: and I was expected to put forward its responses to problems, and deploy arguments on its behalf, with which I completely disagreed.

I haven't changed my attitude at all. In recent times another bone of contention between us is I feel our Church has for far too long gone along with the idea that the Northern Ireland troubles are basically due to sectarianism. They say Catholics and Protestants will always disagree, and any solution must be based on tolerance of each other's different religious beliefs. My own experience flatly contradicts this: I don't see the conflict as being of that nature at all. I'd go so far as to say that in conniving with the idea, the Church has shown itself to be part of the problem itself, and not in any way contributing to a solution. What's wrong transcends anything as simple as difference in religious dogma: and I think it's definitely harmful to allow such an idea to persist. The problem is one of economics: poverty and social deprivation. Until the Church accepts that and insists something's done about it, it's deliberately misleading people. With its power and wealth the Church should be concerning itself actively with social reform: it shouldn't be hiding behind dogmatic schism and pretending that that's what's causing our society's divisions. Some years ago Mother Theresa of Calcutta started a house here: she met with nothing but opposition from our Church and as a result she left. I think it shows the extent to which there's interference from our hierarchy, because the ostensible reason given for lack of co-operation with her was she wouldn't agree to local priests having power over her self-governing establishment.

I'm sad to say that I do see the fact of the matter as the Church having a poor record in almost every respect in Northern Ireland. It's never insisted on the truly important things being discussed. I say it makes me sad, but I should really be more forthright and say what's true, which is that as well as being sad I'm also very angry about its neglect of basics. When the Civil Rights movement began to make its presence felt twenty years ago, it got no support at all from the Catholic Church. Leaders of the movement weren't allowed to speak in church halls for instance, and no attempt was made to change things. Thousands of Catholics at that time had to flee from their homes in north and east Belfast, but there was no meaningful help or defence offered them by the Church.

I very gradually began to see these things and recognise our shortcomings: it wasn't an overnight conversion, but it happened as a result of my own experiences. I became known through the media as a spokesman for a radical approach to attempting to resolve the problems in Northern Ireland: and what I did wasn't at all acceptable to the Church. My main fault in those early days was to think almost everyone concerned was basically benign. I believed all the institutions – the British Government, the police, the Army, the Church – were genuinely and fundamentally wanting to bring about change and a solution to the chaos which existed. But I'm sorry to say that I concluded in the end only the Republicans with their perpetual cynicism about all those people I've mentioned had the realistic approach. They said all of them were concerned first and foremost only with their own position and well-being, and had no real concern about the lot of ordinary people whatsoever. It took me a long time to realise they were absolutely correct about it. When I was interviewed on radio and television and put forward some radical ideas, I was sickened by the lack of response to them. I knew in every interview and discussion, and sooner rather than later, the hostile question would come: 'Oh, you support the IRA then do you?' I'm in fact, and always have been, a pacifist and I deeply resented this. Interviews with me were edited to make it sound as though I said things which were the opposite of what I was arguing, and it even reached the stage of my being accused of being sympathetic to gunrunners. I got no backing from my Church at all: they regarded me as a maverick and a trouble-maker. So I finally decided there was no point in trying to criticise the Establishment any longer. Instead of being answered or having my points discussed, I'd always be personally discredited instead. To try and redress the balance and air at least some of my ideas, I wrote a book.

It's interesting to see the same sort of thing now happening to Sinn Fein. Anyone connected with them isn't allowed to be heard on radio or television, with the reason given that they're in that way denied what Mrs Thatcher called 'the oxygen of publicity'. In fact the reason's nothing of the kind: it's that the authorities don't wish anyone in Sinn Fein to be seen as reasonable and respectable, someone with a point of view that might contain an idea worth hearing and even possibly worth discussion.

Instead all the publicity's being given to bodies such as 'STOP', 'FAIT', and now something called 'New Consensus'. The worthy people who've started these organisations still insist the basic problem is Catholics and Protestants who can't live together: so what they're doing is promulgating the Government's line and the Church's line. The basic problems are still not being recognised or discussed. They're all deluded if they think that if only the natives can be taught to be nice to each other, all the problems will be resolved. But none of them concentrates on the real issues which make the problem intractable, the economic ones. I become very impatient with these new-fangled bodies, and even more so when they're given start-up grants by the British Government. That in itself should be sufficient to make anyone suspicious. And nobody wants to admit how unrealistic they are. Can you imagine how people would react if it was suggested we should visit the Israelis and Palestinians, distribute coloured balloons to them, and organise a mass launching of them to coincide with taking a few hundred children from both sides on a short holiday in America together? What on earth would that contribute towards solving the Israeli-

Palestine problem? You could rightly say to behave like that would insult both sides in its fatuousness. But that's exactly the sort of thing which is being done here.

The only response to the situation here by the British Government is to keep on blaming things on these people called 'terrorists'. What's really happening though – and I'm a pacifist so I don't for one moment condone it – is that desperate people are making a desperate response to a situation that's been going on longer than two decades. You shouldn't denigrate the morals of the people who take up arms: instead you should reflect that the only people in Northern Ireland who actually take up arms for financial reasons to earn a wage are the RUC, the Army, and those described in general as being connected in various ways with what are called 'the security forces'. That's forty-five per cent of the total workforce in Northern Ireland: which means that if there ever was an end to the troubles, almost half the working population would immediately be unemployed!

In the end I believe however long it takes, ordinary Irish people will eventually come to see the truth of the situation: which is that they themselves are the only people who can solve the problems of our country. The British Government could make a constructive contribution by withdrawal of their troops, gradually, but prefaced by a statement of intent. Something like an announcement they'll withdraw completely from west of the River Bann within five years, and from the rest of the north, east of the Bann, within thirty years. I think that might be acceptable to the Loyalists: they do know that eventually it's got to happen. At present neither Nationalists nor Unionists know where they are, and with good reason neither trusts the British. So some kind of statement would help to clarify things. That's how I see it, I think the majority of Irish people do, and I'm sure gradually your people will too.

*

(Father Des Wilson's *An End To Silence* is published by Royal Carbery Books of Cork, and distributed by the Mercier Press.)

14 *A few helpers and triers*

Shirley Carnell, DHSS clerk

P. J. McGrory, solicitor

Mary Caine, prison voluntary worker

Pamela Deacon, youth worker

Brian Spring, youth worker

Chrissy Wharton, women's advice centre worker

Shirley Carnell,

DHSS clerk

A brown-eyed vivacious young woman in her late twenties, in a Laura Ashley dress, she spoke confidently and animatedly, laughing and smiling and gesticulating with her hands.

– You're talking to a happy civil servant. I've been in the local Health and Social Security office here for six years, and I do, I honestly look forward to staying a long time yet. I'm recently married, we don't have children yet, but when we do I'd like to think after a while I could come back again. It's a job wouldn't suit everyone, but it does me just fine, so it does. We have a large and busy office as you've seen, open to the public from nine in the morning till half past three five days a week: after we close we go on until 5.30 with filing and preparing for the next day. In our section there's six of us: we each do a week in turn at the counter dealing with clients, then we have five weeks on the enormous clerical backup work at the back.

When it's your week on the counter, well it is, it's great. You'll see something like forty to fifty people a day: that adds up to between two and three hundred a week, so it's absolutely tremendously varied every minute of the day. And almost all of them without exception, you know, they're very very polite and well disposed to you too. Any idea of a Social Security office being all day full of angry dissatisfied people, I don't know where it could come from: but it's nothing at all like that here. There's an odd person now and again who wants to give you a hard time because you seem to them to be the representative of an unhelpful bureaucracy, that's only natural. They don't want to hear what you have to say about what they're entitled to and what they're not. But I always try to stay polite and do my job as inoffensively as I can, like all my colleagues do. You certainly couldn't stand the work if you were arguing and shouting all day, it'd not be in the least enjoyable. No one would ever want to do it to be sure now would they?

I sound like a spokeswoman for the Establishment don't I? Oh well you know, there are times when you are and you wish you weren't. I don't suppose I'm giving away State secrets if I say now and again you feel a claimant should actually be given something more than the strict entitlement. But you have to tell yourself it wasn't you who decided what should or shouldn't be allowed, nor the rate that's paid. You always have to keep your personal feelings under control while you do your best to explain the situation. And sometimes you know you're taking a subjective approach: you wouldn't be human if you didn't feel a person in a difficult situation being pleasant to you wasn't more deserving than someone who was shouting and angry about it. But it's not your job to let personal feelings enter into it: your job's to ensure everyone gets neither no less and no more than what the correct entitlement is.

My own attitude to my work is that when I can, I try to make it a bit more than giving out money, or not giving it out because of the regulations. There are often occasions when you can help somebody by pointing out things perhaps they're not aware of: so when they make their application, then they can support their case better because of what you've told them. You couldn't say it was exactly social work, but I mean we quite often refer people to the Social Services when they're in need of help. You can point out to someone it'd help their claim to have a doctor's letter backing up what they say about their poor health, and if they could get one then it could certainly be of advantage. You always try to be fair to everyone, and if you can look at yourself in the mirror when you've got home at the end of the day and know you've done your best, well that's what matters, eh?

Here where we are, it's an area where there's great deprivation and poverty: you often learn of some very sad situation, and you feel you'd like to be able to do much more than you're actually permitted to. All claimants have to be treated in exactly the same way, and the regulations are very precise. If you're in doubt you go and consult your supervisor, and he or she'll give you guidance: after all as well as responsibilities to clients we've responsibilities to the Government because we're giving out public money, so both sides have to be kept in mind.

People who come in to make claims are pretty reasonable on the whole, you know. I'm sure I wouldn't like to be in their position myself, I mean having to ask financial help like they do, from an impersonal Government department. However much they're entitled to it, they must almost always feel a degree of embarrassment about it. I don't think it's part of my or anyone else's job here to try and make them feel worse. Everyone has their rights, and there's nothing wrong about seeing you get them. Whether it's from me or any other person on the counter, a pleasant manner and a smile and complete avoidance of any kind of condescension's the very least people are entitled to expect. I do find on the whole because I'm a young woman people are very tolerant of me, even when they get frustrated and feel I'm probably too young and inexperienced to be in my position: and sometimes a person of my own age or older will make it very plain they resent me being in a way in authority over them. I get frightened I must admit by aggressive shouting men, they really make me quake. But in all my experience so far the worst that's ever happened to me's been somebody's got so angry they've demanded to see my supervisor. When it reaches that point, I always immediately agree and fetch the person they want. Just doing that usually reduces the temperature: they have the satisfaction they've gone over my head and it's a useful safety valve.

Because I was born and brought up and went to school in this area, it's a great help to me: it reminds me the people I meet who're on the other side of the counter to me are all fundamentally the same as I am. Sometimes people ask me how I can possibly work for the D Haitch SS. I suppose it's because to them it's part of the Establishment. But that's not quite the way I look at it myself: one of my uncle's been on the brew himself for years: naturally I wouldn't see him or anyone else if I knew them, but it does make you feel claimants are no different from you. 'The Brew'? Well everyone calls it that, I think it's the old pronunciation of Bureau, the Unemployment Bureau.

I wouldn't like to live and work anywhere else but here, the whole area's my home. When I was younger my father involved himself in voluntary work, he drove cars and buses for handicapped people round here. So I got interested in the same sort of activity myself, and I don't know why but eventually it was deaf people I got particularly involved with. From about the age of eleven I learned how to finger-spell, and when I left school and came to work here, it struck me before long that it'd be useful in a Social Security office if there was someone who could communicate with deaf people and people without speech. Both the staff and deaf people themselves always found it awkward and embarrassing to have to communicate by writing on pieces of paper and passing them to and fro between them all the time. I asked my bosses here if it'd be possible for me to go on a proper communications with the deaf course which is done part-time at the university. They took it up with Head Office who said yes, and I'm now in my second year of it and the Department are paying my fees. Someone in the office who can finger-spell and sign is quite an advantage, everyone feels, and if someone with that handicap comes in, I'm brought out to them even if I'm not on counter duty. It's really good to be able to approach someone and start signing, you always see the smile come on their face. Often they think I'm deaf too, but even when they find I'm not, it's a huge help to them that there's someone here with the ability to communicate easily with. I think one day every Social Security office will have someone like me on the staff: deaf people are especially handicapped in everyday life because they're not quickly recognisable like a blind person with dark glasses and a stick. They always get immediate offers of help everywhere, and a lot of sympathy: but deaf people don't get anything like the same consideration.

P. J. McGrory,

solicitor

He lived with his wife and family in a spacious house in a quiet residential area on the outskirts of the city. At the end of a curved drive and secluded by trees, it was invisible from the road and he asked that its appearance shouldn't be described in detail or its exact location specified. In its light airy sitting-room, with ceiling-high shelves of books and paintings and prints by contemporary Irish artists filling almost every space on the walls, he sat relaxed in a deep comfortable armchair: an elderly gentle-voiced man with white hair and a penetrating look, and now and again a softly self-deprecating smile.

– Patrick John McGrory, solicitor: Roman Catholic, Nationalist, that about sums it all up. About to retire before long, well near retirement age anyhow: my wife says she'll believe it when it happens but not before. There's a great deal of work I want to do still though: a little writing perhaps, going to places to talk with people, an occasional bit of legal work to keep my hand in, I don't want to drop out entirely, I'd like to think I can still be of use somewhere. I'll always be one to find something to occupy himself with, I suppose.

My origins? Well I'm just an ordinary boy from the Falls Road. Ever since I was young the law and the courts always had a special fascination for me whenever I heard or read about them. When it came time to leave school and go to university, all I wanted to study for was a law degree. My father made enquiries about prospects for the future in that field, neither he nor I knowing anything very much about it. We found that if I was to try to be a barrister a lot of money would be needed to support me while I studied, and afterwards went into practice and tried to make my own way. And Catholics in the profession in Northern Ireland never got a taste of the cream of the work, because the majority of the solicitors who could give it were Protestants. Obviously it was going to be a long long climb and we weren't rich people, so I decided to settle for being a solicitor. In the legal system here you can work as an advocate in the lower courts, and I was satisfied with that. But also being a Catholic meant civil work was hard to get: so that's how it came about that most of my practice was in the area of crime. It was good grounding and background and I've always enjoyed it you know: in magistrates' courts and petty sessions you come into contact with all types of offenders. From motorists who've broken the speed limit to people who've committed fairly serious crime being passed on to be dealt with at the high level, it's always varied and interesting and I think it's suited someone of my kind of temperament very well.

I've only ever been a defender: and I suppose that's something in my nature. I never took to prosecuting at all: in over forty years of practice it's never attracted me. As a prosecutor, just as you are as a defender, you're concerned with the deed not the man: but though I don't know why, it's always seemed to come more naturally to me to act for defendants. Somehow in all my career I've had this perpetual streak of being not so much anti-authority as never willing to let authority have its say without questioning whether there wasn't another side to things as well.

This has inevitably led to me getting a reputation as someone prepared to take on the defence of IRA terrorists. In the minds of certain people I've as a result identified myself with the IRA's point of view. I don't: I've never agreed with the use of violence. Recently feelings have begun to run higher and higher again on the subject of terrorism: and the point's been reached once more when if people are arrested and brought to trial for terrorist offences, the mere idea that somebody's prepared to defend them is absolute anathema. It's unfortunate but I am afraid it's unavoidable now that my practice has become identified with a political cause. To some extent I've got a name for myself: and it's a very bad one in the view of some Protestants, and a good one as far as those who are on the Republican side. I didn't seek it, but a lot of publicity was given to the fact that I appeared at the Gibraltar inquest for the families of the three alleged IRA terrorists who were shot in broad daylight in the street by the

SAS. I found myself in court on that occasion facing some of the best legal talents of England. Obviously I can't comment on the result: but I thought the outcome was not exactly satisfactory, even though I hope I gave as good an account of myself as I was allowed to. But what a lot of people didn't understand was because of my willingness to represent terrorists or their families, I wasn't in any way agreeing with the alleged offences of those who'd been killed. Since we've chosen to have an adversarial legal system, it's up to the prosecution to prove their case: and the defence's task is to try to show they haven't succeeded. The guilt or innocence of the parties isn't the issue: the proof, or failure of it, is what's at stake.

Ironically, because of some of the successes I've had, I'm now being increasingly frequently asked to handle the defence of Protestant paramilitary terrorists too. So this is now making me unpopular in certain Republican quarters. Yet I feel it's my professional duty to do my best for Protestants just as I would for anyone: and some of them, even more ironically, are people who'd do harm if they could to someone who'd acted for members of the IRA. It's a problem for anyone in the legal profession: over and over again they're identified with those on whose behalf they appear. No matter how many times you repeat that the defender defends the man not the deed, very many people can't or won't accept it. Last year Mr Finucane, a solicitor who often acted for IRA defendants, was assassinated for that reason. And now I've myself been told on good authority, that my own movements are being watched and studied, and information on me is being steadily gathered over a period of time. By whom, by which side, I don't exactly know and so far haven't been able to find out. But I do know this is the usual prelude to an attempt on someone's life. So all I can do is take precautions and hope for the best. But I make no apology, and never will, for the work on behalf of defendants from both sides that I do.

– Shall we talk now of other things? Certainly, fine, by all means, yes. How did I become a Nationalist, well I suppose in the same way most other Nationalists do – by growing up in the Falls Road and seeing as a young man the constant discrimination in the north against Catholics for no other reason than that was their religious faith. For decade after decade since Partition in the early 20s, Northern Ireland was ruled by Protestants and for Protestants. Catholics didn't get a fair share of anything: not housing, not education, not employment nor anything else. They were persecuted and in thousands of instances driven by violence out of their homes in many different areas of Belfast. They felt, and they were, powerless: and got no protection from the British Government. It turned its back on what was going on, ignored the situation, and didn't wish to know. This is the one and only origin of the troubles now and the bitterness ever since. Even if only thirty years ago the Government had taken steps to end discrimination, two generations of people wouldn't have grown up with all the feelings of fear and antagonism towards each other which they now have. Catholics in the North had legitimate demands for protection and equality of opportunity: and when there was no sign of them coming, finally in despair many of them turned to violence. And then even the judicial system itself became embroiled in trying to enforce the idea all activity of that sort was actually nothing but crime. That brought the judiciary into disrepute. And now you see the results: violence continuing, mistrust and suspicion, obduracy and obstinacy, and bleakness and hopelessness everywhere.

The English people aren't informed about the truth of the situation, and I think this is because English MPs in Parliament only represent constituents on a local basis. An MP from Lincolnshire for example, he's going to earn no thanks from those who voted for him if he spends time in Parliament arguing the case of Irish Catholics in the North of Ireland. They're going to say to him 'We put you in Parliament to represent the interests of Lincolnshire people, what on earth are you doing making speeches about Catholics in Belfast?' And the ignorance is perpetual: English voters don't want to know what happens here. We who are far away over this narrow stretch of water are only a whimsical people, never to be taken seriously, not often even to be very much thought about.

So you see to many people here the British Government tries to do nothing constructive about the situation. They become more and more exasperated and exhausted by the impossibility and dangerousness of the IRA. The Government dissembles, and meantime the IRA are increasingly resilient. They continue to resist,

they arm and re-arm, and however many members they lose
through death or capture there's no shortage of new recruits to join
them. The Government plays right into their hands because it can't
think or won't think of any response to terrorists but terror. There's
a nod and a wink to the SAS for example that the behaviour of their
wild men will be tolerated and in extreme cases covered up. The SAS
have shot a number of other people besides those they killed in
Gibraltar, and given the justification that they thought they were
about to be attacked themselves. But in no case yet have they simply
arrested anybody to prevent them doing whatever they were alleged
to be about to do. Time and again people have been shot down
without warning. It's surely a very worrying thing indeed that
certain people are allowed to go out and to murder people, and
afterwards don't have to fear serious enquiry into whether what they
did was justified. They can simply say they shot someone because he
or she was a known member of the IRA and was about to attack
them or run away. I don't know any other country in Europe where
such a thing would for one moment be allowed, because what it
illustrates is the breakdown of law and order everywhere, on every
side.

Both Protestants and Catholics in the North are becoming more
and more disillusioned, because no British politician can be seen who
has the vision or the will to end this situation. It attracts the obloquy
of the whole of the rest of the world, and it's being continued at
fantastic cost to the British taxpayer. No problem's insoluble,
especially with the political expertise of the British: but allowing
things to drift is inexcusable. It's wasteful of money: and worse it's
wasteful of lives. Soldiers, IRA men, innocent civilians in bombing
incidents – they're all being sacrificed by the ineptness of politicians,
and it's a very shameful thing that it's so, it truly is.

Mary Caine,

prison voluntary worker

Her modern house was on the outskirts of the city: inside in her open-plan sitting-room were books and records and colourful prints by Klee, Mondrian and Miró. In red trousers and a white blouse she sat cross-legged and relaxed on a big settee, her long fair hair falling loosely on her shoulders.

– Yeah I suppose my slight American accent does show up now and again: but I'm genuine Northern Irish. When I was around nine or so my parents emigrated with me to the States, but I came back here on my own when I was twenty-two. I'd several times returned for holidays and to stay with relatives, and I never lost the feeling I belonged here and would come back permanently one day. My parents though, still they live in the States.

My education in the US was up to high school level: it was the time of the great growing of the Civil Rights movement there and the war in Vietnam, and those two things had a greater influence on me than the educational system. At the same time I was reading and discovering the Bible and the New Testament in particular, and very curious to discover what Christianity was about. The one thing that came most clearly of all through to me was its pacifist message. I didn't see how you could profess to be Christian without being a pacifist then, and I still don't now.

It was something that puzzled me greatly about all the churches, that they didn't accept that. Their leaders talked endlessly about peace on earth and goodwill towards all men, but never took any fundamental stand against war. It wasn't until I began reading about Quakers that I found compatibility between my idea of Christian faith and any religious body at all. So, since Quakers were and always have been pacifists, that was why I became one myself. It wasn't until I came back to Belfast, and I was helped along by the fact I was doing community work and shared a flat with a girl who was a Quaker herself. I found much in common with her and became an attender for two years before actually becoming a full member of the Society of Friends. This was in the early 1970s at the start of the troubles.

When I returned to Belfast it reinforced the strong feeling in my mind that this was where I belonged. I've never lost my love for this country, I've a very strong emotional attachment to it, and I identify with it more and more every day. I come from a Protestant family, and I was most disturbed by what was going on: it's difficult to put it into precise words, but I felt strongly this was where I was meant to be. I guess that some people won't identify to the same degree, or do it in a different way. I'm not sectarian, and I feel I must do all I can to help. It's my interpretation of what Christianity is fundamentally about, peace, that makes me feel I've a duty to be here and work for that.

At first when I came I didn't know exactly what I wanted to do. I'd no job, so I stayed with a friend and looked into the prospects of taking a qualification for social work. In the States for a while I'd worked with Puerto Ricans and I had a degree in Spanish: but that wasn't strictly relevant to social work. But the degree was accepted for teaching in secondary schools here, and so that's what I did at first. I was only a temporary teacher in a temporary post though. Then I did community work in the Shankill area, and while doing it studied for the social work qualification. In fact I've now married, and I haven't quite yet finished my studies. Meantime I'm still doing voluntary work with a small group of Quakers and others who go into two of the big prisons, Long Kesh or the Maze as it's now called, and Maghaberry. Most of what we do is involved with life-sentence prisoners convicted of terrorist offences.

Naturally as a pacifist I've always absolutely abhorred the use of violence. When I first went into the prisons, I felt the sort of people I was being asked to work with would be so alien to me that I probably wouldn't be able to come to terms with my pacifist stance and their actions. They'd used extreme violence, they'd killed people. My attitude was it didn't matter whether they were Loyalists or Republican, but if they'd taken their belief to such an extent that they were prepared to kill for it, I couldn't see any way in which I could possibly empathise with them.

To begin with I was only a worker helping in the family visitors' canteen, so my ideas weren't tested much. Then after a while I started to involve myself more with the prisoners' families when they came to visit, and I began to learn what sorts of situations they were in. For all of them, their lives had been totally traumatised by the offences their husbands were in prison for, and were going to be in there for a very long time still. I began to want to try to understand the prisoners, which isn't the same thing as agreeing with them: but at least I did at last see them as individuals, not just men lumped together and labelled 'terrorists'. Each of them was somebody's husband and somebody's brother and somebody's son, and all of them human beings. And they were all in despair: they desperately wanted to talk about how a man could have any sort of validity as a husband and father, when he was spending a life sentence in prison. It forced them to think most painfully about themselves. And you find trying to help a man is of far greater importance than your own feelings about him as a person. It gradually teaches you more understanding of everyone's common basic humanity.

When the point's reached at which the man's given a definite future date for release, that brings a whole new set of quandaries to be talked through, both with him and with his wife. Before long it strikes you very clearly how desperately men and their families cling to the prospect of getting a release-date, however far ahead. It's almost all they have to live for, being told exactly when it'll be, when the suspense of not knowing it is over. And when it happens the whole situation changes radically: husbands and wives become obsessively nervous about changes they'll both have to face when the man goes home, what adjustments they'll have to make. In talking with them you try to help them identify what some of the problems may be, and how they can be dealt with by talking through them. The fears and expectations on both sides are often very exaggerated, naturally enough: so you've to bring them out in the open and discuss them in advance so far as it's possible for the different people involved.

Even though we're only voluntary workers, we get a great deal of co-operation both from the prison service and from the probation service. And in some ways it's an advantage for us to be a voluntary group not connected with the powers-that-be. It means we don't have any official status and can be seen as what we are, just ordinary people. Also we meet prisoners and their wives and families while they're still in custody, and then continue contact with them after they're released as well. Officials can't do that: their connection with them in prison has to finish when they're released. It's voluntary contact with us on their part, they can break it off any time they wish: but I'm surprised how many do still want to keep in touch.

When a lifer finally gets out into the community, it's after a long period of years, and he usually feels himself to be a powerless person. In prison all decisions have been made for him: what time he eats, what time he sleeps, gets up, whether he works and if so where and when – every single thing. So when he goes out he has to re-learn the whole business of living again. It's similar for his wife if she's still with him: she's had to do all the decision-making in the world outside, and it's difficult for her to share it again and help him regain self-confidence about it. In many ways that's when the real effects of a prison sentence begin.

Life sentence men usually haven't a criminal record of any other kind when they come into prison. Terrorists, fanatics and extremists or whatever they are, they're different in nature to the ordinary type of offender whose life outside has been connected with simple crime and aren't in that sense criminals at all. The offences they've committed have resulted in appalling suffering to their victims' families, and during the long time they spend inside, most of them come to realise that. It's almost as though they were sentenced to death and then years later resurrected again as different people. I've come to believe now myself that there's no room for continuing recrimination on the part of society against people who've done such long terms of imprisonment, and I hope somehow a time will come when most people agree with that.

Pamela Deacon,

youth worker

The housing-estate community centre she worked at was an ugly single-storey concrete building on a piece of derelict ground at the end of a street. Her office in it was a partitioned-off area at the end of its draughty central corridor. Tall, in her fifties, with an angular face and large hornrimmed glasses, she wore her hair scraped back from her face and held in place by a large tortoise-shell slide. Her voice was low and hesitant.

– Talking's not something I think I'm very good at, I'm more of an organiser really. At one stage in my life I used to be a teacher but when my husband died ten years ago and our three children by then were old enough to make their own way in the world, I felt I didn't want to go back into that any more. So instead I enrolled at university as a mature student for two years and took a diploma in community studies without much idea of what I was going to do with it. I enjoyed studying, did various things like working with mentally handicapped people for a while, and then finally decided to try my hand at youth work. I was fairly comfortably off and I didn't have responsibility for the children to face any more, so at first I worked on a voluntary basis as a youth club helper in different parts of the city for a couple of years. After that I got an administrative job in the social services sector, and then finally about two years ago came here. At that time there wasn't anything in this area for young people at all, so I had more or less a free hand to do whatever I wanted. I talked to people and listened to people and soon discovered the only youth activities there were were all church-centred and denominational and therefore divisive. So obviously there was a great need for something of a more general nature.

In the back of my mind I wanted to attract not only young people from this Protestant area, but also from the surrounding Catholic estates further up the hill. But it didn't work: they all keep themselves to themselves and so what I'm in charge of is still an almost entirely Protestant youth club. We function chiefly in the evenings: I have as helpers two excellent young women plus a temporary young man who's waiting to go to university, and we make quite a good team. Our activities are mainly of a social nature, with a disco and table-tennis, and we have a snooker table which a local business concern donated to us. All our members are between the ages of twelve and sixteen: the upper age-limit wasn't our idea in the first place, but when young people reach school-leaving age they seem to want something more exciting than a youth club, and they go down to the city-centre places.

It disappoints me to say it, but although we've tried hard not to make this just a place for young people to come to if they've nothing better to do, we haven't made a great deal of progress yet. At first we arranged weekly debates and discussions on such subjects as the present political situation in Belfast, but the idea never really took off. I think we've still got a lot of thinking to do about this. We went so far as to invite Catholic youth clubs to join us in that sort of activity: I feel the more young people meet and mingle with others from a different section of the community, the more hope there'll be for improvement in relations between Protestants and Catholics. I hope I'm not being biased when I say though that the only initiatives of that kind so far have come from us. There's definitely a reluctance in those running Catholic youth clubs to take part in things of that sort, almost as though they don't want their own young people to learn about other points of view. Anyone hearing me say that would probably think I'm prejudiced: but if they do I can only answer it's because of what I've actually experienced.

Our young man that I mentioned, Steve, has arranged things like football matches between teams from here and some from Catholic areas, and they've been a great success. They've brought youngsters together who wouldn't ever have met under other circumstances: but there's still a strong element even in sporting competition of religious factionalism. The games aren't played in a truly sporting spirit at all, and some of the jeering by the spectators is very distasteful.

Working in a deprived area like this one has made me realise one thing very clearly. It's that the deprivation in working-class Protestant areas is just as bad as that which we've all heard so much about, for so long now, in the Catholic parts. There's a great deal of resentment here when people read in the local newspapers about various new housing developments which are specifically for Catholics. I could take you to any number of parts of the city where Protestants are living in very poor housing: and although I'd be the first to agree in the past that Catholics were discriminated against in such matters, I think the pendulum's swung now rather too far the other way. There's a good deal of strong feeling about enclaves where Protestants still live in poor housing in the middle of areas where Catholics have had their houses rebuilt and refurbished. It's not exactly improving community relations.

I do think myself that the whole idea of forced mixing of the two different religious factions, in housing or in schooling or anything else, is a bad one. Their differences and antagonisms are so traditional and so deeply ingrained that lumping them together and telling them to get on with one another simply won't work. It's like apartheid in South Africa: I know it isn't a popular thing to say, but people do have different histories, different ways of life and different attitudes. To pretend they don't and try to force them to mix with one another in the hope they'll all eventually live happily together is a very simplistic view, and time and time again it's been shown it doesn't work: in South Africa, in Cyprus, blacks and whites in America, the Baltic States in what used to be the Soviet Union, the Croats and Serbs – their differences are so great that the only realistic attitude is to recognise it and let each race or part of the community live its own life and order its own affairs.

What I'm saying is a long way from talking about youth work I know. But I've found I've had to rethink all my woolly liberal ideas since I came here. The Protestant youngsters on this estate feel threatened and hemmed in, they feel nobody cares very much for their ideas and opinions. I was really surprised at the strength of feelings about this at one of our early discussion evenings before we gave them up. Boys and girls of thirteen or fourteen felt very strongly that their part of society was misrepresented on television and in the newspapers. They complained Protestant children were always shown in an unfavourable light, there was endless talk about what had been done *to* the Catholics but very little said about what had been done *for* them. When the boy or the girl who's saying it lives in cramped and overcrowded housing that should have been pulled down years ago, no one can be surprised if they feel angry at Catholic rehousing taking precedence now as it always seems to.

And the other thing that worries them, and me too I have to say, is the tolerance which seems to be increasingly extended towards Nationalists and Republicans. I think it's now got completely out of hand. Just a few weeks ago for instance another youth centre decided that as a contribution to widening young peoples' understanding of the present-day situation, they'd let them hear all points of view: so they approached Sinn Fein and asked them to send someone to this particular youth club to talk about Republican ideas, with a question-and-answer session afterwards. Our SF friends couldn't really believe at first that this was a serious suggestion, but they said they'd consider it and let the youth club know. Meantime an approach was made to one of the Loyalist organisations, a perfectly legal and legitimate one, to invite them to send a speaker on a separate occasion and do more or less the same thing. When this was discovered by the authorities at City Hall, they immediately said it wasn't to be allowed, it was likely to lead to accusations of political influence. Sinn Fein had never given a firm answer so it was taken they wouldn't come: the Loyalists would, but the whole thing degenerated then into an argument and the idea was dropped.

A lot of what I've said will sound highly contentious, so I'd prefer you not to be specific about who I am and where we are. But I hope something of what I've said will be taken notice of.

Brian Spring,

youth worker

He sat on a frosty morning close to a single-bar electric radiator, with his feet up on a chair in the cramped and damp room which served as his office round the back of a block of soon-to-be-demolished council flats. A burly middle-aged man with thick dark hair and a ginger moustache, in a torn grey tracksuit, a faded green turtle-neck sweat-shirt and a pair of old trainers.

– Sometimes I feel I've been twenty years on this estate, not what I have, which is two. And then other times I feel like it's only two days you know, I'm just starting and I'm right out of my depth. You'd think by the time someone was forty he'd a fair idea what youthwork was all about. But I don't, I seem to change my attitude once a week. One day I'll think what I'm doing's the most important thing in the world: then the next one I think it's all a complete bloody waste of time. It depends on what happens or what doesn't happen: a spring day, the sun shining, everything going well, it makes you think everything's all right with the world. But by afternoon it's raining, the police have been riding round everywhere in their pigs looking for trouble, lifting lads right left and centre, and you wonder what's going to become of civilisation. I used to think when I was young the older I got the more level-headed I'd become in my approach to things. I have to say it's not turned out that way at all it hasn't. I'm more and more of the attitude I'm against the whole apparatus of the State and society's structure, and really bitter and unChristian about people's indifference and lack of understanding towards teenagers. I go round a lot giving talks to civic bodies, churches, educationalists, social science people at the universities: and in all of them there's a distinct hardening of attitudes, a real lessening of interest in the welfare of young people. People are simply giving up on the young of Belfast today, they feel nothing can be done or they feel they don't want to try to do anything for them any more. Maybe it all comes down to money in the end and they think it's being wasted: certainly young lads on this estate at least are more and more often being written-off as trouble-makers, and no real attempts are being made to understand their problems.

This part of the city's got a reputation as a very rough one: and OK, in some respects it's justified. It's a Catholic area, a Republican area, and it gets its fair share of attention from the authorities. But not in any way what you might call constructive, it's oppressive more than anything else. In other areas of the city there's been much more attempt at improving housing conditions for a start: but round here there's a feeling we've been forgotten or given up on. Once it was designated a priority development area, but no one'll believe that until they see it starting to happen. Now it's looked on like a zoo full of dangerous wild animals: every night there's a cordon of road-blocks and barricades sealing-off the whole area. In case anyone breaks out and starts terrorising – that's the impression we have.

I work for an organisation funded largely with money from America and Canada. More than once I've thought it'd be better if we had a direct grant from Government, but that's got too many conditions attached. It's going in that direction too now though even with financing from the States. Everything we do's got to have this stupid label 'Cross-Community' stuck on it, whether it's relevant or practical or has any real meaning to it. If you want to get up football teams for kids of eleven and twelve, you've got to make them into a league with teams from Protestant areas. That sort of thing may be all right in an ideal world, but in Belfast today it's unrealistic. Last winter we started a martial arts club for boys: when we applied for a grant for equipment, we were told we couldn't have one unless we held matches against lads on a Protestant estate. When I enquired around, I found there weren't any martial arts clubs on any Protestant estates. Who I'm aiming my main criticism at is the authorities in the Catholic church. Most priests round here won't let us use their halls or any of their facilities unless we can show them what we're doing is what they call 'bringing the two communities together'. They say the best way to do this is to get youngsters to have friendly rivalry in sport. To put it mildly I think that's bloody stupid. I can't see that playing a football match between a team of Catholic boys and a team of Protestant boys does anything at all. I've known several times when our lads have gone over to estates in east Belfast in a coach to play a game, and they've had stones thrown at them as soon as they got anywhere near where they were supposed to be going. Ambushed, they were. And yes, the same sort of thing happens the other way round, don't let's pretend about it. But all that kind of thing does is make the situation worse, because it's false, it doesn't work, and everybody knows it doesn't.

Well now: yes, so long as you'll not use my real name or say too much about where I work, I'll tell you some of the things which our mutual friend said you'd be surprised to hear about. I suppose they'll be a wee bit surprising in the eyes of a lot of people and not just exactly what they'd imagine someone did who was called a 'youth worker'. My main concern, to describe it very simply, is to protect the young lads of hereabouts from getting themselves lifted, that's pulled in for questioning by the police. They can be taken in to Castlereagh and held for seventy-two hours, without any reason as soon as they reach the age of eighteen. I could introduce you to two dozen or more from here who've been taken in within forty-eight hours of their eighteenth birthday. The police come cruising round and they've got all the details about the lads, names, addresses, dates of birth already on the records, and they're quite frank about what they're doing. I hear the same story over and over again: a lad'll be taken into Castlereagh and he'll be told he's not going to be charged with anything. The police simply want to let him know he's on their list, and they can pick him up any time they like. Some of the threats made aren't exactly what you'd call subtle: he's told if at any time he gets any information, he'd best pass it on to them before they find out he hasn't and come looking for him. And if he doesn't want to have something really serious happen to him, he'd better not ever get himself mixed up in anything.

The police aren't talking to him about crime of course: they're talking about Nationalist and Republican activity. I think it's harassment and I think it's disgusting. Everybody knows it goes on, and nobody protests about it because they're afraid to. It's as though we were living in an occupied country. Certain lads, especially those who come from traditional Republican backgrounds, they have fathers and brothers and uncles and grandparents who are all in the Republican movement. They'll be the ones who're particularly targeted and their lives made a misery. When the police have an idea who such a lad might be, if they can't find him they take in his mates to try and get them to give information where he is, whose house he's living in and so on.

I've to be careful here and not be too specific. So I'll put it like this: if things are getting hot for somebody to the point where he feels and we feel it might be better if he wasn't around for a while, we do have a system for getting him to disappear. We can get someone out of Belfast and a hundred miles away within five hours or six at the most: we can put him somewhere he can't be touched, and where he can stay a few weeks in peace and quiet among friends and not be afraid to go out.

So that's what being a youth worker means today in parts of this country of ours. Where you come from it'd probably be called something different: obstructing the course of justice perhaps? I don't make any apology for it though. Here on a Catholic estate there are only two sides: and you're either on one or the other, you can't be neutral. By birth I'm myself a west Belfast Catholic and that makes me one of a minority: I grew up as a member of it, and all my ideas and attitudes were formed because of that. All my life I knew and heard nothing but discrimination: and so you grow up either one of the oppressors or one of the oppressed. I see my job as a youth worker to be that of giving practical assistance to lads and young men of my own kind. What I've been talking to you about, helping people disappear when the police want to question them, is against the law: but I don't consider it to be criminal activity. It's a law that bears down heavily and unfairly on one particular vulnerable section of the population. I believe it's right to do what I do: and I trust you to present what I've said in a way that makes sure where it comes from isn't identifiable.

Chrissy Wharton,

women's advice centre worker

She lived in a small flat on the top floor of a four-storey terraced house in one of the city-centre roads. Small, with black curly hair and blue eyes, she sat at the table in the kitchen, smoking and drinking coffee from a dark brown basalt mug.

– I'm twenty-two, my boyfriend Bob's a year younger and we've lived here for eighteen months. He's a student and he's very nice, or at least I think so, and we're very happy together. We get on well together, we're young and we enjoy life. I work two and a half days a week at a women's advice centre in the Shankill Road area, and three nights a week as a waitress in a restaurant in a hotel. Bob's at the moment in a solicitors' office in the city, and next year he hopes to take his final exams for his law degree. We've no plans about marrying yet, we're content to go on for a while as we are. Both our parents seem to be quite happy with the situation: my mother divorced my father when I was very young, so I suppose she doesn't want me to make what she thinks was the same mistake as she did and marry the wrong person. Bob's parents are always very nice to me when I go there, and I can't imagine they'd treat me any different if we'd actually been through a wedding ceremony. They're Catholics but not very devout ones, or perhaps I ought to say they might be devout but it doesn't stop them being fairly liberal-minded. And they apparently don't mind Bob having a girlfriend who's from a Protestant background as I am.

It's always noticeable isn't it how quickly the subject of religious origin comes into every conversation? That's one of the facts of life in Northern Ireland: you want to know almost with everyone you meet whether they're Catholic or Protestant, and you presume other

people'll be the same about you. As far as middle-class people are
concerned I don't think it makes any difference to how they behave
towards you, but all the same they like to know. Sometimes you
wonder will it ever change or will it always go on being like that?
Don't ask me the answer because I don't know: but it's hard for
young people like Bob and me to grasp its importance still to some
people. To us it's not important, it doesn't matter what anyone is:
but perhaps that's because basically we're both agnostics.

One of the things I notice at work which I think's a hopeful sign is
when women come into the advice centre, most of them don't ask us
about our religious affiliation: and they don't seem to feel either it's
necessary for us to know theirs. When the subject they're enquiring
about is say abortion or birth control, we don't ask questions about
whether there'd be a religious objection from anyone including
themselves: we just tell them what they want to know freely and
openly. The Shankill area's predominantly Protestant and well-
known to be, but it's obvious some of the women who come are
from Catholic areas: and you can tell by the way they express their
relief at finding out what it is they want to know, that they come
from somewhere where it's not easy even for them to talk about such
subjects. And before long they often start to talk to other women
who are there too.

Maybe I'm not explaining myself very well, but I say it makes me
feel hopeful because I think it shows the women who come to us
have found some kind of common ground in the mere fact they're
women: and people like me who work there are gradually starting to
see it too. I think if this can be realised and stressed, it's important for
us all. We're women first, and Protestant or Catholic a long way
second. I don't think I'm being idealistic in saying that it's hopeful
that we realise it. I don't know whether what I'm saying makes me a
feminist: I don't think terms like that are important. What's
important is that women in trouble see they're not alone and are able
to identify with other women in trouble. And if we can gradually
learn that matters of social deprivation are things that'll never be
changed unless we all work together to change them, that's what's
important, not what sort of religious allegiances we have. I don't
mean we should all march in the streets carrying banners: but I do
mean we ought to discuss them and start to think about things that a

lot of women never thought about at all when they were young. If a woman's pregnant when she doesn't want to be, because she's already got more children than she can cope with, or if she's in a situation such as being knocked about by her husband or boyfriend, then this is a matter of her fundamental rights in life as an individual.

Oh Lord, sorry: I'm afraid I tend to get carried away on the subject. But when I listen to men politicians and religious leaders on the television or radio, I feel these are the subjects they should be addressing, not so much things like discrimination against this religious denomination or that, and threats of Northern Ireland being overrun by the Roman church and that sort of nonsense. I can't help feeling religious sectarianism is a diversion which everyone, not just women, are wasting their time indulging in. It prevents them doing anything really meaningful about poverty and social inequality. The poor Catholics in the Falls and the poor Protestants in the Shankill are never going to break out of their deprived backgrounds if they spend all their energy in fighting each other about Protestantism or Catholicism. They're both in the sub-class of the deprived, materially and educationally, who've never had a proper chance to better themselves. Politicians won't ever talk about this: instead they go on and on about the troubles. But I think there's only one trouble: which is the division in our society, split in pieces by social deprivation, not by religion.

A deserted woman like the one I talked with last week, trying to cope on her own with four children, two of them in trouble with the police and one a Down's syndrome eleven-year old, said she wasn't so much worried about her kids' religious upbringing, which she'd just had to fill in a form about from their school, as she was about the fact her local supermarket had last week put up the price of cornflakes. She said that was all they ate mostly, and feeding their souls the right food wasn't something she'd much time to bother about. I think that summed it all up for me.

15 *Everyday lives 2*

Alfred Gridley, bookseller

Angela Meadows, school teacher

Victor Taper, unemployed

Carol Marsh, shop assistant

Alice Jordan, housewife

Sandra Brown, prisoner's wife

Simon Shore, emigrant

Alfred Gridley,

bookseller

The bomb warning at the railway station resulted in the area round it being sealed off for most of the morning. When it was declared a hoax at midday, people began to go again into the nearby old brick market hall. On a trestle table near the entrance, he was tiredly pulling dust sheets off the rows of second-hand books which were his stock. A fat man in his fifties, with a bald head and a grey beard: he wore an open-necked check shirt and old corduroy trousers, and had an unlit pipe clenched between his teeth.

– Oh hello, I didn't think you'd come today when we were turned out at five past nine this morning. We don't usually have scares as early as that: they usually wait till there're a lot of people in so it'll cause the maximum amount of trouble. That's the fifth time this month it's happened: ruinous, that's the word for it. I've been in this hall thirteen years and this is the worst time I remember. Who wants to come in browsing round books when they think the roof might fall in on their heads any minute? and I only came here in the first place because I had a little shop in an arcade off Crown Street but it was always getting its windows blown in. I thought if I came here there wouldn't be any windows to worry about and it'd be a better prospect. Some hopes. If it wasn't for the postal business I'd have given up long ago. These days I seem to be buying more books than I sell: people keep bringing things they want rid of and if it's rubbish I won't have it. Not unless it's what you might call high-class rubbish, Jeffrey Archer and Jackie Collins and Margaret Drabble and stuff like that. All my best things though I keep at home. I come here more for the people than I do to earn a few bob. There'll usually be someone to talk to: since the wife passed on three years ago I don't like being too much at home on my own.

How I began funnily enough was in Scotland. I'm Irish not Scottish, but my parents'd gone over there when my father was looking for work before the war. I was born in Glasgow but I never liked it. They say we and them are more or less the same people, but I can't see it. I think the Scots are a miserable lot, most of them. I suppose I shouldn't say that really though, the wife was Scottish: she used to get cross when I said it even if it was true. When we had our two girls though, that was a funny thing: they felt Scottish more than they felt Irish. They came from their mother's side you might say, and both of them've gone back there to live in Glasgow. One's at university and the other one's a nurse, and they're nice girls, they come over once a year. They say they wouldn't live here, though, it's too rough. God knows what they mean by that: I mean have you ever been to Glasgow? You'll know what I mean then.

There's been a lot of rubbish talked by those who think they know about the Irish and the Scots. How different they are or how they're the same. Some say this, some say that. Ever since I can remember. Reminds me of old Omar Khayyam:-

> Myself when young did eagerly frequent
> Doctor and Saint, and heard great Argument.
> Something something, and came out by the same door as
>   in I went.

He knew what he was talking about all right didn't he? When I was a young man I could recite nearly all that poem. Funny nobody asks for it these days: yet a few years back I couldn't keep a copy of the Rubaiyat for a day. Buy one in the morning, by the afternoon it'd be gone. Fashion in books and writers, you never know do you why someone's in demand this week and then next week nobody wants to know. I can think of a lot like that: Warwick Deeping, James Hilton, Francis Whatsisname, Hugh Walpole, any number of them. They all used to be top of the tree in their day. Mention them to people today, they've never heard of them. Howard Spring, he was another one, he used to write great books: and that *Magnolia Street* man, Louis Something. As soon as you start thinking of them, there's dozens

whose names come back to you. Whatever became of them, why did
they drop out of fashion? Some of these modern ones you know, you
think forty years from now will they be forgotten the same way too?

Tell you another thing I always think's funny as well. A lot of
people read books but they don't notice who the author is, do you
know that? It was only yesterday a woman came in and she said
'Have you got a book called *The Scented Veil*?' I said 'Who's it by?'
and she said 'I've no idea, it's the same person who wrote *The Golden
Lamp*.' I said 'Well you must have some idea what her name is
haven't you?' She said 'Oh no I only remember the titles. You must
know who I'm talking about though, she's very well-known, she
wrote *The Side of the Brook, Tempest in the Desert, City with No Name*
and a lot of other ones, you can't mean you've never heard of her?' I
said 'Look, it isn't me who hasn't heard of her, it's you: you've read
her bloody books, if you'll pardon the expression. Why don't you go
home and look up her name on the title page?' 'Oh' she said 'I can't
do that, when I've finished them I always give them away to the
hospital.' Honestly, she must be mad. And you know what she said
to me at the finish? She said 'You can't be a very well-read person if
you can't tell me the name of a well-known author like she is.'

Still, I suppose it was company of a sort for me wasn't it? I'll tell
you another one I had, last week. Elderly bloke with a big overcoat
and a scarf wrapped up here all round his neck. He looked like a
professor from the university or something. He stood there by that
table and he ran his finger like this all along that line of books there
very slowly, one by one. After a bit I said to him 'Excuse me, are
you looking for something, can I help you?' He said 'Yes, I'm
looking for things by H. Brown.' I said 'What sort of things does he
write?' 'Oh' he said, 'all sorts of things. I'm interested in everything
he's done.' I said 'Well there must be a million Browns who've
written books – what are they, fiction, history, biography or what?'
'No' he says, 'they're detective stories, and he wrote poetry too.' I
don't know why, it just came to me like in a flash: I said to him, 'You
wouldn't by any chance be thinking of G. K. Chesterton would
you?' I mean detective stories and poetry, there aren't all that many
who combine those are there? 'Yes' he said 'that's the chap!' I said
'Well his name's not "Brown" is it?' And this bloke looked at me and
he said 'Of course his name's not "Brown", what on earth are you

talking about?' I said 'You asked me if I've got anything by somebody called H. Brown.' He said 'There must be something wrong with your hearing, how could you mix up "Brown" with "Chesterton"?' I mean some of them, they do, they drive you crazy.

Funny folk people are, aren't they? I get one or two, and you know, they don't think I know who they are. I do though, they're the police. They're not just looking for books for themselves you know, they're looking what sort of books I'm offering for sale. Anything that looks as though it's to do with politics and they'll be on to me, asking me to let them know who buys it. That happened to a friend of mine in the trade: two of them came up to him at his stall at the other market, and they picked up one of his books and they said to him 'Who buys this sort of thing?' You know what it was? It was the Bible.

It makes you sick, I mean how crazy can you get? What sort of lives are we leading here? All my life all I've been interested in is books: all my life all I've ever wanted from do was buy books and sell books, I don't mind what kind and I don't mind who from or who to. Only I tell you, these days you're not even allowed to get on with something that's doing nobody any harm. There's always a political or a religious dimension that somebody can find in it. Books you know, books are harmless aren't they? You wouldn't think so though. Some people think there are bombs in books don't they? Perhaps there are: there's a thought, isn't there?

Angela Meadows,
school teacher

Tall and dark and in her mid-thirties, she sat at the kitchen table
drinking a glass of wine. She wore a brown T-shirt and green jeans,
and her voice was firm and quiet: she screwed up her eyes thoughtfully from time to time.

– I come from an Irish Catholic family background, but for most of
my childhood and youth I was brought up in Liverpool which was
where my family lived. Largely as a result of that, I've never got used
to defining myself by my religion or my family's religion, like
everyone here does almost automatically. I'd say I haven't really any
religious belief at all: but I do identify a bit with what Quakers call
having a concern about things, and that was what aroused my
interest in social work. My husband was a social worker in the same
sort of field, community work, which was how we met.

It was in England where Roger was at college doing his training,
and I was teaching at a nearby school. He's a Belfast man, brought
up Catholic but not practising: and when we married fifteen years
ago we decided this would be the best place to be.

We bought our first home in what was largely a Protestant area
here: but this hadn't been something either of us had consciously
given much thought to. It's not the first thing that comes into your
head anywhere else in the British Isles, when you buy a house. You
don't think that you're saying something about yourselves by
choosing where you live. You don't think of it, your mind doesn't
work that way. But here of course it's very different. Perhaps Roger
was more aware of it than I was, though he didn't say anything about
it at the time.

To me, my main concern was I was troubled by the troubles. As they got worse I felt I wanted to do something within my own limited capabilities to help. I'd temporarily given up teaching to stay at home and look after our two young children, but I started to take an interest in women's advice centres and devoted a lot of my time to that. I enjoyed it, and I also felt in some vague kind of way that the solution to the troubles might be through women coming together as women. I wasn't politically active, but I did gradually find myself becoming drawn more and more into the problems of wives of long-term prisoners, so that was what I chiefly specialised in.

You can go on doing something and become involved and engrossed in it to such an extent that it never strikes you how it looks to other people. The women we offered support to at our centre were both Catholics and Protestants, and we didn't differentiate between them in any way. They were prisoners' wives having a hard time, and we did all the usual things: laid on transport when they went to visit their husbands, helped them out with advice about what social security benefits they could claim, arranged for their kids to be looked after for a couple of days so they could have a break, encouraged them to form self-support groups and so on. I thought that what we did was worthwhile and it never occurred to us that some people might not think so, or be suspicious about what we might really be up to and start feeling hostile towards us. The only hint we had that not everyone would understand what we were doing was when Roger tried to join the local Residents' Association and was met with a complete blank wall everywhere. But at the time we didn't particularly construe this as meaning anything. It's easy to see now that we were considered to be Catholics: and up to no good, whatever we might happen to be doing.

As the troubles got worse, because of the way we looked at things ourselves we weren't aware of exactly what was happening: and we didn't understand the real strength and depth of feeling that was beginning to spread everywhere. We'd truly no idea we'd been identified in the minds of some people as Catholic Republicans. And like most other people, when we heard of acts of intimidation which had been performed against people in other areas of the city merely because of their suspected religious affiliation, we never grasped it might happen to us. So the first indication we had of it was therefore all that more shocking and frightening. One night there was a crash at the front door and we found a petrol bomb had been thrown through the glass into the hallway. It was a very crude home-made effort at a petrol bomb, some rags stuffed in the neck of a milk bottle with petrol in it, and it hadn't been lit. Nevertheless, it was a petrol bomb: and without a doubt it was intended as a warning.

I was very scared, I was very very scared: but after a few hours thinking about it, I gradually began to get very very angry instead. I surprised myself: because what I did the next morning was I went down to where I knew the local UDA had their headquarters, and I demanded to see whoever was in charge. If I'd given it a moment's thought I'd have been far too frightened to do anything like that, I really would. And I think the men who were there, equally if they'd been expecting anything like it, they'd not have done what they did which was actually let me in. I wouldn't accept anybody's assurance that if I left a message it'd be passed on: I said I wanted to speak face to face with the person at the top, and I wasn't going to leave until I did.

Eventually I was taken upstairs and shown into a little office where a man was sitting behind a desk. I was in a furious temper and I immediately let fly and told him what I thought of him. I said the work I did at the women's centre was for all prisoners' wives, both Catholic and Protestant it didn't matter which, and I thought it was disgusting that someone should try and frighten me into giving up and going to live somewhere else. As far as I knew I'd never seen him before in my life: but I had the feeling he knew perfectly well who I was, which house I lived in, and what had happened the previous night. I'm sure he didn't know how to deal with the situation, so he asked me to wait. He went out into another room and made a short telephone call, and then he came back and to my astonishment he was profusely apologetic. He said the persons responsible would be told such behaviour was not acceptable: and he also tried to suggest it could have been a mistake and the petrol bomb was intended for somebody else. I didn't believe him and I told him I didn't: and he just sort of shrugged and apologised again.

I think I was optimistic and very very naive to imagine an impression could be made on people of that calibre just by one individual's protest. But I was sufficiently aggrieved about it at the time to delude myself I'd spoken my mind and made it plain to whoever'd been behind it that whatever they'd thought, they'd been wrong about me and Roger, and to threaten us had been outrageous. Roger and I discussed whether we should stay in Belfast or not: but months went by, nothing else happened, and so we didn't actually take any action, thinking on the whole we'd probably be left alone from then on.

When you don't have any particularly strong religious or political ideas it's difficult to accept that for certain other people you must always still be on one side or the other, and that there's no such person as a neutral. Or it may have been there was a change in the command structure of that particular branch of the UDA. I don't know how these things work, but I know that in nearly all paramilitary organisations there's a power struggle going on almost all of the time. Anyway, I'm not sure how long it was afterwards, perhaps a year or so, but by then we'd begun to feel confident it'd all been satisfactorily resolved and we'd be left in peace. Up to that point we hadn't been out often on our own after the incident, and things don't always stick in your mind in the way they should. But we gradually started to feel all danger had passed and we could live more or less normally.

One night some friends asked us to go out for a meal to their house, which wasn't very far away from ours: and we did, and the consequences were almost fatal. The young teenage daughter of some friends came in to babysit for us at eight o'clock, and Roger and I went off. At nine o'clock another petrol bomb came in through the front door and into the hall: and this time it was lit. That there weren't any casualties and no one was hurt was sheer good luck, that's all: the ground floor of the house was very quickly ablaze, and the girl got the children out of the back only just in time. Neighbours rushed round for us at our friends' and brought us back: the fire brigade came, the police and all the rest of it, and the house was badly damaged and the children badly shocked.

We still can't appreciate even now the sort of feelings behind it, and what sort of people would do such a thing. It didn't matter at all that we weren't really Catholics. The point being made to us was that in some people's eyes we were, so we were not welcome in that part of the city either as residents or anything else. We immediately packed up and moved to furnished accommodation on the other side of the city, and then after a few months there we moved still further out and bought this house where we are now. We discussed whether we should allow ourselves to be intimidated, because it seemed like giving in. If it had only been to do with Roger and me it would have been different: but the children's lives had to be considered too. So putting it simply, we did give in, and we ran away.

That was three and a half years ago. We still talk about it and sometimes we still have a feeling that we ought to go back again and make a stand. I ask myself very often whether we should. Even when we take the children into account, there's still always the question as to whether it's right or wrong to take them away from a situation like we did. Fortunately financially we were able to do it, just: but a lot of people aren't able to do that. They have to go on living their lives in fear: and their children are brought up in an atmosphere of fear for the whole of their lives, or will have to unless everyone takes a stand. We wonder is it right or is it wrong to bring your children out of a situation like that? If you do, isn't it giving in to those who've created the division situation and want it to continue? How will it ever improve if no one takes a stand? If people run away then how can there ever be any hope of improvement?

Religious belief or lack of it in no way controls our own lives, so shouldn't we try and do our best to spread the same kind of attitude through those who it causes to hate other people? People are complacent here about what's going on and feel nothing can be done: but it's only ordinary people who can do anything, and unless we take a stand and make our voices heard, there's no future really for anybody is there? Sheltering children from prejudice and danger, when the reality's prejudice and danger . . . is that right?

Yes we say, yes of course it is, yes. But there's still a niggle sometimes . . .

Victor Taper,

unemployed

He sat at one of the battered fold-up tables in the empty youth-club canteen at four o'clock on a darkening Tuesday afternoon. Thin face, sparse grey hair, bushy eyebrows and a low voice. He sipped moodily at a thick white porcelain mug of tea.

– I don't know there's much to say about myself. I've lived on this estate here fifteen years, but I wasn't born here, I was born in the Shankill. My father worked in the shipyards. He died when he was a young man, only just gone forty-four. I was sixteen then at the time, the oldest of three. I'd a brother older and a sister younger: she died when she was thirteen. My mother was always ill herself, we've none of us had good health in our family.

I went to school till I was fourteen but I didn't take to it, I wasn't one for books and reading and learning. I don't think there was anything special about my childhood, not that I remember: and I'd no special ideas or ambitions about myself. When I left school I did odd jobs, mostly not the sort that were going to lead anywhere. When I was eighteen I joined the Army, I joined the Royal Enniskillen Fusiliers, I signed on for six years. I went to Germany, then the Persian Gulf, then Kenya. For my last two years I was at the stores depot at Ballymena.

The way I looked at it was the Army'd give me an opportunity to get away from Belfast. It was a good period, it learnt me the difference between right and wrong, taught me how to stand on my own feet and to get on with life of my own. I worked most of the time in the stores and never got any promotion, I stayed an ordinary Fusilier all the way through. At the end of my time I could have signed on again, but I didn't: when I think back about it, I think I should have done. You don't always see chances when they come along and that was one I didn't. The two reasons that influenced me to come out were first I didn't like Ballymena, neither the place nor the people there: and second I'd got married to a local girl from Belfast here, and she didn't want to live away from her family. She had a job in a meat-packing factory so we decided it'd be best for her to stay there and me to come out. She didn't fancy the idea of being married to a soldier and perhaps having to go away from home some time.

They gave me a small pay-off, and most of it went towards furnishing a flat and paying for things we needed when the first baby was coming along. I had a fair long period out of work, and life wasn't easy: we talked about going to England but the wife didn't want to leave here, she never felt ever that she wanted to be far from her family. In the end I got a job in the shipyard as a storeman, but it wasn't much of a job, it'd no kind of future to it. If I'd had the sense I'd have learned myself a trade in the Army that I could have earned a living with when I came out into Civvy Street. I didn't though, I was stupid.

I worked at the shipyard ten years almost, then things started to go down and I got paid off. That was eleven years ago now, I was forty-one at that time, and I've not had any kind of job since. I've all the time been unemployed, I shouldn't think now at the age of fifty-three I've got no chance of having a job again ever. Once you come to a certain age, no one wants to know you if you're not a skilled man. The only sort of work I could do now would be the kind of thing a lad in his teens could do, and he'd do it for a less wage.

Last year I was on a Government scheme for people who'd been unemployed a long time. It was on the estate here, I think it was mainly to try and keep you occupied. I did painting iron railings, I did tidying up the park gardens, and then they put me on a project of cleaning up the riverside. That was for the new development scheme there which they dropped in the end anyway half way through. None of the jobs trained you for anything and what you got paid in the end came out at ten pounds a week more than if you were just signing on. Some days there was no work they could find for us to do. Another restriction on it was you could only be on the scheme a year, then you had to step aside and make way for somebody else. I think it was all a waste of time myself: it was just something the Government did to make it look they were trying to help the unemployed.

You'll find a lot of people on this estate here with the same story to tell you that I have: there's no future here for anyone. For the young people, there's nothing: and for older ones like me, we've no prospects and not anywhere to go. When me and the wife got rehoused here just on twenty years ago, it was all clean and smart, everybody felt good about living here. But it's all gone downhill, look anywhere you like: everything's rough and broken down, paint sprayed on the walls, broken windows, everywhere completely neglected. But nobody cares about it. There used to be a local shopping centre down at the bottom there, where you came in off the ring road. Now there's only three shops that's still going, just the post-office and newsagent's, a grocer's and that vegetable place. Everybody says they're all too expensive and poor quality, it's better to get your things down the market.

Nowadays you get all the kids running round too: they've got no jobs or prospects, all they do's hang about and have fights, break up things because there's nothing else to keep them occupied. Could never have happened like that when I was a youngster, we didn't behave like they do. I don't know whether it's the parents or the schools or what. I saw some of them a couple of weeks ago, they were pulling down a fence at the end of the street there, just for the sake of doing it. I was going by so I told them they were breaking up things that belonged to everyone, but all they did was they laughed. Even if you was to phone the police about it, they wouldn't come, they don't care either. I asked two of them once, they were sitting having a fag in a patrol car up at the top: I said why didn't they patrol round the estate like they used to any more? D'you know what they said? They said they'd got better things to do than chase after kids. If the police themselves take that sort of attitude, what can you expect?

It's all a big question, I couldn't tell you what the answer should be. I think it's the Government and the politicians myself. You see them on TV and all they're doing is arguing whether there should be a united Ireland, whether Dublin should have a say in our affairs and all things like that. I don't see what it's got to do with the conditions on this estate whether we're governed by the British or the Irish or

the Japanese. What's needed is put back people's pride in their lives
and give them something to live for, a future. I've one son's never
been employed, and another one went to England seven years ago
and we've not seen him since. He said before he went he didn't think
there was anything here for him and he was right. I'd not feel any
different to him myself if I was his age. I wouldn't feel pride living
here and I wouldn't feel there was prospects for anybody no more.

The heart's gone out of this estate, the heart's gone out of
Northern Ireland, that's how I look at it. I'm not a church-going
person me, but I think there's a lot more the churches could do to try
and improve things. If they took more interest in the lives of
ordinary people and all that sort of thing, instead of all this arguing
and ranting they do. It's a big question for anybody, to say where
they can see any hope of improvement. I know I can't.

I wish now I'd stayed in the Army I do: at least there'd have been
security and a pension on the end of it.

Carol Marsh,

shop assistant

A bright spring morning, the sky light blue, the sunshine glittering on the water by the riverside walk. At lunchtime she sat on a bench eating her sandwiches: a well-built young woman, with straight dark hair in a neatly trimmed bob. She wore a black trouser suit, a plain white blouse and a man's wristwatch. She was in her mid-twenties.

– It's good to get away from the shopping precinct and come down here for an hour on a day like this. I like working in the shop, I like it that there's lots of people all day. Now and again though it's nice to sit on your own so it is, and have a think or read a good book. What I read mostly are things for my studies: I'm taking a degree in anthropology, it means a hell of a lot of reading just to keep up. I can't remember how long it is since I last read a book for pleasure. I enjoy studying but it'd be good once in a while to read something purely for enjoyment.

I don't know why anthropology, it was just a subject that caught my interest when I was at school. Another advantage is when you're looking for a university place like I was three years ago, there wasn't all that many people wanting to study it: so there was more chance of getting accepted than if I'd wanted to do something in greater demand. I've not the faintest idea what I'll do when I've finished. I've an offer of part-time research, but I think there's a danger you can get into a groove and become a perpetual student if you go on too long on those lines. I don't know, I might do something totally different: perhaps go to the Pacific islands somewhere, Papua New Guinea, get some direct experience of tribal cultures. I'd like to work in a team rather than just drift around on my own: some of the American universities offer that sort of thing if you guarantee them two years.

I'd be willing to do that, but I'm in a state of uncertainty right now about which direction I'm going. After my degree this summer I'll really have to sit down and start thinking: twenty-five's a kind of watershed in your life, well it will be for me.

I've been working at the artists' materials shop since Christmas. Originally it was only going to be till the end of the winter vacation, but they couldn't get anybody else to take my place. They were paying me quite a decent salary so I decided to stop on for a couple of months because I needed the money. I have to support myself: I get only a very small grant, otherwise no help from anyone and things are very tight. I share a flat near the university with four other girls: they're all younger than me and I don't really fit in with the sort of lives they lead. They're rather a Bohemian lot, but I'm not. They're into all the student political things: two of them are ardent Republicans, one's a Nationalist and the other one's an absolutely dyed-in-the-wool Unionist. They stay up till the small hours of the morning arguing and discussing, they get quite heated at times. I'm afraid it's not something that concerns me very much. They keep repeating the same things over and over, and I just can't be bothered with it.

You can't help getting the feeling sometimes that the whole of Northern Ireland is preoccupied to the exclusion of everything else with sectarian and political divisions. Someone who didn't live here, reading about it I'm sure they'd get the idea everything revolved around that, and people never talked about anything else whatever. The idea that people might go to work, have friends, listen to music, read books, make love: you might think people never did any of those things, they were too occupied with fighting and arguing. I went to see some people over in London last summer, a girl I'd known when I first went to university who'd got married and settled over there. They'd arranged one or two dinner parties for me to go to with their friends: and after a while I said to them I'd much sooner stop at home with them. I can't tell you how fed up I got with having to have the same questions and the same conversations every time. As soon as anyone knew I'd come from Belfast, all they wanted to talk about was the situation here, whether there were bombs going off always, what ought to be done about it and all the rest of it. Nobody treated me as an ordinary person, and when I said I wasn't interested and I didn't know anything much about it, they didn't seem capable of believing it.

The truth is if you keep yourself to yourself and lead your own life, do your work or your studies or whatever your thing is, you can shut most of it out of your life most of the time. The impression people give you in England is it's as though they think everybody here's got the same illness, flu or something: and you must have it too because they've read about this epidemic that's sweeping the country and everyone's got it.

What I was saying earlier on about being a bit cloistered in my studies at the university and going on possibly into research, that's one sort of protective barrier I've erected round myself. Strangely enough, the other one's working in the shop. People who come in want paints or brushes or paper or crayons, and I can go from first thing in the morning till closing time without anybody who comes in ever mentioning anything else. It's because they're people who're only concerned with their own way of looking at the world, they see things in terms of faces and landscapes and pictures rather than just thinking about words. I didn't put that very well, did I?

You know, I don't think I've ever said as much about it all as I've done today. I'm afraid it means I've not left much time for the other subject before I'm due back at the shop. We'll talk about it tomorrow shall we, rather than start now? One o'clock here again then, OK?

– Being a lesbian in Belfast isn't really as difficult a life as a lot of people might think. We've a very rigorous evangelical Protestant-dominated society for the most part, and I wouldn't say people are any more liberal about this subject than anything else they consider has to do with morality. I suppose one of the ironies is basically the idea's so far out they don't even acknowledge its existence. They're hot and strong about gays, but they never even mention the subject of same-sex love between women. The idea probably so horrifies them they'd sooner not mention it, so of course that makes things a bit easier. Some people might think it's extraordinary, but the telephone book actually has an entry under the heading 'Lesbian Helpline'. There it is in black and white for anyone to read, but with a PO Box number rather than an actual address. Anybody who rings gets an answering machine which tells them what hours somebody'll be there to talk to them. That's more than gays get: there's no similar entry in the phone book for them, so we do better than they do on that score.

The Helpline's run by volunteers: at the moment there's eight or nine of us who put in an hour or so on a different night in the week. We're kept pretty busy usually. How people hear of us in the first place might be because they've read an ad we have in the personal column of the evening paper: it's ages since I've looked at it, I think it says something like 'Lesbian? Ring 2468' or whatever the number is. Women ring in from all over Northern Ireland: most are from the Belfast city area, but we get people from as far away as Derry or Galway, and we sometimes get calls from Dublin too.

It's not so much a counselling service, it's more a means of letting people know they're not on their own, they're not the only ones who are the same as they are. That's the most common fear women have, if they're lesbian this makes them complete pariahs and no one else is in the same position. We have social evenings from time to time in the city at different pubs where we hire rooms: discos, discussion groups, all sorts of things, and any woman can come so she can meet others and find out she's not on her own. Some don't make it a regular thing: they just want the contact and friendship and understanding. We put out a newsheet too now and again, it's got information in it and dates of social evenings and so on.

We don't have a formal organisation as such because we don't feel there should be one. If there was there'd be a danger that some kind of official line was being suggested: but one of our most important messages is lesbian women are all different individuals like everyone else. So obviously there shouldn't be any sort of announcement the press could get hold of, suggesting all lesbians think this that or the other.

I was one of the first who began it. It was about four years ago, because I felt lonely and isolated and didn't know anyone else like I was. I come from a small village in County Armagh, no one else I'd ever heard of in my whole life had been lesbian. In fact I'd never even heard the word until I came to university. It was an absolute revelation to me when I first found out there how many other people were like myself. Lesbians are very supportive towards one another, they have to be because they're a small minority group: and they're intensely understanding and friendly once you join them. The important thing is that their sexual orientation transcends all classes, politics and religion. You recognise your basic nature for what it is, and those other things are almost what might be called trimmings. You can choose which of them you like, but what holds you all together is the fact you both give and receive acceptance. It's a tremendously lonely life before you find out how much a part of ordinary society you are, and how big that part of society actually is. I couldn't ever go back now and live in the community where I grew up, in that small village where I was born. Here in Belfast I live a fairly ordinary life, and most of the time with my friends I can be myself. But if I went back home again, I'd immediately feel a stranger: I've never even mentioned the subject for example to my parents, or my brothers and sisters. Here I'm a happy person: there, I'd be a stranger in my own country.

Alice Jordan,

housewife

Both times we met she sat by the window in the front sitting-room of her first-floor council maisonette, looking out at the sun setting over the big civic park on the opposite side of the main road. A plump soft-voiced woman, she had untidily-kept short fair hair. While she talked she sometimes slowly laced her fingers together, holding them out in front of her and looking at them thoughtfully.

– Oh I'm just a plain ordinary woman from Belfast, I wouldn't say more than that. I'm forty-two and I've lived in Belfast all my life. My father died when I was seventeen, I've two older sisters married and living now over the water, one in Birmingham the other in Lincolnshire. And my mother died two years ago when I was forty. From when I left school at fifteen I spent all my life looking after her: she was permanently an invalid, she had a disease they don't seem to know much about called multiple sclerosis. It took them a long time to find out what was the matter with her. Sometimes she seemed almost as though there was nothing at all wrong with her, but that never lasted longer than a month or two, then she'd have a bad relapse. It must have been awful for her to live her whole life like that, thinking she was getting better and then finding she wasn't. I'd have liked to have worked when I left school, but I realised I had to always be ready to look after my mother, that took first place, so I never got the chance.

I was a very plain-looking girl, I was always well aware of that. Boys never seemed to be interested in me if I went to a dance: my sisters were the ones who got boys. I think I was a very dull person too. My mother and I were good friends and we got on well together. She wasn't a great one for reading, but she liked me to read to her: mostly romances and things. I can't remember any of their titles. Living like we did, it might sound strange to say it but it was almost as though we were in a different country. We read in the newspapers or saw on television about things that had happened only perhaps a few hundred yards from this street, things like fighting and killing and shooting, yet it was like they were taking place miles away. Once a week I went shopping at the supermarket, but that the furthest I ever went away from home. We weren't concerned with what was going on outside, it didn't seem to have anything to do with us. It didn't mean we didn't have friends though: people were regularly popping in to see us and chatting, so we always felt as though we were part of things in the neighbourhood and area. That was how I met Bob: not by meeting him but by hearing about him.

His cousin was a married girl about the same age as me and she was the one who told me about him. He was in prison serving a life sentence, or rather a number of life sentences. He'd been a member of a Protestant paramilitary organisation: it happened when he was eighteen, and he'd been in prison ever since. His name would seem to come up in conversation with this girl quite normally and naturally now and again: no more than in an odd phrase or two, but somehow at least once a week without fail his name would occur. I don't think she was doing it deliberately and I wasn't either at first: but then gradually it got to the stage that if she didn't mention him, I did. I don't know why it should have been, but I felt somehow drawn to him. I suppose it was because all his life had been spent in prison from when he was very young, and all my life I'd spent in a kind of prison too, only a much more comfortable and happy one. I'm not making a very good job of explaining it, but I used to think about him a lot and how similar our lives were.

One day she asked me why didn't I write to him: he'd no family, no one he was really close to, and she said she felt sure he'd like it if I did. When I wrote he replied, and the correspondence between us gradually grew till we were exchanging regular letters about once a month. I don't remember much about what we wrote to each other about: but it went on for a good four or five years before we ever met. In all that time we never set eyes on each other. Then one day when I was writing I said would he like me to go and see him?

When we first met in the visiting-room it was very strange: both of us were very shy, and yet neither of us felt embarrassed about being shy. Sometimes we spoke and sometimes we didn't, but it didn't seem to matter that there were long silences. Neither of us felt awkward about it somehow. The next visit was easier: but I didn't go and see him very often, only about twice or three times a year for round about two more years. Then one day on a Wednesday afternoon, though why I remember it was a Wednesday I don't know, I asked him if he'd marry me when he eventually got parole. I remember very clearly the expression on his face: it was surprise that I'd asked him something so obvious and it'd been already agreed a long time before. He just nodded and said 'Well yes of course.'

– After you'd gone the last time I was thinking about what you asked me, about what was the most important thing that drew Bob and me together. It must seem strange to a lot of people: me a Catholic, him a Protestant paramilitary. I can only say that everything that happened between us from when we started writing to each other, to two years ago after he came out of prison and we got married, everything always seemed perfectly natural and normal. It was like it was inevitable we should come together. It was late in life for both of us to marry: I was forty and he was thirty-nine, but we were in love with each other, and there it was. I'd never felt like that about anyone before, because I never really thought much about anything but my situation, which I accepted, of being here to take care of my mother. Even if she hadn't died when she did I'd have married him: I'd told her all about him, of course.

The religious aspect never came into it for either of us. That I was Catholic and he was Protestant was only just a name of a section of the community we came from. It didn't mean fanatical belief or anything of that sort. I think Bob must have changed a lot too: when he was eighteen he was wild and adventurous, and thinking there was something exciting and heroic in what he did. To go from that to the man he is now is a huge change. He's very quiet, he doesn't talk much, and mostly he likes to stay at home and watch television. He's always anxious to know where I am: if I go out to the shops or to see someone he can't settle till I'm back again. I once asked him

why, but he said he couldn't explain it, he just felt the house felt
wrong without me in it.

I'm the same about it when he's out, and I've got more reason to
be. He was told to his face when he was in prison that whenever he
got out, he'd be a marked man. It does happen, that: someone serves
a sentence and people are angry that he escaped what they consider to
be proper punishment. They believe in the death penalty and nothing
less. Bob and I discussed if we should still go on living here in Belfast
or whether we ought to move somewhere else: mixed marriages
aren't popular in certain people's view, and we thought there could
be trouble. So far there hasn't been any, because where we're living
now is mainly Protestant but as near a neutral area as you could get.
There are very few Catholics round here, and I don't draw attention
to myself. I very rarely go to Mass or have anything to do with the
Church. If I did want to make my confession I'd go over to the other
side of the city.

It's hard for me to sum up the feelings I have. If I ever thought of
marriage when I was younger it was of marrying a Catholic I
suppose. I think the most important thing is to forget your background and pay no attention to what sort it is that you come from.
My one big regret is my mother died without meeting Bob: I know
she would have liked him, and I know she wouldn't have had any
problems about him being Protestant, because she wasn't like that.
Towards the end of her life she talked a lot about religion: but she
talked about it as though it was a personal private thing to her. When
I asked her once if she'd like to see a priest she said she wouldn't: she
shook her head at the idea, and said religion was not something she
thought she needed. Not long after he came out of prison, Bob
mentioned to me somebody'd once asked him if he'd like to go to
some particular church. He said he wouldn't because he felt churches
were inside people and the one he went to was inside him. I don't
really know what he meant, but I do know he and I love each other
very much. We met when we were grown-ups, so it wasn't a
childish romance, and I feel very secure about it. The fact he was
helped by a Catholic uncle of mine to get a job when he came out as a
long distance lorry-driver, that somehow seemed again to be
something that was inevitable. When he comes back tomorrow
evening it'll be a very happy time for both of us, because when it

happens he has to go away it always reminds us of when we were permanently separated by our situations.

I wish very much something could be done that could stop people thinking about what religious background someone else comes from and they're all just human beings. I'm sorry, I'm not very good at explaining things. I've never tried to do it before, it's not been necessary with Bob: neither of us needs to explain anything to each other, we just know what we feel about each other that's all.

Sandra Brown,

prisoner's wife

Her voice was quick and nervous at first. She sat at the kitchen table smoking and drinking tea, with a plate of digestive biscuits and some freshly-made iced buns. As she began to feel more at ease she talked more slowly and laughed sometimes in amusement at herself. A lively delicate-featured woman, with brown eyes and sandy hair and a freckled face, she wore a white pullover and red jeans.

– Well to be sure there's not much I can think of to tell you about myself so there's not. I'm an ordinary woman, with two children in their teens, that's Colin and Gordon: and then there are the twins, they're seven, two boys again, Tom and John. I'm forty, I was born in the Shankill Road, I left school at fifteen, and the only thing I remember learning at school was they were always after us about our manners: don't be cheeky to your elders and always be polite. They weren't a great success with me though, I wasn't very bright. There was five of us children, all girls, and I was the youngest. My mother was a very quiet person, not one for being hard on you if you got into scrapes. My father I remember as being mostly unemployed. And he was very keen on all the Protestant things, the Orange Order and the parades. To us kids those were like carnivals I suppose: marches through the streets with the pipes and the big drums and the flags. I don't think we knew what it was all about. But we did know there were certain streets if you went along them you'd get stones thrown at you by the Catholics. So of course we liked the parades best that followed those routes, they were exciting.

I remember the British soldiers coming: they appeared on the streets suddenly one day, their uniforms and their armoured cars. They didn't seem real, they were like tin soldiers, they didn't talk to us and we didn't talk to them. Now and again you'd hear about a girl that you knew, she was going out with a British soldier, but you didn't know what to think about it. We weren't a political family so there was never much talk about that sort of thing. Live and let live was my father's idea. I never met a British soldier, I wasn't interested. The first boyfriend I ever had was when I was sixteen: his name was Ian, his family lived in the next street. He was the one and only boyfriend I ever had, and he's my hubby now: all my life he's been the only one for me. He was always very shy when we first met: if we went to a dance or the cinema he never tried to kiss me even, for months, nothing like that. He was tall and a lovely looking young man you know? He still is too, I've never known another man could make my tummy turn over, just by looking at him. Sure, he's always been able to do that: and that's a fact, still after all these years so he is.

Him and me, we were always very close to each other. I think it must have been two years or more of going steady before anything went on, if you know what I mean. Sometimes on a Sunday in summer if it was nice we'd get on the bus and go anywhere out of the city into the country: we'd take sandwiches and perhaps cider, and just lie together cuddling. It never seemed there was anything wrong to us in making love.

When I was just eighteen I fell pregnant. I didn't tell anyone except my mother, and she was very understanding about it like I knew she would be. I didn't tell Ian about it either, because somebody'd told me once your boyfriend knew a thing like that he'd start cooling off. I didn't grow big ever. Ian's job with an electrical goods company meant he had to travel around and go away a lot on different jobs. Then there came the day he told me he'd have to go away for two months because the firm he worked for had a big contract in County Fermanagh. When he told me I wanted to tell him I was going to have a baby, but I was too frightened of it and I couldn't. So when he went I thought I'd never see him again: the way I pictured it, I thought he'd find out about it while he was away and wouldn't want to come back.

I still don't know how he found out, but apparently he knew exactly what was happening. I went in to the Mater Hospital and had the baby, and the very first evening Colin was born there was Ian, by the side of my bed. I'd been dozing: I did, I thought it was a dream. He just stood there and smiled at me, then he stretched out his arms towards me like this. I cried and cried. He told me he'd come to see his baby: that was how he put it, he said he'd come to see his baby and make arrangements for us to get married. A lot of people will tell you you shouldn't get married because of something like that, but I didn't argue with him, I was just happy and he told me he was happy too. It was about a month, not more, after Colin was born that we married: and what people said about not marrying is wrong, at least it was for us.

In his job Ian was earning enough for us to put down a deposit on a small house, and within two weeks of me leaving hospital we were set up in our own place. It was like a wonderful dream, a fairy-story come true: and when he said he thought only one child wasn't a good idea and we should plan on having another one, well then I really knew what he felt for me was true love.

I suppose it's funny how you can be very close to someone and love them very deeply, and yet there are still things can surprise you when you find them out. That's how it was with me. One night about a year later there was a knock at the door and when I opened it his sister was standing there. She was as white as a sheet and she just said 'They've taken Ian into Castlereagh.' I asked her in and made a cup of tea and asked her what had happened. What she told me was the biggest shock of my life and I couldn't take it in at all. It was as though it had happened to somebody else, not Ian: neither of us could believe it. She kept saying 'It must be a mistake, it must be a mistake.' I remember I kept nodding my head agreeing with her because I couldn't believe it either. He'd been arrested and charged with murder.

I truly hadn't any idea he was a paramilitary at all: and it wasn't just I'd been blind, because neither had Joan his sister or his parents. He'd never spoken about political things, not ever: and to me the whole idea was well, just simply unbelievable. We'd read about things like that in the paper, but never did I imagine what was happening so close to home. The only thing I could think was that like Joan had said, it must be some kind of mistake.

I used to go and see Ian on remand of course while he was in Crumlin Road awaiting trial: even then he never said anything to contradict me when I said obviously it was a mistake and they must have got the wrong man. So it was an even bigger shock at the trial when I heard him plead guilty. And to three murders too: guilty of that, my Ian: I can't describe it, how I felt. It was like something what wasn't possible: yet he was admitting it. The reality of it took months to sink in. We had one child and I was pregnant with our second who was born after the trial. Ian got life sentences on each of the charges, which meant for as far into the future as I could see, he'd never be living with me again.

And well, in a way it's true, in a way, he never has been. It's almost sixteen years he's been in for now so far. Last year, for the first time, we heard there was a possibility fairly soon now he might be considered for parole.

What do I mean by it's only in a way he's not been living with me? I don't know how to put it exactly, except to say that right from when he first went inside, I've always tried my best, for my sake and the children's, to include Ian in all our lives all the time. I write to him once a week every week without fail, I visit him without fail once a month, and of course birthday cards and Christmas cards, Easter cards, Valentine's Day, Father's Day and all the rest of it. And the children are included in everything. I do everything I can think of to make it like he's here with us, like he's just gone out and he'll be back again soon. We have games about him: if there's something special on the news we talk about what we think he'll be thinking about it, if there's a family decision to take we make a point to remember to ask him what his opinion on it is next time we see him. Things like should we go to Auntie Paula's this year for Christmas, or Granny's, or just stay at home like last year? If a school trip's coming up, how much will it cost and can we afford to start saving up for it? Every day we talk about him over and over again: we remember things to tell him about, little silly stupid things, then afterwards we talk about what he said about them and whether we made him laugh or not.

I've always been honest with them about him. I've had to tell each of them in turn, as soon as they were old enough, why he's where he is, in prison and can't come home. I say Daddy was the same as a soldier: it was like he was fighting in a war and soldiers killed people. But I say what he did was wrong because it wasn't really a war, and so he was punished for it by the Government and put in prison. I try to be as truthful about it as I can, and I tell them what I believe myself: that he's a good man and has always been a good man, but just as bad people sometimes do good things, so good people sometimes do things that are bad and wrong.

I'm not bitter, no, I can truthfully say I'm not bitter at all. To keep my marriage in existence is the most important thing of all in my life: and to let myself be sour and bitter wouldn't help me do that. I tell myself I'm lucky, I've got lovely kids and a lovely husband. And I'm even luckier now, because at last now I can even think and talk about him soon coming home. To a lot of people being a life-sentence prisoner's wife might be something to be ashamed of, but it isn't to me. I don't excuse what he did, but that doesn't mean to say everything about him is wrong: he has some very good sides to him and it's important he should feel he's important himself to me and the children. He knows he did wrong, but he knows as well that all of us are looking forward to having him back with us. He's still my lovely good-looking young fellow and he knows that too, as well as what a lot of men in prison don't know, that for his wife there's never been anybody else but him and never will be.

Now they're older he's still young, so Colin and Gordon look on him not just as a father but as their friend. They tell him about school and what they hope they'll do when they leave, and they ask his opinion about how to look for jobs and where. They've a very good relationship, sometimes they go and visit him now on their own. While I was carrying the twins, we made sure Ian knew every detail about how things were going, and after they were born Colin took a photo of me in bed in the hospital holding them in my arms. He and Gordon took it up to the prison for him two days later, even though they weren't due a visit, and handed it in for him at the gate. It all brought us all very close as a family.

I won't let myself look at it as a tragedy, because it's not. How could it be, when we've been in love with each other for as long as we have? It's no use eating yourself up with regrets thinking about how things might have been: it's best to see them as they are and carry on as normal as possible. Next month Ian'll be coming home for his first-ever period of home leave. It'll be perhaps three days, but he says it won't feel strange, and it won't: he'll recognise everything in the house because he's heard about it so often in a letter or we've talked about it on a visit. If he walked in now and saw that blue vase of flowers on the window-ledge, he'd know it was there because I've told him about it in a letter: so everything would be as he'd expected it, and if something wasn't he'd ask what had happened to it.

No no, he's never been home yet, he's not had any leave at all during his sentence. Seven-year old twins, how did they come about when he's not been out of prison for sixteen years? Well to be sure it's really quite simple so it is. On a visit with a lifer you can sometimes sit nearly an hour you know in each other's company in the visiting-room. So all you need is a long coat and a little bit of imagination, isn't it now?

Simon Shore,

emigrant

A stockily-built young man with a thick beard, he sat by the window of his ground floor flat in an old house in a southern suburb of the city, looking out at the afternoon rain. He wore a short-sleeved sports shirt and light blue trousers. His voice was hard.

– I'm twenty-one, I have a degree in French and I'm also qualified to be a teacher of English as a foreign language. And this time next week I'll be in Thailand, in Bangkok I'm glad to say.

I'm going to work for a French company, one of the largest exporters there, and they've offered me a three-year contract. I'm looking forward to it very much: I hope it's the start of a completely new life. My girlfriend is coming with me, we're due to have a baby in three months' time, and we hope we'll have at least one if not two more children after we've established ourselves there. It's her idea that she'd like to work as well: she's a graphic designer but what openings there'll be for her we don't really know till we get there. Both of us feel this is too good a chance to miss. In career terms it is for me, but also for more than a year now we've been determined that if an opportunity arose we'd leave Northern Ireland and make a fresh start somewhere else. We met at university and we've lived together long enough now to know, as far as it's possible to know such a thing, that we want to be together in the future on a permanent basis. Both of us were born here: I come from a Protestant family and she comes from a Catholic one, though neither of us would say our religious beliefs played much part in our lives.

It's been for both of us a very carefully thought-out decision to emigrate: and understandably it's caused a certain amount of dissension in our families. Her mother and father live quite near mine: and it's ironic they did little more than merely acknowledge each other's existence till we told them six months ago we were going to leave. Both of them wanted then to try and dissuade us: they met together and talked about it on several occasions at some length. It ended up with us having to face a kind of united front committee, with them both asking us to think again. I don't want to sound cynical about it, I'm sure they felt it was in our best interests: but they couldn't see it was far too late for any kind of change of mind on our part, or that to some extent their previous stand-offishness towards each other might have had something to do with it.

I can't say whether Eileen's feelings or mine are the stronger and which of us has most influenced the other. The main thing was we both felt deeply we wanted to be together and to have a family, and to lead the sort of life which would have some meaning both for us and for our children as we had them. Emphatically we've no regrets about going: we don't feel Belfast is any kind of place that offers a future for people like us.

Well, neither of us is the sort who wants to involve ourselves in trying to change things. I'm only speaking for myself now, not for her: but if you look back over the past ten or twelve years, there can't be any argument about the complete failure of people with all the good intentions in the world to bring about any improvement in the situation here: attitudes haven't changed for as long as I can remember. To be the child of parents who are liberal-minded in every way and then one day to have to face the fact they still have a kind of residual prejudice against another form of religion, is really quite a shock. I'm quite sure in my own mind that if Eileen had been a Protestant girl, my own parents wouldn't have been so distant towards hers: and her parents wouldn't have been towards mine, even though they too are what could be described as liberal-minded Catholics.

Even in the most trivial way our present-day society functions on the level it's hard for outsiders to grasp at or even believe. For example we live in this flat which is near the university and between us Eileen and I just about manage to run a car. We've lived here over a year, and it's happened to us not just once, but over and over again, that when we've been coming back home in the evening, perhaps after going out to see friends, we've been stopped at a road block by the police. If I'm the one who's driving I produce my licence with my Protestant name on it, and invariably all that happens is I get a polite 'Thank you sir, that's fine, goodnight' and then waved on. But with Eileen that doesn't happen, ever: she has an obviously Catholic surname, and if she's driving when she produces her licence the questioning's always much more rigorous. 'Where have you been this evening? Why are you coming back at this time? Is this your permanent address, or do you live in another part of the city?' It might sound trivial: but it does, it happens every single time we're stopped. When that kind of treatment always occurs, you can't help knowing what's being demonstrated is a fundamental rift, which'll never be overcome.

Nothing has improved the quality of life here for as long as I can remember. From time to time organisations come into being and what brings them into existence is usually a reaction to some particular incident: but before long they always run out of steam. Even organisations like the Peace People who were given the Nobel Prize: for a time they received endless publicity on television and in the newspapers, their founders went on worldwide tours speaking about what they were doing and what they were going to do: but what happened to them? Today you never hear of them at all. And there are plenty of others – every single one of them fades out of sight. Then there's another horrifying incident, people spring into action again saying it can't be allowed to go on: that dies down, and on and on everything goes in the same old way.

To me the principal people at fault are not the politicians, though criticising them is usually an acceptable alternative to actually doing anything. But it doesn't stop those same politicians being re-elected time after time. Most of all I blame the churches, I mean both Protestant and Catholic. It's incredible they don't use what influence they have, not just to condemn atrocities but to force their own communities to take positive action. They should all join together and give a lead, all at the same time: there are no other organised bodies who could make such an impression. I don't want to criticise one denomination more than the other, but I feel they've all totally failed the people of Northern Ireland. I know the churches didn't get far in Germany at the time of the Nazis, and I know they haven't achieved much in South Africa: but there've been outstanding individual men like Pastor Niemöller in Germany and Trevor Huddleston in South Africa, and just a few others here and there, who've stood up to the authorities and denounced them. Nothing like that's happened here: not one churchman has done anything but keep on wringing his hands and say how much he deplores the use of violence.

I can't speak for Eileen because she's not here, and if she was she'd have several things to say for herself. But nearly all our attitudes and opinions are the same: she agrees that there's no hope whatever in Northern Ireland today for anybody who wants to live any kind of a decent family life. It starts the very moment you choose where your child is going to be educated: you have to choose, and the decision in most cases follows sectarian lines. There are a few worthy attempts at mixed religion education, but for them to have any real impact they'd have to be extended and made universal. Church schools of any denomination would have to be abolished: but it doesn't need much imagination to see what little chance there is of that happening.

And the whole pattern of daily life that's become acceptable here, it's really now quite unbelievable. Where else in the British Isles would you find barriers across the main streets, armed police in body armour driving round all day in armed vehicles called 'Pigs', soldiers pointing guns in the streets, helicopters whirling overhead, Army checkpoints when you drive into the city in the morning, 'Control Zone' signs everywhere with no explanation of what they mean because it's taken for granted everybody knows, women going into department stores having to have their handbags searched and their toddlers and babies in prams body-searched, your car being stopped every night and you being made to get out and open your engine bonnet and boot and stand at the side with your hands up? What other capital city in Europe does this happen in every single day, and nobody so much as think it's unacceptable?

It's a state of anarchy, it's a state of war. But it's not Eileen's and my war, we don't want any more part of it: by next week we'll have turned our backs on this whole society we've both grown up in. To us it's a positive step: the only alternative would be to stay here and hope for the best. To do that we'd have to ignore the truth of the situation.

16 *Terrorists*

Edna Hanson, Loyalist
Terry Dodd, Loyalist
Marie Jones, Republican
Eamon Collins, Republican
Geoff Mitchell, Loyalist
Eddie Boyle, Republican
Willy Burns, Loyalist
Roy Walker, Loyalist
Peadar O'Donnell, Republican

Edna Hanson,

Loyalist

– A dancin' priest! Now tell me did you ever in your whole life hear anything so ridiculously stupid as that? He came here last summer at that wide part of the road where the shopping parade is, and he holds up his fat little hands over his head like this, the idiot, and starts dancin' and cavortin' all round everywhere would you believe? A grown man wearing a kilt and a black shirt and a dog collar – and round his shoulders in a good Protestant area like this, he wears an orange and green sash! 'I've come here from Dublin' he's telling everyone, 'And I'm dancin' for peace over the whole of Ireland I am.' A dancin' priest dancin' for peace, what a blethering fool! Sit yourself down while I finish making us this cup of tea.

Scarcely five feet in height and wearing a pleated grey skirt and a magenta blouse and a double-stranded necklet of pearls, she fumed round the kitchen recess in the sitting-room of her pristinely-neat council flat, her words rattling out like automatic rifle-fire.

– It makes me mad, it's an insult to decent God-fearing people they should have to suffer an exhibition like that. My next door neighbour this side is a poor wee woman whose husband had been murdered by the IRA men exactly two months before: when she heard what was going on she came into here and she said 'Edna' she said, 'Edna do I have to put up with it and my husband only eight weeks in his grave?' I said to her 'No you do not Mary' I said, 'Come on now, let's you and me go and tell him to get back where he belongs.'

So we went straight down there and confronted him we did.

There's a crowd of people gathered round watching him, you'd think they'd have known better: and him still jigging around and waving his arms in the air and whistling a tune. So I went up and stood right in front of him and stopped him, and I said 'Who are you?' I said, 'And what the hell do you think you're doing?' 'I'm a priest' he says, 'And I've come here dancing for peace, I'm dancing for peace through the whole of Ireland.' So my friend said to him 'And how do you think you're going to bring peace then, by making an exhibition of yourself and dancing in the street? My husband was murdered by your IRA' she says, 'Dance to them if you want to bring peace.' 'Oh' he says, 'I'm very sorry' he says. 'Tell me your name and I'll pray for you.' I said straight out to him 'She doesn't want someone like you to pray for her. She can pray for herself, now go away and leave us in peace.'

That they should let priests come on to a Protestant estate and stir up trouble like that is wicked I say, wicked it is. And only the next day after that some people calling themselves Peace People, they came on the estate and tried to talk to people too. Do you know who they were? They were all nuns: nuns coming on to this estate where only Protestant people live. If that isn't trying to cause trouble, then tell me what is.

Look I've poured your tea, don't let it go cold. You people in England, you don't get a proper picture at all from your television and newspapers of what we have to put up with. Never mind what happened in the past, that's history. But now, the Catholics get all the houses, there've been laws to make sure they get the best jobs, they get new schools, new shops, everything done for them they want. And all the while most of them are drawing state assistance money you know, money for their kids which they go on and on having. All this money for the Catholics: and it comes out of our taxes. Ours – loyal Protestant people's who look up to the Queen and respect the flag. But they don't, the Catholics, oh no. They're not loyal to Britain or to the Queen, yet they'll take the Queen's money when it's offered to them won't they? They can murder and kill, destroy our homes, put firebombs in our shops, and yet nothing ever happens to them except we go on passing laws for them and giving them money. They go off to their priests who tell them to say a couple of Hail Marys and all their sins will be forgiven, then they can go back and carry on exactly as they were doing before. I'll tell you what I think it is: I think it's a disgrace.

I'll tell you how it could be stopped tomorrow too. If the Government would let the Army and the police loose to really get in among them, they could have them all out of the way in two days. They know very well who the top men in the IRA are, the authorities do: and so do we all. And they're walking the streets all day with smiles on their faces because they know they won't be touched. It shouldn't be allowed and it's got to be stopped, and it will be. I know honest people, decent people, who're ready if it's necessary to give up their lives to make sure it doesn't go on.

I've nothing against Catholics, if that's their religion let them practise it. If that's what they want to do, then they should do it. Only not here: they should go across the border and live in the south, where they can be Catholics to their hearts' content. Where we are now is Ulster: it's part of the United Kingdom and the United Kingdom isn't a Catholic country. That's what we've fought for and suffered for and stood up for over hundreds of years, not to be a Catholic country, not to be under the thumb of Rome. You people over the water don't realise what our situation is. You don't stand by us and you let all the Catholics have everything they want. What do we get in return? We get fine decent men put in prison because they had the courage to try and do something which the Government won't allow the Army or the police to do. Men who are heroes, treated like criminals by the country to which they give loyalty.

You've made the UVF illegal and now you've made the UDA illegal, but not Sinn Fein. Yet if it wasn't for Sinn Fein and the IRA, there'd never have been the UVF or the UDA, they wouldn't have been necessary. All you do's let dancing priests in here, and nuns come among us.

Have another piece of cake and I'll tell you another thing the Catholics have started doing now. A clever little scheme this one is too: and that it goes on is a fact, as anyone'll tell you. A Catholic family decide they'd like one of them nice new houses that are being built, and they don't want to wait for six months for their turn on the housing list to come up, so what do they do? This is a fact I'm telling you, a well-known fact. They set fire to their own house and go off to the authorities and say the Protestants have burnt them out. It's disgusting it is, isn't it now? And it's the IRA that sets fire to their houses for them, that's well-known as well. I'm not saying there aren't any decent Catholic people, I know there're a few. But all of them have to do what they're told by the IRA: they have to let their houses be used by people running from the law, give up space in them where bombs and guns can be kept, and everything. If they don't, they're punished, things happen to them they do, and that's another fact too.

What it all comes down to is this. I'm glad you've come to talk to me because I'm an ordinary working-class woman, and our voices aren't listened to as they should be. I think the solution would be better left to me and people like me, who really know how things are. We're not afraid of taking on the Catholics and the IRA: we know who they are and what they do. We'd be prepared to clear them all out if the Government and the police and the Army won't do it. Sometimes I think there ought to be a women's army to deal with the women Catholics, because they're frightened to lay a hand on women, the police and the soldiers are. But they're just as bad as the rest. The only way Ulster'll ever be made into a better place to live is if they're all, men and women Catholics I mean, cleared out and sent across the border to live in the south. I'm telling you exactly how I feel, and I'm not ashamed to do so: I'm for the Royal Family and the Union Jack, I'm a true Orange Loyalist, I always have been and I'm not ashamed of it.

All my uncles were in the war fighting for the British, and so was my father. My grandparents too, they were upright religious people who wanted to lead good Christian lives. I was brought up to believe that the twelfth of July was the greatest day in our calendar, when we always paraded with bands and flags and drums and Union Jacks, to celebrate King Billy's defeat of King James at the Battle of the Boyne. He made sure for ever afterwards that we were not going to be under Catholic domination, so just tell me what is wrong with that? The proudest date in our history, and yet now when we want to celebrate it by having parades and showing how proud of it we are, people say we're being provocative. It seems to me the only people being provocative are the Catholics who are protesting about it.

I'm a Protestant and a Christian, though I don't go to church: I don't think that's anything to do with what you feel inside yourself about your religion. I was brought up Presbyterian, and I love Mr Paisley because he stands up for all us Protestant people and our rights. He says to the British Government what needs to be said, he's not frightened of them and he speaks for all ordinary working-class people like me. He says, and he's right, that Catholics are always trying to interfere in Ulster affairs, and it needs to be said. People on the mainland should back us to the hilt, not have secret discussions with Dublin about Ireland being made eventually into one country. I'll tell them this: that is never going to happen ever, there's far too many people like me who won't allow it and who'll die if necessary to stop it coming about.

Oh yes if necessary we'll sacrifice our lives. And others'? Well, what do you think? Don't misjudge the heart of Ulster men and women: we can't be frightened and we won't give in: there's nobody braver than an Ulster person. I have friends who've been in prison, I have friends who are in prison now: and I have friends who're ready to go to prison tomorrow. Do you understand what I mean?

Yes, all right, I'll see what I can do.

Terry Dodd,

Loyalist

Slightly built, sharp featured and pale faced, he had short red hair, a thin moustache and pale blue eyes. He wore clean newly-pressed stone-washed jeans, a bomber jacket and a black polo-necked sweat-shirt: while he talked he chain-smoked, pinching the cigarettes out half-finished with nail-bitten fingers and putting them carefully away in his breast pocket. His voice was clipped and his speech staccato: now and again a muscle fluttered in his cheek when he paused to think about what he should say.

– Edna says it'll be OK to talk to you so I suppose it will. I can't stop for very long though because there's a man I've got to see at the club in about an hour. It's Geoff actually: he knows I'm seeing you today, he says to tell you he'll meet you next Wednesday night as arranged.

I'm seventeen. I left school last year, the ordinary secondary school, and I have five GCSEs: English, History, Geography, Chemistry and Metalwork. I've not worked since I left because the employment situation's very bad round here. You stand most chance of a job if you're a Catholic, they'll go a bit out of their way to help you if you are. If you aren't they don't bother. A lot of people working in the Employment Bureau are Catholics themselves: it was Government policy a few years ago to recruit as many as they could into the Civil Service. They did that and now the result is the Catholics help their own.

I come from a Protestant family: we're all Protestants and we always have been. Where we live is on an estate at the top of the Shankill Road: it used to be a fairly decent place when they first built it twenty years ago, everyone says people were proud to live there. They're not now though: not sufficient money's been spent on the upkeep of it and so it's got very run down. All my friends live round there who I've known since school and we all feel the same about it. There's hardly anything for young people to do except hang round the buildings or play football in the street. There is one youth club but it's right over the other side of the estate: I don't go to it, I don't know anyone from our part of it who does, because it's so far.

My family is my dad who's unemployed, two brothers who're older than me and they're both in the Army and both of them in Germany: and two sisters, one of them's living over the water and has a job there in a bank and the other one's a nurse. My mother left home ten years ago, and I think now she lives in Armagh. She went off with a man: somebody told me he was a Catholic but I don't know that for sure. Myself, I don't have a girlfriend at the moment, but in fact the last one I had, she was a Roman Catholic. I met her at a disco in the city centre: it's where a lot of young people go. It broke up because things started to get very awkward for both of us. Her friends didn't like me and my friends didn't like her, so we agreed we wouldn't see each other any more. I went to her house sometimes: about three times altogether, and I met her parents and they seemed to be decent people. I never asked her to my home, I thought that my father wouldn't approve if he found out she was a Taig. I was going out with her after I'd joined the paramilitary organisation I'm in: which was funny because she had a brother who was an active member of the IRA, or I was told he was. I'm only judging from what I heard though, she never told me it herself.

I'm not allowed to say which organisation it is I belong to: I'll just say it's one of the largest ones there is. There's nothing unusual about being in it: a lot of young men of my age are connected with things like it in one way or another. One thing is you never know exactly who's a member because you don't have a membership card or anything of that sort. I've been surprised sometimes when I've gone to a planning meeting and seen someone there who I knew quite well. Up till then neither of us had any idea at all the other one was into anything of that sort. It's only common sense: the principle is that the less you know about the structure of the organisation and who's in it, the less you can tell somebody about it if you're picked up and questioned by the police.

I think how I came to join isn't something I should say much about. There's not really much to say anyway. I was in a pub one night and there was a group of us talking, one of them was a friend of mine whose brother had been shot two weeks before. No one was caught for it and there was a lot of high feeling about. I don't remember now what I said but it was to the effect everything was against us, the police weren't on the side of the Protestants any more and I felt bitter about it. A lot of people there felt the same way: I don't know how it came about I should be picked out by somebody, but that was the result of it. An hour after I'd gone home there was a ring at our front door, and when I opened it a man asked me could he come in and have a talk with me. I had a feeling I'd seen him before but I couldn't remember where: when I asked him he said he didn't think so that we'd met.

I took him in the kitchen and I made a cup of tea for us. He sat at the table without saying much at first, but then he said he understood I felt strongly about the shooting of the boy that had happened the week or two before. I said yes I did, I felt very strongly because no one'd been arrested. He said he understood I'd said in the pub something ought to be done about that sort of thing. I said yes again, I did. Then he asked me had I heard of this organisation whose name I won't mention, and I said I had of course, everybody had. He said did I feel I'd go as far as being a member of it? I asked him what it would mean, and he said some of what they did was connected with the various incidents like we'd been talking about, but on the whole the members were just ordinary people who'd swear they'd be ready to fight for the defence of Ulster if it ever became necessary. He said it would be like being in the Army except that we'd all be civilians. I thought for a minute and then I said yes.

He was drinking his cup of tea, and in a very natural way then he produced a Bible from his raincoat pocket and a revolver, and put them on the table. He said if I was ready to swear the oath for it, he could join me into the organisation there and then. I said I was ready, so he told me to put my hand on the gun which was on the Bible, and repeat certain words after him. They were to the effect that for the rest of my life I'd be loyal to the organisation, to God and to Ulster. Those were the things that I swore allegiance to, three things in that order. His next words to me straight after that were I was now a member of the organisation for the rest of my life, and the only way I'd ever get out of it was in a box. I'm not sure if I should have told you that much.

Yes, I was perfectly happy to do it, and I still am that I did. I think I was almost in a way flattered that I'd been taken as a member so readily. I felt it meant I had real importance then, and I was regarded as reliable and someone who'd grown up and people would trust. To me it was very serious that so many people were prepared to say if it ever became necessary they'd all join together and fight.

After a while I felt I wanted to do more and be more active in things. It's better I don't describe too much detail of day-to-day activities, but I think it's all right to say we obviously have training. Older members give it on a regular basis at meetings arranged for that purpose. Training is of two kinds: one in how to handle weapons, and the other in how to operate in small units of four or six people. So far all I've taken part in myself is operations in which I've been a car driver: I've not yet fired a weapon except in training.

You're never told in detail where you're going on an operation or what for. The most I'll get is a telephone call telling me to be at a certain place at a certain time. Then usually there's a car standing there, and waiting by it two or three people I've not seen before and know nothing about. One of them simply says to me the name of a road: because my job at present is to be a driver I'm expected to know where it is. I usually do because I've lived all my life in Belfast. I drive to the road and stop where I'm told to stop. What usually happens then is I'm given the name of another road, and the men get out. I go to the road that I've been given the name of, on my own in the car, and I wait there. It might be ten minutes, it might be half an hour: then the men come to where I am and get in, and I drive them back to some other road they name. Then they tell me when we get there to get out of the car and go home. That's the full extent of what I ever know about it. I might read the papers the next day to see if anything's happened or I might not. The less I know the better as far as I'm concerned. What the men do when they get out of the car at the place I've driven them to, I've no idea. I think often it doesn't amount to much more than going to have a discussion with other members of the organisation. It could possibly be to do something more, give someone a warning or something: I don't know and I don't ask.

I'm not actively seeking work now, because being a driver and being ready at all times is now my job. They don't give me a lot of money, but they look after me financially so that I'm never short. What I'm doing is a justified thing to do, because I don't think the Government takes steps to combat the IRA properly. The police have their hands tied, a number of well-known IRA people are walking about the streets and they can't do anything about them: unless they can be caught actually doing something, and evidence produced which is sufficient to get them convicted, they can't be touched. People like me are defending our country, because the IRA want to overthrow its Government. They don't fight their war out in the open, because if they did they'd be beaten. So they have all the advantages: they fight in an underhand secret way, blowing up buildings, setting fires and actually killing people. They shouldn't complain if we organise a force to fight them with their own methods: there's no other way of fighting them that will succeed. If there wasn't such an organisation as ours, the IRA would have a free hand. They've got to be shown they can't behave as they do and get away with it, and if the Army and police can't do anything there are plenty of people like us who are ready to.

Yes, I would go further than I do. If it became necessary and if I was asked to, I would because I gave my oath.

Marie Jones,

Republican

She worked behind the counter at the warehouse of a wholesale builders' supplies merchants; in overalls and with a kerchief tied round her head she laughed and joked all day with customers and exchanged bawdy remarks with the rest of the staff. But in the evenings in her home she was a different woman: she sat slender and long-legged in jeans on the floor, elbow propped on the seat of an armchair, her voice quiet and slow, drinking whiskey from a small glass while her long fingers played languorously with errant strands of her long black hair and her big green eyes half-closed in thought.

– I don't know if you think anyone who's been in prison is a bad person Tony: if you do then for sure I can't do anything about it can I? And I wouldn't be wanting to, I'm not ashamed to tell it to you, I'm proud of it so I am. I was sentenced to four years for possessing explosives and bomb-making equipment, and I served three and came out on my twenty-third birthday. That was ten years ago next week. I still say now and I always will that I don't regret it: it was one of the great experiences of my life so it was. Does it shock you to hear someone say that, and for a woman to be saying it too? They think us IRA people are all savages Tony: barbarians eh, isn't that what we're supposed to be? But going in prison makes you twice as determined as you ever were before, you know: not for a day since then have I ever changed my views. We're fighting a war which one day God willing we're going to win: and we'll win because we've got a cause, and so long as it's one people believe in, it'll triumph in the end.

Before I was inside I lost my cousin shot by British soldiers, and inside I lost my Catholic religion which I'd believed in all my life.

But the thing I lost most of all there was my innocence about what was really going on in the world. It's something I don't regret that I had my eyes opened, I don't regret it at all. Everything that happens to you, you can gain something from it you know, if you think it out for yourself. Ten years on, I'm married and with two children, my husband a volunteer and away now on the run. But I haven't changed: I tell my kids what he's doing and they're proud of him, and so am I.

I've been a Republican all my life, or sure that's how it feels it does. I'm the youngest of five children, born into a working-class family who lived in a two-up and two-down terraced house in the poorest of the poor parts of west Belfast. I went to a Catholic school, all girls, I wasn't bright so it wasn't a very happy period in my life. From almost when I can remember my father was out of work and no use to anyone, he spent most of his time drinking and gambling and never at home. My mother was the breadwinner, she did cleaning most of the day, she was a domestic at the Victoria Hospital. There was nothing special about my childhood, I enjoyed my friends and we spent most of our time playing in the street and whispering about boys like silly girls do. I wasn't politically aware, and I'm saying that because some people think your ideas get put into you by your parents. My father wasn't interested in politics at all, nor was my mother either.

The first inkling I had of any kind of a Republican feeling was one day in the street when I was coming home from school. Two British soldiers suddenly jumped out of an armoured car with rifles and pointed them at me. I was terrified, I didn't know whether they were going to shoot me or take me away in their vehicle or what. One of them very fiercely asked me my name and where I lived: when I told him he told me to eff off and I shouldn't be hanging about in the street. I wasn't, I was going home. I was only a hundred yards away from where I lived: and I remember as I walked that short distance my feelings changed from fear to anger at the way he'd treated me. Strange isn't it, something as trivial as that starting someone on a life dedicated to Republicanism? It left me for evermore seethingly angry about the presence of British troops on our streets.

When I was sixteen and not long left school, then two things happened which were much more important than that. One was I'd got a boyfriend, and he was in the IRA. He had very strong views, and he and I used to stay up into the small hours talking about politics and the situation in Northern Ireland and what could be done. I knew enough to know by then you don't ask questions of somebody about being a volunteer: you don't discuss the rights and wrongs of it, and most of all you don't mention it to anyone else. He shouldn't even have told me. The other thing was probably even a greater influence on my life: soon after, when I was seventeen, my cousin was killed by the Army. He was only two years older than me and he was shot in the back by soldiers in Derry. They said he was a known terrorist, they were questioning him and he was trying to escape from them so they fired. I still to this day don't know whether it was true or not that he was in the IRA. I didn't know him that well, but I know he often travelled to and fro between here and Derry. I'd never an idea until then what for. Him being killed though made me think about him more, and the most important thing I learned from knowing both him and my boyfriend was that the idea of the IRA as mindless terrorists always given out by the media is absolutely incorrect. They were young men, both of them, who cared deeply about Ireland, and wanted it to be united and rid at last from hundreds of years of British occupation and exploitation. They and hundreds of others like them are brave soldiers: I could arrange for you to meet any number of them who see fighting as the only way left of bringing about an end to division and social deprivation.

You know, it's naive of people in Britain to think the IRA will ever give up or can be defeated. They won't and they can't, not by military means. And it's wrong to talk of them as criminals: despite all the media says, they are not. In fact if you do have a criminal record, however trivial, the IRA won't have you. They're people of principle who want to see an end to injustice and the harassment on the streets of Irish people by foreign troops. What they stand for is superior to that of those who oppose them, who're motivated politically and have no ideas other than retaining their own power. But is there anyone in Britain who tries to understand that, and why the IRA exists? If you really want them not to exist, isn't the best thing to do to listen to what they say and consider their point of view? Why won't British politicians even try to reach agreement with them, by discussion and negotiation? Everyone should be heard, not just those selected as acceptable by the British Government. Isn't the only alternative to it that the whole situation drags on and on for ever?

I read in a newspaper the other day the latest casualty in our war's now brought the total of deaths on all sides up to 3,000 in a period of just over twenty years. But in the oppression which has been visited on Ireland and the Irish people by the British over five or six centuries, it's caused not a few thousand but millions of innocent Irish people to die from brutality and starvation. Britain brought the gun to Ireland to suppress the people: so is there any other way now to fight back? Your Government's said hypocritically that they don't negotiate with terrorists, even though they've done it more than once in other countries. But Tony who are the terrorists? Look back through history: you'll see all the terrorising has been done to the Irish by the British. They've never hesitated to use force to keep the people down: yet these are the same people who shout in outrage when force is used against them in return.

– I didn't say much the other night about prison, except that I learned a lot. For an ordinary person like myself it was, really it was, a very valuable experience. I was a political prisoner, but not many others that were there were: they were women in for petty crime, shoplifting, stealing, prostitution, drug offences and other things like that. Mixing with them made me think about things I'd never given much thought to before. The main one was to see how much crime is a result of deprivation. Nearly all who'd committed theft did it because they'd no money. Often they'd been abandoned by men and couldn't see any alternative: and yet it was men who arrested them and prosecuted and punished them without offering them any understanding at all. Instead they treated them harshly, brutalised them in spirit, set them against society, and made them think of themselves as an underclass. So they were by then, but it was men who'd put them in that position. I'm not a feminist, but I learned a lot in prison about the inequality of women in society. I found I could identify with them, and I don't think I'll ever look at criminal women in quite the same way again.

Another thing I learned about women's position was it was due to the domination of the Catholic church. I'd been a practising Catholic since I was a teenager. But in prison you have a lot of time for reading and thinking, and I started to see how rigorous the church's attitude towards women is. It prohibits divorce, it prohibits contraception, and it teaches that abortion is sin. But these are all man-made rules to keep women in their subservient place. The Church threatens sin and damnation for those who don't obey its laws, but it's a totally masculine and patriarchal authority. No one must even question the Church. And this by the way is something the Loyalists pretend not to recognise. When they say they want freedom to live without being under the authority of a state that's run by the Church, and have freedom of speech and the right to such things as divorce and contraception and abortion, well so do we. All Republicans want to get rid of the domination of the Catholic church: it's something we firmly unite with Protestants about.

The third thing I learned much more about when I was in prison was the fundamental idea of Republicanism. Because I didn't have much else to do but sit around and wait for the date of my release, I read a lot and had long discussions with the other girls about Irish history. A couple of the other women there were Republicans too: they were older than me and they could teach me a lot and they did. Everything I read, everything I talked about and heard, it all deepened my resolve to commit myself fully when I came out to the cause.

– It's not possible is it to condense all your ideas and say all the things you want to about yourself and your life in a few meetings and a few hours? I've not changed much in the second half of my life, since I left school. I'm more aware, I hope more understanding, and more determined in my views. I'm married, I love my husband and our children: but I've not let that stop me doing what I do, which is help the movement all I can. What happens to me is less important in the end than what kind of a future our children have. I'd like to think they're developing their ideas, and they and other people's children will have the chance to grow up in a better country than those of my generation have.

What I'd like to do most now is travel to England and talk to women's groups. Then they could see a Republican isn't someone with two heads and cloven feet: and we could find out how much we had in common as women, and where there'd be what you'd call a meeting of minds. I don't think all English women are idiots who believe everything they're told: they don't unquestioningly accept what their Government says, that the IRA are menaces to the fabric of society. Do English women know for instance that a middle-aged person like myself can be walking down the road in the Lower Falls and be stopped like I was today and asked by a soldier who's not more than eighteen 'What's your name and address? Where are you going to today, you Irish whore?' But it's not personal insults like that that I'd mainly want to talk to them about: I'd want to try and explain to them why men in this country resort to the actions that they do. Occasionally the IRA do bad things, yes, and they do unjustifiable things. But so do the police, so do the Army and the UDR, so do the Ulster Loyalists and their paramilitaries too. These things happen in a war: and this war's been going on in our country here now for more than twenty years. It won't stop until the mass of ordinary people in Britain ask the British Government to rethink its ideas and set up meetings of people: not the same old politicians, and perhaps not even always men but women too, and have discussions where all points of view will be listened to and treated with respect.

I can go on forever, as you've found out since you started coming here, about the injustices perpetrated against the Irish people by you British for hundreds of years. I expect the Loyalists will carry on in the same way to you about how they've suffered because of the Catholics for many years too. But if you put the two lists side by side, one would be very long and the other'd be very short. A point in the Protestants' accounts would be reached when it'd have to take off into realms of fantasy and imagination about what the Catholics would do to them if the British Army went away. But it wouldn't happen: what they say wouldn't happen, but what the Catholics say has. I don't think anywhere in the rest of the world Protestants hate Catholics in the way they hate them here: and I don't believe any Government in the world except the British would go on for so long burying their heads in the sand and pretending it isn't like it is. Northern Irish people are friendly and warm and hospitable, and they'd show it to English visitors any time, readily and gladly they would. So why don't more people come here to meet us and visit us, and talk to us and take an interest in what our problems are?

God help us, we're only ordinary people, and the IRA are only ordinary people too. Only how many English people will accept that? They condemn us without knowing or trying to find out even the first thing about the situation, and they've never met anyone at all who is in the IRA. No one will meet with us without having a condemnatory attitude already firmly fixed in their mind.

I'll do my best for you, I promised I would and I will. I'll speak to some people: but give me a bit of time.

Eamon Collins,

Republican

– Everyone's a story aren't they Tony eh for sure? And depending on who's telling it, it'll look different different ways. If you're telling it about yourself you're the one who knows the most, but you might be the one who sees the least too. Well I'll leave it to you to make of it what you can, that's the best way. An outsider looking at me sitting here in my own little flat, I wonder what he'd imagine was my tale d'you think, eh? What'd he see? A small roly-poly man, sixty-three years of age, going bald, looking for all the world like a living example of an ordinary guy who'd never known much about life. And how wrong he'd be about that, how very very wrong. If you want to hear it, it's an enigma: the story of an enigma, that's all I can say.

I was born in a village in County Armagh: my father went round with a grocery van, calling at people's houses and selling them whatever they'd buy. I've a brother younger than me, a clever one so he followed a different path. After school he went to university, and he's done very well for himself all his life since as an engineer. Not a gaol bird like me, to be sure. My mother was a nice woman I'd say: she wasn't well educated, didn't take much interest in things except her children and her husband, but she was none the worse for that. She'd have liked both her sons to do well, but I was the disappointment to her. When I was a lad my ambition was to be a brain surgeon: don't ask me where I got that from because I can't remember. I left school at fourteen and went as an apprentice in a local barber's shop, so cutting men's hair was the nearest I got to becoming a brain surgeon. It wasn't so far off you might say though, eh?

I was a prolific reader, as a youngster, and what I liked reading in particular was books about the American Civil War. I think it must have been due to that fella Longfellow and that poem of his, what was it, 'The Midnight Ride of Paul Revere'. That was what started me off. Then I went on to reading about what was done to the Indians, how they were robbed of their lands by the settlers. I didn't put it together in my mind with what was going on here in Ireland though, I wasn't politically minded at all. I was an ordinary young lad who didn't think about things very much, associated with local boys and girls his own age, went to dances and such things as that. I went to the fillums a lot too, I liked the cinema: particularly Fred Astaire, I wanted to be like him, I fancied myself as a dancer I did, at the local hall on a Saturday night. It was there I met my late wife: at the time I was seventeen and she was twenty-three. Her speciality was the tango: she was magnificent to see, and I learned how to do it myself, so one night I could pluck up courage to ask her to do it with me. She did, and from then onwards we were permanent dancing partners, we were the two best ballroom dancers for miles around.

We got married, and I could find no work in that part of Armagh so we had a very hard time at first. When I was twenty we had our first child, a boy: we had another son then who died a month after birth, after that a daughter, then another son, and the last was our youngest daughter, she's now aged thirty-four. After our first son was born we went to Glasgow where my wife had an auntie living: I took odd jobs, I worked in a factory for a time, and at least I made a living on the whole. Finally I got a good position at a bakery, it was one belonging to a famous company, and I became a supervisor on the production line.

Up till that time you can see can't you an ordinary man living an ordinary life? A steady job and a wife, and I think it was then at that time with two children. But Jenny my wife had bad health: heart trouble she had and spent quite a bit of time in hospital, and a long period of convalescence when she came out. She wasn't happy at all really in Glasgow, so finally we came back to Ireland and lived in Belfast. The early 1960s it was, and the troubles were growing: Civil Rights marches, Bloody Sunday, riots and street fightings and all the rest. You'll have heard about those times.

Let me say to you this: till then I wasn't interested in it all at all I wasn't, not one bit. I was just an ordinary apolitical man, concerned with my wife and family and nothing outside. And then one morning all my life suddenly completely changed. We had a small house in a small street, and at six o'clock that morning the front door of it was broken down and soldiers and police came pouring in: they came through the windows, in at the front and in at the back, so many of them it seemed as though they were even coming through the floor. Our eldest son was sixteen years of age and it was him they'd come for. They told him to get dressed but they only gave him time to put on his shirt and a pair of jeans: in front of my eyes four of them dragged him with a great deal of force down the stairs, banging his head on the wall, out through the front door through the snow that was covering the front garden, and they then threw him into an army vehicle and drove him away. It was the most terrible shock and the most terrible sight there'd ever been for me in the whole of my life. He was held in an interrogation centre, and I couldn't get to see him for five whole days: and when I did, he told me he was to be charged with belonging to the IRA.

I'd never dreamed until that moment of any such thing: I thought I'd never met any such person as an IRA man. And here one was, and he was my own son. I didn't ask him about it, if it was true or not: I frankly didn't care. The image in my mind was of my boy being dragged out of the house like that through the snow, and thrown in a patrol truck by the British Army. I wasn't political, but from that moment onwards all I wanted was to fight the British, that was the only thing in life that mattered to me. And when my son was given a prison sentence of five years, it can be looked on that I determined to take his place in the Republican Army. I read like I'd always done: only history this time, Ireland's history, and I saw how I'd been blind. In time people came to see me and talked with me: my past and present were very carefully examined, because you can't just become a member on your affirmation that you wish to. There are standards you've got to come up to. I'd no history previously of being even faintly involved in any kind of politics, so that made me a good candidate because I wasn't known: and I wasn't political, all I wanted was to do what I could to drive those people who'd treated my son like that off Irish soil.

At their request, and with people putting in a word here and there for me, I changed my job: I became a milkman delivering milk round one area of the city, driving a float. An ideal person to be a carrier for the IRA. I knew who lived where and the police never even thought to look at what was in my float besides milkcrates: they wouldn't would they? I had no narrow escapes because nobody ever suspected me of anything at all. I went on like that five years, and only through my own fault eventually I was caught. But I'd done a lot of damage by then: I'd been an active fighting man in the end, which is what I'd wanted most of all. But never political: never, and that was my strength, do you understand? Discussion and argument and stance: none of them was of interest to me.

I was captured in an attack on a police barracks in the city. In the fighting I was cornered in the back garden of a house: no one could come to my assistance, and at the end my only choice was being shot dead or surrendering. I thought the second one was the better option. They took me to an interrogation centre, and for seven days I was kicked, beaten, starved, threatened and shouted at and all the other interrogation methods which they use. I gave no names, but there's a limit to what the human frame can stand and I reached it, I couldn't take ill-treatment any more. So I signed confessions: I never bothered to read the papers put in front of me, I just signed. No names or information to harm anyone else, but more than sufficient to be the end for me.

I was on remand in Crumlin Gaol for fifteen months before trial. Thirty charges against me there were: killings, murder attempts, explosives, arms possession, being a member of the IRA. They made up things to add on too, that they wanted in their records as clearings-up. They knew they could do that because I wasn't offering any defence: I'd said from the start I wouldn't recognise the Court. I had no consultations with solicitors or counsel, and at the trial I stood in the dock with my back towards the Judge. He gave me twenty years each on some of the charges, a couple of fifteen years, and some life sentences as well for a few other things.

I was in Long Kesh in the H blocks: on the blanket protest with all the others for a time, and there my only concern was personal survival. When I was in, I was the oldest IRA lifer there was, but we were all equals in a group together, serving our sentences as prisoners of war. All the time there was a feeling of absolute solidarity: talk was always about 'us', you never spoke about 'you' or

'I': it was what 'we' would do to aggravate authority, what would 'our' response be to this or that. At the height of the protest there was something like three hundred men all on the blanket at the same time: that's a lot of bodies it is, and it meant it gave you a great strength to resist, far more than you could ever possibly have had had you been an individual doing it on your own.

The majority of the prisoners, the majority of them without a doubt, they were idealists who saw themselves as fighting for the cause of a United Ireland. I wasn't one, as I've said: I was just one hundred per cent anti-British because of what had been done to my son. It's ironic when I look back on it of course: he got five years for what he'd been involved in and my reaction to it earned me much longer imprisonment for mine. Until they heard I was on remand in Crumlin Road, not a single member of my family, including my son in prison, had had the faintest idea I was involved with the IRA. I'd kept my feelings inside me and never talked to my family about it. When my wife came to see me on the first visit after I was sentenced, I remember her saying to me she'd never had any idea I was a Republican: but I didn't bother trying to explain to her nor to anyone else what my motivation had been. And I never changed. When I'd been in some years, one day a prison officer said to me with a disbelieving sort of shake of his head 'You know Eamon, I haven't you know, I've never thought somehow this was really your scene.' A shrewd man: he'd been watching me, and seen I'd never taken part with enthusiasm in the political arguments and discussions all the others were for ever always talking about.

My wife hadn't been well a long time with her heart: she had a stroke and that left her incapacitated, so she couldn't write or come to see me any more. After I'd been in prison five years she passed away. The authorities wouldn't let me out to go to her funeral, and I took her death hard. The children were growing up and two of them were married. They all came to see me regularly though: even my eldest son, he did too after his release. It wasn't supposed to be officially allowed, but he managed to do it somehow.

So there we are: and that was it, for me that was all. I stayed in prison altogether for fifteen years: a loner and an enigma to everyone, and most of all to me. They finally let me out a year ago last May. I was moved for the last part of my sentence from Long

Kesh to Maghaberry, which is what you might call a less oppressive regime. When they send you there, it's accepted as an indication that you've changed your attitudes, and that when you come out you're not going to continue in the same way as before.

My son had long since been released from prison, and over the years it's true, I'd begun to feel I'd played my part and had my say. I knew before they did that there was no other future direction for me than starting a new life. When I'd been moved to Maghaberry my mother came on a visit: she was a frail old lady and didn't come often, and that day when she was leaving she said to me: 'Now Eamon, you're sixty-one now so you behave yourself in future, be a good boy and do as you're told, and don't forget to keep yourself always nice and clean.' So that was what I did.

From prison after a few months they started letting me go out in the daytime each day to work: a small party of us did house-painting and things of that sort. But another thing that happened was more important: it was that one day an American lady came to visit me. There's always been a connection between Ireland and the USA, and this lady came from Boston. She was in an organisation there which took an interest in prisoners in Northern Ireland, sending them small gifts and occasionally writing them letters and things of that sort. She and I, we'd been in correspondence for a year or more, and then it happened that she came to Belfast to see some distant relatives of hers. And while she was over she came to see me. She knew a good deal about my family because I'd written about them in my letters often: so she went to see two of my children too, and liked them and they liked her. When she came on her visit to me she asked me if I'd like when I was released to go over to America for a visit, and stay with her. I didn't think with my record it would even be considered: but she said she thought it could be arranged. I don't know how it was done, I really don't. But I was told before I was let out on parole that I could go and stay with her in Boston for a week, and I did.

I know it's easy for a man in prison to get romantic ideas about a woman who takes an interest in him: and it's easy for a woman to get the same sort of ideas about a prisoner too. But it wasn't like that really at all with us. The first thing she asked me when I went to stay with her was to give her a promise: that I'd never do an act of violence ever again in the rest of my life. When I did, she said that

that perhaps was where we could start: and we have started for sure, I know that I've lost all my hate, through her.

The week I spent in her home was one of the richest ones I've ever had in my life. She's interested like me in American history, and we talked and talked together for hours about the American Civil War. We liked the same kind of food, the same kind of books, and the same kind of music. I'm sixty-three years of age and she's a widow of fifty: and we're getting married to each other next year in July. And so there you are, that's how it stands. She's a nice lady and a special one: she says until we're married, there's no question of it, it's single beds. I go along with her on that. I don't know how to express it, but somehow both of us feel at this late stage in our lives God or whoever's responsible meant us to spend our time together.

My dear first wife, I don't need to say it, she's someone of course I'll never forget, nor the love we had for each other and the having of our children, which gave us so much happiness. This is something quite different and I don't compare or contrast the two. I've family living all around: the total's sixteen grandchildren now, with ages from fifteen down to five months. The American lady who'll be my wife knows all of them already by name, sends birthday cards and Christmas cards, and she's been back over here twice again and by now met almost all of them. I don't think it'd be possible for me to emigrate to America with her, but we've not talked much yet about that. She's hardly any family of her own and she's never had children, so she's no reason to stay there: she says she wants to live here, and maybe we shall have to anyway, because of the regulations which apply to me and always will. We shall see, we shall see, and how it all turns out for the future, well who knows? Wish me luck if you can, and tell me I'm an old fool which I am for sure. But I'll tell you this Tony: I'm enjoying it.

Geoff Mitchell,

Loyalist

A foreman in charge of a garage repair shop, he was a quietly spoken man in his early fifties, with a mass of wiry fair hair and humorously twinkling blue eyes. He sat in the comfortably furnished front room of his small modern terraced house, casually dressed in a fawn jacket and trousers, and an open-necked corduroy shirt.

– You'll have seen on your way coming, you're in a hundred per cent Protestant area. These are new houses built four or five years ago and we were one of the first to be given one of them because our street was scheduled to be demolished: it was just over there on the corner, so we didn't move far. The first thing we did was painted all the kerbs and lamp-posts red white and blue to let everyone know what sort of an area it was and make it feel like home: that's how everything in the other street was painted before. Not a single Catholic family's been given a house around here and never would be. They just wouldn't risk it.

We're all ordinary working-class people and always have been. My father was a fitter for the city gas company, and he and my mother had four children. There was never much money, but that didn't matter: it was a great community feeling to live round here, and even though it's all been rebuilt, a lot of that's still been kept, thank God. You still feel you're living among your own and that's what matters. The important thing isn't how much money you've got, you won't find that in these parts, everyone all trying to outdo one another all the time. And for as long as I remember, that's how it's been, it's always been that way. Right from when I was a kid, if you didn't have enough for food at the end of the week there was always Uncle Ted who lived over there or Auntie May: and they'd lend you a couple of quid to help you over. At first I used to feel ashamed a bit, going out and asking to borrow money for the family. Then when I got older I realised everybody else did it: we lent to other people when they needed it too, so there was nothing to be ashamed of at all. They say a lot of that feeling has gone out of life nowadays, everyone helping one another: I don't know how it is where you come from, but it's still alive and well all right in these parts.

My main memory of being a kid though is that like every other boy round here, I was football mad. Locally we were all Linfield supporters, Linfield being the Protestant team: but our great heroes were Glasgow Rangers. They say there's as many Ranger supporters in Belfast as there is in Glasgow, and I should think it's true. We've always felt it's just as much our team as it is theirs. A fine club and as good as any team in Europe, Rangers are. You might read sometimes about something called 'Northern Irish Protestant culture' do you? Well as far as kids are concerned round here, what that began and ended with and does still, is Glasgow Rangers. I could never afford the money to actually go over to Scotland to see them, and thought I never would, it'd just be a dream. But then one day for my birthday when I was sixteen one of my uncles gave me the fare to go over on the boat to Scotland to watch them play. It was the most fantastic experience of my young life, standing on the terraces at Hampden Park and actually seeing Rangers in the flesh. The only thing that soured it a bit if I remember it right was they were playing Celtic and they got beaten. Imagine the humiliation of it: to be beaten by Celtic, who're the Catholic team! Ah well, football, football eh? We could go on for hours!

I'd no great educational achievements when I left school, and at first all I had was a number of little jobs doing this and that. But finally I got work as a cutter in a clothing factory, and that began a good time in my life. I'd money in my pocket and I'd started taking an interest in girls, so things were fine. Except that the troubles had started. It mightn't have meant much and you tried to let it not interfere: but the thing you did know of course was you were a Protestant and it was as simple as that. I don't mean going to church: just that Protestants were 'us' and Catholics were 'them'.

Yet you know, the first serious girlfriend I had, she was a

Catholic. She came from the Falls Road, and we went steady for two years. I met her at the factory, where she worked as well. We were very fond of each other and went out regularly. But it always had to be places where no one knew us: not dances or cinemas, but to fish and chip shops or walks in the park. If we'd been recognised together there'd have been trouble both in her family and mine: it just wasn't on for a Protestant boy to go with a Catholic girl. But going with someone for two years, it was definitely more than a flirtation. I've often thought it's not impossible we might even have got married, she was such a nice girl. She came from a strong Republican family, she supported the IRA, and she used to sing Republican songs to tease me. We both knew there was no future in it, and we never got as far as talking seriously about marriage or anything because something happened that made us split up.

It was a bomb in a pub: a Protestant pub, put there by the IRA. There was two or three people were killed, and a lot were injured: and one of them, badly hurt, was my sister who'd been having a drink in there with her boyfriend, and was taken to hospital cut about by flying glass. I went to visit her the day afterwards: and I remember sitting by her bed and thinking I'd never go out again with someone who was a Catholic. I told my girlfriend about it, I said her people were a lot of murderers and I could have lost my own sister because of them. She just nodded: it wasn't she was unsympathetic or hard-hearted, but what could she say? It wasn't an occasion for her to sing one of her Republican songs to me either: she knew it and I knew it that we were finished from then on.

Other things had happened too. By then I was involved with the paramilitaries, though she didn't know it of course. I was only young, and the most I'd ever done was set off a few explosions and fire a bullet or two in the general direction of Catholic houses, that sort of thing. But the very next night after I wound up with my girlfriend, still very angry about my sister, I went out with three others and took them to the street where she lived and fired bullets through her windows. I didn't tell the others what it was all about, why I should have picked out this one particular house: but from then on I had, I'd really changed.

Then the troubles escalated, and things developed fast. Before long I joined an operational unit and was given proper training in how to use weapons. Catholic young men were doing the same thing, and soon it got to the point when every night you went out to attack places you knew Catholics frequented. You were disappointed if there wasn't any action, because it'd taken over your whole life.

There was never any great philosophising about it all. In the Protestant community we saw the Republicans as threatening our way of life, and there was no question about it, we had to show them we'd fight back. The police and Army were hampered in what they could do, they had to operate within the law: but we weren't, we could do as we pleased. We had a good intelligence network, and gathered all the information we could as to who exactly the IRA members were. The authorities couldn't arrest and charge them unless they'd hard evidence, but restrictions like that didn't apply to us. We knew their names, we'd photographs of them and we could identify them by sight in the streets. We targeted individual people as they did, and didn't wait for them to attack. If you got a tip-off a certain man was in a certain pub on a certain night, you went straight after him there. If it was a well-known Republican pub as it often was, that made it more exciting because it was like you used to see in films about the war. A commando raid: that's exactly what the feeling was.

As time went on our information got better: we began to get co-operation, you see. I'll not be too specific, you won't expect that: but those in the police who felt their hands were tied knew ours weren't and they'd give us some help now and again. Information, or something more than that once in a while: there were instances weapons went missing, let's not say more. Can you imagine how that made us feel?

Then when I was twenty-eight I got myself a different girl, and this time a Protestant one. There'd been others, but this one was special and of a different kind. She worked as a clerk in a bank, and lived with her family in north Belfast in what was one of the better class areas you might say. She'd no idea what I was into: and one night there was an unlucky incident, some people burst into a pub where we were and shooting began. I knew the place and knew what to do: I took her out at the back where she'd left her car. She drove us out by one of the city ringroads towards her home, then suddenly she pulled up in a parking bay, switched off the engine and turned to

look at me and asked me straight: had it been me who was the one
the gunmen were after? I told her truthfully that as far as I knew, it
wasn't, no: and it was a slip I made, to say as far as I knew, because
she was on to it in a flash and wouldn't let go. As far as I knew – so it
could have been? Finally I had to tell her: it could have been possibly,
and in the future it might be still. She gave me an ultimatum: either I
had no more to do with my organisation, or then was going to be the
last time I saw her. I liked her very much, and I asked her to give me
a day. I surprised myself, because I decided in twenty-four hours she
was more important to me than anything else and met her the next
night and told her so. I asked her to marry me, she said yes, and that
was fifteen years ago. We've our home and three children, and from
then on I was never active again in Protestant paramilitary affairs.

At eight o'clock two evenings later, he was sitting on his own in his
fluorescent-lit office in the far corner of the garage's deserted service
area, glancing through a newspaper and sipping from a polystyrene
beaker of tea. The badge on the breast pocket of his white overall
jacket said 'Workshop Foreman' underneath his name.

– Good, found your way all right then, fine. Everyone else's
knocked off, we'll not be disturbed. Sit there, that's the most
comfortable seat: no no, it's OK, I'll be all right here.

After you'd gone Tuesday Penny asked me what we'd been
talking about so long: history I said, you were writing a history
book, I'd been telling you about the bad old days. It's true all right I
always think, that's what they really were. You can't have made
much sense of it, you'd have thought I was some sort of crazy
gangster I suppose. The English always do, they don't understand
history isn't in the past in this country: they can't see why we can't
just bury it and let it die. But you see I took an oath when I joined,
like everyone did: not just for then but for now. And history looks as
though it's happening again if you see what I'm trying to say.

If some kind of call comes again like it seems it's going to, I'll have
to think seriously whether to respond. The way things are going's
not good: violence increasing and it looks as though it's going to go
on. Around our part I can see a lot of youngsters who remind me of

what I was like. They react to the present situation and what's being done by the IRA: and they feel like we did, that nothing effective's being done by the security forces. I talk with them now and again, and I know what they're looking for: a lead. They want someone to help them organise and be effective. And who do they look to? Obviously an older person don't they, like me? A lot have their own fathers in prison and to them they're heroes, people who've done something if it needed to be done.

I can tell you this: no one I know in the Protestant community trusts the British any more. All we see's compromise with Dublin, and everyone's worried about the outcome. Make no mistake: for the first time we're genuinely afraid. I'm no political person, but I am a Protestant: I'm not willing to live in a state dominated by the Catholic Church. In Ulster we've our own way of life, British currency, loyalty to the Queen. On the mainland English people don't understand. We're the only part of the United Kingdom which has a land frontier with another country: and it's as foreign a country as any country in the rest of Europe'd be to you. Catholic statues by the roads, road signs in Irish, everything. The Republic's a foreign country, and want the whole of Ireland under their control. Ulster people'll no more accept that than people who live in south-east England'll ever accept being handed over to France.

What's happening here every day now is people who have no allegiance to our Government are blowing up buildings. They're causing deaths and injuries and destruction right in the heart of our capital. So how would English people react if this was going on in London? Say it was being done by French people, creating havoc so that the south-east of England will eventually fall under their control? That's how it looks to us: don't your people on the mainland understand it at all?

I'm not an educated man but I'm British. How can I stand by and watch those growing up after me without telling them my feelings when they ask me for guidance? Should I tell them to trust the British Government and say it'll never relinquish Ulster? If you feel that's true then tell me: and I'll tell them.

The Protestant people feel it's essential for their own safety's sake to have an armed and trained paramilitary force: which is a well-equipped one that, if it really comes to it, is ready to fight. Well I'm telling you no secrets: there is one. It's called the Royal Ulster Constabulary, and many of them would be loyal to their own people here, not to the British Government if it tried to hand Ulster over to the Republic. I hope it never comes to the test, but I know enough to know what I'm talking about.

And there's a personal dilemma as well, for someone like me. I never imagined when I was the age of some of these boys I know round east Belfast that this all would still be going on. I thought we'd have had it all solved years ago, and know for ever and for certain who were our friends. I've got a loyalty to my family and the promise I made to my wife. But your family isn't just your children: it's your father and mother, your grandparents, everyone. You can't ignore what they stood for always, you can't put aside what they'd still expect of you if they were alive. I'm finding all these thoughts coming back that I had when I was young. I wish they weren't, but they are: and I'll tell you, I'm a worried man. You'll maybe think me a prejudiced person, an ignorant man who can't see or listen to anybody else's point of view. That's how us Loyalists have always been seen. Perhaps we are, I don't know: but if so then that wasn't how we all always used to be. People are hard on the UDA but it put out its own pamphlet once, did you know that, about solving the troubles by talks and discussions between the two sides?

But nothing came of it and time's running out. People've lost patience, they won't listen any more to talk about compromise. It's getting to be the time for the wild men again now. You'll find it confirmed in some places, I think, I'll pass you on those when it's been arranged.

*

(Beyond The Religious Divide: Papers For Discussion is published by the Ulster Defence Association.)

Eddie Boyle,

Republican

Tall and well-built, he came out of the darkened sitting-room into the brightly-lit kitchen, closing the door firmly behind him to shut out the sound of the television. He looked round for the waste bin, dropped the empty lager can he'd been carrying into it, shook hands, searched for an ashtray, and sat at the table when he'd finally found one behind the drawn curtains. It wasn't his house. He wore a thick brown sweater and jeans: his voice was strong and firm, his manner friendly and smiling. He was thirty-six.

– Sure now and didn't I read a book once of yours Tony, *Soldier, Soldier* was it, about the British Army? And wasn't there a fella in there, a British Army major, and didn't he say something like if he'd been born in Ireland he'd have been a terrorist himself? That's right so he did, I remember it well: though I can't say I care for his word 'terrorist' much, it's one you Brits use for anyone who's fighting for his country when you're occupying it. But if he's fighting for his country against somebody else when they're occupying it, you call him a 'freedom fighter' isn't that right now? This fella the major or whatever he was, I remember the point he was making was he could understand how we felt: and well you know I can understand him too. We're both soldiers aren't we, the business of the both of us is war?

And another thing I think I remember in the book is it said you were a pacifist yourself Tony, is that right too? Well well everybody has a right to their point of view I suppose: but I never thought I'd be one day talking to a Brit who was a pacifist I didn't: and I don't suppose you ever thought you'd be sitting talking to an IRA man either did you, eh?

So well now then what can I tell you that you'd like to know? You wouldn't expect me to be telling you anything much very personal about myself I'm sure. I'll just say I'm a soldier in the Irish Republican Army, but naturally not one who's going to give you personal details that anybody could identify me by.

For how long have I been a soldier? Oh for as long as I can remember, I have. My father was an IRA man, and two of his brothers: so I always knew I'd be one too, I knew from when I was a boy. It was my only ambition it was, to be a volunteer. That's something Brits don't understand: we're all volunteers you know. You don't join the Irish Republican Army for the same reasons soldiers join yours, like a settled career and good money and good housing. It's not like that with us, it's the opposite so it is. Those are the things you give up when you join the IRA: you give it all you can from your life, not take all it can give you. You get no medals for it and you won't be given a pension at the end of your service either.

I wonder if he'd understand that, your British soldier major man? He might enjoy the fighting part, but I don't suppose he's thought the rest of it through. It probably wouldn't make sense to him, and it probably doesn't make any sense at all to you being a pacifist like you are. Only someone like myself sees it as a war to be fought and a war to be won: not as a career to be finished and done with at the end of a set time.

Now let's see where they keep the drink before we start.

– Sure I'll try to describe how I look at it for you, sure. Without any sort of feeling of apology for carrying it on, that's the first thing to say: I'm fighting for the freedom of Ireland against the occupation of a foreign power. If the Germans had won the last war and they'd come over here and occupied Ireland as well as mainland Britain, I'd be fighting the Germans now in exactly the same way. If you understand it or not, if you believe it or not, is a matter for you: but that's the way it is to me.

And second I don't ask or expect to be judged by your rules: if Brits do that, then they'll see the IRA as a lot of ruthless maniacs which by their definition I suppose we are. Ruthless, definitely yes: and maniacs if that's what people are who're never going to see sense as you define it, well yes that'd be an appropriate word. The IRA has its own logic and oh no it's not yours. I can't explain too much about it either for you in concrete terms, because one of our strengths is there has to be a part of us which other people don't understand. 'Know your enemy'? No, we won't try too hard to explain. If you don't know our aims or how we justify them in our thinking, then it's that much more difficult for you to combat us. You'll not know where we've come from or the direction in which we're going, do you understand what I mean? Our secrecy and our willingness not to be understood by those we're fighting, our capacity to confuse and cause frustration because they lack that understanding: those are some of our best weapons and always have been.

Another thing too you don't understand is how strong we are, and how behind our Army there's an invisible infrastructure. The British Army has more people engaged in supporting it than fighting, from storekeepers to soldier's wives: well so exactly in the same way ours has its support system too. There's the actual soldiers we call 'active volunteers': and a much bigger number still providing the services that keep them going. It might be someone who provides a safe house or someone who does even less: keeps watch, gives warning, passes on information, and things of that sort. No Army exists in a vacuum: it needs supporters and suppliers, and we've those in abundance. Probably many more than the British do: and nothing like as expensive, because all of ours, like our soldiers, are volunteers. And for every volunteer, helper or soldier, who's killed or put in prison, there's always another five ready to take that person's place and step forward. Any success claimed by your side, remember on ours it multiplies every time the number of people ready to prove that you're wrong.

You read sometimes in your newspapers the IRA's finished, it's been dealt a severe blow because it's lost its top men. Well that's just a joke. Your press tries to present the IRA as a small number of thugs without support or proper organisational basis. Who're they kidding? If you read all the press reports of the end of the IRA, ever since twenty years ago, you can't help wondering how it is we're still here.

Our definition of who the enemy is isn't one which follows the same line as yours either. We regard all people who support the armed forces of the British Government in any way as legitimate targets. We don't define it as people who wear uniforms: someone who might be working for the Post Office, to give you an instance, or as a supplier to the armed forces, or as a civilian in part of the Civil Service, is every one of them part of the oppressive system we're fighting. A hairdresser who cuts a soldier's hair, a barman who serves a policeman with a drink in a pub: to us every one of them is a collaborator, helping to keep the presence here of the enemy. Every time somebody like that's attacked or killed, you'll hear an official statement saying that he had no connection with the security forces: but in our eyes they did you see. We'll define whether someone's helping the security forces or not: it's not for you to make the definition and criticise us for not agreeing with it. I don't know if I make that clear: probably not and if that's so then I have to say it doesn't greatly matter to me.

Places you know too, as well as people: as far as we're concerned they're legitimate targets if it disrupts in any way the enemy's world. Maybe just repairs, or something like increased surveillance of similar buildings: the basic idea is to keep the occupying forces constantly preoccupied with trying to think what's going to happen next, where it's going to happen, and who it's going to happen to. The aim's the inconvenience and disruption of the economy of the Six Counties and to keep everything under threat: police and Army barracks, businesses, shops, hotels, everything. You could best compare it to an air raid: but instead of it happening in a night it's spread out over a year. So when people talk about it all being 'mindless', as they do, they're not seeing it as a bombing raid by enemy aircraft would be seen. When the RAF bombed Hamburg they killed more German civilians in a night than the IRA has killed in twenty years. What we're aiming to do and what we've so far been successful in doing is making life uncomfortable for the British and that part of the community in Northern Ireland, which an official estimate says is in the region of 100,000 people, who're engaged in either fighting us or repairing the damage that's caused by the IRA. I think we're doing well, couldn't we say?

Can I point out to you something else too? When it comes to accurate or perhaps we should say truthful reporting of what's going on, you're not well served. There's a lot about the shortness of time in the warnings we give to the authorities before there's an explosion of a bomb, isn't there? Well the truth is there's a dangerous propaganda game being played here. Because it's not true. I've known of several instances where warnings have been given an hour in advance: yet after the explosion the police claimed they had only twenty minutes' notice, and they were lucky in being able to evacuate people from wherever it was the device was set. This is done to suggest the IRA are irresponsible, and the police are heroes. But those aren't the facts of the situation at all. The police have had warnings for much longer in advance than they claim: and if they don't take action to evacuate as soon as they're warned, they're playing with people's lives. Shortage of time makes them look good, and us look bad: but it's not true, in fact it's part of a propaganda war. I'm not saying there aren't some operations which go wrong: there are, but as a result of human error rather than deliberate intent. The result may be the unintended death of civilians: it happens sometimes, yes it does. But I return to the comparison with an air raid: the target may or may not be hit, the raid may or may not be a success. And if there are civilian casualties, that's what you'll hear about because it's good propaganda against us. I've brought this book for you: read it, it's good, you'll find it all in here.

What does it all come down to in the end? It's a war we're fighting that's not under rules and regulations made by the British, but by us. The only way a small body of people can defeat the well-organised power of a determined oppressor is not by fighting in the oppressors' way. There wasn't any organised opposition by the Germans within their own country when Hitler took over: there should have been, and if there had been Hitler'd have been overthrown. Here in Northern Ireland it's clearer to us though: we are in the right, this is our country but you and your people are occupying it. We're never going to beat you by fighting the battle you would have us fight: but you're never going to beat us while we fight it our own way. We will win, and you will have to go.

To a person such as yourself Tony, a pacifist, all war yes is wrong. But in a little of what we've talked about, I hope you'll find some understanding of our point of view.

*

(Liz Curtis's *Ireland: The Propaganda War* is published by Pluto Press.)

Willy Burns,

Loyalist

– It's been agreed someone'll meet you for a talk and tell you our
position, and I've been asked to be the one. I'm not all that happy
about it, from the start I'll make that clear: and before we begin let's
just run over the undertakings again so there won't be any
misunderstandings. No description that'll identify who you talk to,
and nothing about when or where or how the interview was
arranged. OK, understood?

Right then. And well before we go any further, I want to say
something about my own position, which is that to be frank with
you I've no great desire at all at the present to talk with anyone from
England. You've just banned our perfectly legitimate organisation,
the UDA: yet you've still not touched the IRA's party, Sinn Fein.
For over twenty years now we've remained loyal to you, yet never in
all that time have you treated us fairly or reported us properly. When
it comes to you seeing our point of view or trying to understand it,
we're fighting a losing battle: and we feel you'll abandon us
completely in the end. That's why the point's been reached when it's
not worth talking any more. It's over a hundred years since Lord
Randolph Churchill said 'Ulster will fight and Ulster will be right',
and as far as I'm concerned that's correct: it shouldn't have been
allowed to drag on like it has, it should all have been settled long ago.
I know it's not very hospitable of me to talk to you like this, but I
don't often have an ordinary English person sitting right in front of
me and listening to what I say. So what I'd like to get over to you if I
could is I'm an ordinary Ulster person, and because the two of us are
British I think we should back one another up. Never mind that
you've put me in prison for ten years when my only crime was to be
loyal: let's forget that. I've been out two years now, but it's not

altered what I think and maybe it'll happen you could do it to me again. But I'll take the opportunity of telling you how it came about so you'll know what sort of person I am: and I hope you'll listen and understand. And I'm saying what I'm saying is the point of view that's hardly ever heard: it's the view of the ordinary Protestant working-class man.

I'll begin at the beginning. I was born in Londonderry and I'm one of eight children. We lived in a small estate of prefabricated bungalows on the east bank of the River Foyle, in a district known as Waterside. My mother was a Roman Catholic, she died when I was eight: my father was a Protestant and a member of the Presbyterian Church, and he died when I was fifteen. I had what I'd say was an ordinary happy childhood: where we lived was almost out in the country right at the edge of the city, and we played in the woods and fields, not like a lot of city kids who've only got the streets.

There's a feeling among people who don't know any better that the Northern Irish are divided into two separate communities, Protestant and Catholic, and never the twain shall meet. It isn't true, and it was even less true when I was young. My father and mother had different religions, and I've two sisters and a brother who are Protestants but both married to Catholics. As a young lad in my teens, and a Protestant young lad too, I spent my spare time in the evenings over on the other side of the river, in an entirely Catholic area called the Creggan Estate. I was doing what most young lads do at that age, chatting up the girls the same as the rest of my mates. It didn't matter talking to a Catholic girl: most of the Londonderry girls were, and they knew you were a Protestant.

What did matter most was that in Londonderry like everywhere else, when you left school work was hard to find. I went to technical college because I wanted to be a plumber, but I soon had to face there were no jobs going there. All this propaganda about Catholics never getting a chance of employment: when I hear it, it does, it just makes me laugh. Protestant lads couldn't get employment either in Londonderry: that's one myth I soon found out had no truth in it for a start.

I didn't like what was going on in Londonderry that I saw all the time in my teens: the Catholics were rioting and marching, and a lot of people from outside the city were coming in and fomenting trouble. They were coming there from all the outside Catholic areas, from Fermanagh and County Tyrone, and even from as far as Armagh. All they wanted to do was stir up trouble. They went to the Creggan and into the Bogside which was another Catholic estate, and were always organising rallies and marches and demonstrations. The police did their best to keep control, and I'd half a mind myself to join the RUC. My brother though was living in Belfast at that time and said there was a better chance of work there, so I went to live with him.

But it was the same picture in Belfast where employment was concerned: there wasn't any really unless you were properly qualified and I wasn't, so I had a hard time. Then I was stupid, I got married to a girl I hadn't known very long: it didn't work out, we separated after only a few months and then we divorced. My brother told me about a paramilitary organisation he was in, and said he'd introduce me to people who'd give me odd jobs now and again so long as I showed I was reliable. I was keen to do it, and not just for the money. I wasn't politically minded but I was beginning to think for myself. I could see how much propaganda the Nationalists and the Republicans were putting out and the effect it was having. When the politicians and newspapers talked about discrimination, they always meant against the Catholics by the Protestants. What never got properly aired was the discrimination the Catholics practised themselves: they had their own little cliques and clubs, and there were parts of Belfast it wasn't safe to walk in at night if you weren't of their particular religious persuasion. I got in one or two fights and experienced it: as well as all the time this drip drip drip that was going on about their demand for civil rights.

I thought so then, and I still think so now, that all that's a load of bloody nonsense. Talk of a United Ireland, it's all based on myth. The Nationalists go on and on about Irish culture and Irish history, but when you come to examine the situation, there isn't a hope in hell of there ever being a United Ireland and I'll tell you why not: simply because it's the last thing in the world the twenty-six counties of the south would ever want. Our living standard up here is far higher, and the freedom of people here to do what they like with their lives is not something that's opposed by the Church. There can't be any serious comparison by someone who takes an objective view. One country's British and the other is foreign, and it's as simple as that.

Another thing is that when all the civil right business started, who was on the marches demonstrating? Middle-class Catholic students, that's who: they'd taken the State's money for grants to get themselves educated at university, and repaid it by fomenting trouble. One of the biggest mistakes of all at the time was that the Protestants didn't demonstrate demanding their own civil rights as well. If only they had, the world would have got a far more balanced picture. But all people ever saw in those days on the telly was the brutal RUC beating up people, and the brutal British Army shooting unarmed people on the streets. I'm not saying there weren't one or two incidents of that sort, that happened and shouldn't have done: but what I'm saying and it can't be denied is there were never any pictures of the Catholics rioting and burning Protestant people's houses, nothing of that was ever shown.

The prejudice and the lack of balance still goes on, that's the terrible thing. You can't switch on the TV any night without hearing about the poor Catholics and what the wicked Protestants have done to them in the past. The Nationalists or what they should more rightly be called the Republicans, because that's what underneath they all are, they're given hours of time to put forward their case. When do you ever see or hear a Protestant being allowed to do that? All you get's always only the same thing: Ian Paisley bawling out two sentences and then people suppose that's all there is to be said by the Loyalist side. There are other people besides Paisley, and others who could put forward better arguments than him: but they're never heard, because the picture the media wants to present is of us Protestants being plain downright unreasonable, that's all.

But we're not. You and I are sitting here, and in the last forty-eight hours there've been two massive explosions in Belfast city centre, right? Everyone knows who did it, right? They've proudly claimed it themselves, it was the IRA. Well, we could retaliate if we wanted to, we've enough explosives to blow the whole of the Falls Road up ten times over. But we don't do things like that. Instead we pay our taxes to repair the damage they cause. More people are out of work and out of business, and still we put up with it. How long are we expected to though? Tell me because I don't know. When we go out it's not to cause indiscriminate destruction. It's to hit a legitimate target, an individual, that's all: someone we know it's justified to remove because we've taken the trouble to find out about them in advance. We don't make mistakes either, we don't kill innocent people: yet they'll kill anyone at all, civilians or police or Army, it doesn't matter who they are. But did you ever hear of a member of the security forces in a battle with Protestant paramilitaries? Did you ever hear of Protestant paramilitaries destroying shops and businesses, just because they were owned by Catholics? But these things are never taken into account by your newspapers are they? They give us no credit, they picture us as bigots and lunatics who kill for no reason, just like the IRA.

There's increasingly talk every day now about the British Government withdrawing its troops from here. From where I sit, that looks very much to me like a softening-up process, preparing us for it. So you tell me: is that what it is? Ten years ago you wouldn't have even heard discussion of it: now you can't go ten days without someone or other talking about it and putting the case. Well what I think ought to be put over to people in Britain is that if such a thing as that happened, then something else would happen too as inevitably as night follows day. It's called by some sometimes 'the Protestant backlash'. Well make no mistake about this either, friend: if the British withdraw their troops, that's what you'll get. The increase in violence you've seen in the past two months, that's nothing it isn't, believe you me: you ain't seen nothing yet.

Would you like me to spell it out? The Provos are better armed than they've ever been: they've got supplies from different countries I don't need to name, and now they've very sophisticated weaponry indeed. OK then: and so have we. We have the technology, the expertise and the manufacturing capacity already in place. And we're not a third world country, we're a highly tooled-up and skilled western country which makes some of the most advanced armaments in the world: they're produced in our factories right here. We know how to make things, whether we're talking about hand grenades or whether we're talking about radio-controlled missiles. So we have the means if necessary to defend ourselves from being overrun by the Catholics and having to submit to the Catholic government of the South. We have the means and we have the knowledge and we shan't hesitate to fight if we have to. If all our legitimate fears and feelings are ignored, then the more determined we'll become. People in mainland Britain know what it's like not to have any friends or any allies because they learned it in the war. What it came to then for them, that's what it might come to now for us: and we're well prepared if it does. The time's not very far off now, if you want my honest opinion, when all the talking will stop. We'll go so far but no further: never so far, let me tell you, that discussions about the future of our country should include Sinn Fein. We'll never talk to them. What is there to talk about? Surrendering ourselves to the twenty-six counties of the South? That's all Sinn Fein are interested in, and the honest ones of them admit it.

I want to say this to you most of all. I didn't put my life on the line and do ten years' imprisonment for something I didn't believe in: and going to prison for that length of time hasn't altered my belief that what I did was right. The man I was after was a killer: I tried to kill him but I failed. Details would identify me, but doing something of that kind is not something you take on lightly and without thinking a lot about it first. You know there's a fair chance you'll be killed yourself, or if not that then you'll get caught like I was and go inside. It's a reality and you know it's there: and the other part of the reality is now I'm out, because of what I did I'm a target for the IRA. I was a trigger man: their trigger men if they get the chance will do the same to me. I'm well-known to them, and I live with it.

So there's one very simple question for you to ask me isn't there? Not would I take up the gun again, but when again would I take up the gun? The answer's simple: when it's time. And I make no apology for saying it.

Listen to me, and hear me what I say. Tell it to your friends in England. I hope the message is clear. Give us your thoughts, give us your sympathy, give us your understanding. Don't use the term 'Loyalist' about us as though it was a derogatory description: let's be able to talk about you as 'Loyalist' to us too. And don't call us terrorists because we're not. You've nothing to fear from us, we shan't be coming to London to blow you to pieces, ever. The only people we want to terrorise are the terrorists: and we will. When they stop so shall we: but not until.

Roy Walker,

Loyalist

He sat at one end of the settee by the curtained window, screwing his eyes up in the light from the standard lamp at his side: he held a small velvet cushion on his knee, and turned it round and round in his big hands while he talked. A thin-lipped pale-skinned man with a hesitant low voice.

– This is my sister's house, I'm staying here on ten days' home leave out of Maghaberry: I'm due back again there on Monday. I don't like going out in the evenings but if you don't mind coming here we can have two or three talks before then. I'm not very good at talking to people outside of prison though. I've done fifteen years so far of my life sentence, and after that length of time, wherever you are if it's not prison you feel you're in strange surroundings and you don't find it easy to express yourself. I wasn't much of a talker anyway ever even before I went into prison: but I'll do my best. This first time I think it'd be best if I just tried to outline things in a general way if that's OK with you. As I get more used to it we can go into things more deeply if you like.

It's actually two life sentences I'm serving: they're running concurrently, that means in parallel at the same time. One's for murder and the other's for attempted murder. There were other lesser charges too, and I got fixed sentences for those: I don't exactly remember what they were for or their length. They were to do with possession of arms and explosives which they found in my house when they searched it after they'd arrested me: the longest sentence of any of them would be about ten years, but they've all been served during my life sentences so they're run out by now. It's easy to forget the detail of the smaller things: that's because naturally you tend to spend your time inside thinking about the future rather than dwelling on the past. I'm forty-one now: when I went into prison I was twenty-seven, and my mind was full of memories of what I'd done in my life till that age. Then there was the long period in which there was nothing but prison life, and they faded. In about the last two years though I've been able to start to turn my thoughts forward, because now there's a possibility of some kind of future outside of prison to think about again.

I don't have a definite date for release yet: it's not been given to me so far. To some extent it'll depend on what arrangements can be made for me, or ones I can make for myself. The most helpful would be a definite offer of a job for when I came out: but the employment situation's bad even for people who haven't been in prison, it's not going to be easy to find something. Nothing's in view at all at the moment: several people are working on possible things on my behalf, so I do have some hopes. Another positive is if you can show you've a settled home to go to on release: in my case I can do that, I'm getting married. It's to someone who's already got her own house, which'll count a lot in my favour. The third important thing they take into account is if you show there's been a change in yourself and in your attitude. It's taken a long time for that to happen to me, but now it definitely has done. That's why I was moved to Maghaberry last year from having been in Long Kesh so long: it's just as much a top security prison, but it's regarded as a positive step forward towards rehabilitation if you go to Maghaberry. If I hadn't been there the privilege of home leave, which I've had twice now, wouldn't have been considered so favourably. In my case it was a problem that I'd already served an earlier sentence to the two lifes I'm doing now. It was a previous ten-year sentence for attempted murder, and it was while I was out on parole from that that I committed the current offences I'm doing time for now.

I'm finding it difficult to tell you things in a backwards order, as it were, because I'm not feeling so good. If you don't mind, it'd be easier for me if I started again at the beginning. I'll tell you what you might call the bare bones of it, and we can fill in what more details you want to ask me about when you come tomorrow night, is that OK?

I'm forty-one now as I've said, and I was born into a Protestant

family in a Protestant area of east Belfast, I went to a Protestant
school and I left it when I was sixteen. I'm the oldest of four children,
with two brothers and two sisters, and my father was a foreman in a
paint factory and my mother was an ordinary housewife. We weren't
a particularly religious family or in any way particularly Loyalist
either. If you describe yourself as Protestant, its main meaning isn't
that you were a regular church attender or anything of that sort. You
could say it was almost more of a descriptive term like Welsh or Irish
or Scottish. Above all what it meant was a negative: it meant that
you weren't a Catholic. The twelfth of July was the big day of the
year, but it couldn't be described as a religious festival at all: it was a
political one. There were street parties and bands and parades, and as
a kid you watched it and took part in it without any idea of what it
was all about: it was a Protestant celebration but you knew nothing
of the historical context of it. I don't remember ever that there was
specially taught anything to us by our parents about religion. I had
an uncle who was one of my mother's brothers, he was something
big in the local Orange Order: and I remember he once said to me
when I was still a kid 'Never forget, Roy, you're as near to God as
the Pope is.' But why he said it or what the occasion was, I don't
recall, except knowing it wasn't anything to do with church. In
every way you were brought up to feel there were people called
Catholics who you shouldn't have anything to do with. That wasn't
difficult: you didn't know any and never met any, they lived mostly
in west Belfast and that was somewhere you didn't go. But as you
might say doctrinally, no one ever told you what was so terrible
about them.

In my teens in the 1960s and 70s, there was always trouble between
Catholics and Protestants. You heard about it and read about it and
were told about it by your family; and it was always in terms of
Catholics causing trouble rioting in the streets and making raids on
areas where Protestants lived, smashing the windows in their houses
and setting fire to them. You never knew why they were like that
and you never knew who they were or what was so different about
them: you just knew they were very bad people.

You grew up in those days perfectly used to seeing armed police
and troops on the streets, tanks and guns were part of the normal
scenery of everyday life. And so was fighting, that was part of

ordinary activity. The most enjoyable thing was rioting: there were certain streets you could go at night where you'd be sure to see people jeering and throwing stones at each other. Sometimes you'd go with a gang of your friends and you'd all join in. It was fun, it was very exciting. It might seem a strange expression to use, but for me it was true: I was in love with it. Especially in the dark winter nights I couldn't wait to get home from school and go with my mates round the parts where we knew there'd be trouble. In the end I was fairly notorious for it: and at seventeen, after several warnings I got six months' imprisonment for riotous behaviour. I was sent to Crumlin Road prison, and it was something I was proud of. It gave me higher status than most of my friends and it confirmed my standing. I was one of those who'd actually been picked out by the police in street fightings: I was a leader.

I did four months: and then less than six months after I'd come out of prison I was back inside once more. Only this time it was with a ten-year sentence for shooting someone: I'd definitely moved on up the scale. They let me out from that on parole, after I'd served five years: then it was a year afterwards that I got these life sentences that I'm still serving now. By then you see I was nothing else but a fighting man: a paramilitary in the true sense, and it was something I was proud to be. I was in my middle twenties, and I was known as someone to be respected, someone with a very big reputation, a hard man. I was in an organisation known as the Red Hand Commando: in those days that was really something to say. The Red Hand Commando was the first of the Protestant Paramilitary groups to be specifically outlawed by the British Government.

Look I'm sorry, I've not felt too good the last couple of days: I've been most of the afternoon in bed but I got up because I knew you were coming. I think I've got a temperature: I'm sorry, if you don't mind that's about as much as I can talk about tonight. What I really want to do's go back to bed with a couple of aspirin, and a whiskey and hot milk. I'll feel better tomorrow, come at the same time again will you? Right: sorry, right, OK?

– No really I do, no really tonight I feel great. The whiskey did the trick, I slept like a top for a change. Funny thing you know: you come on home leave, you sleep in a comfortable bed and what happens usually is you don't get a wink, it's too soft. All you want is to get back to your own bed in the prison. People wouldn't believe it would they?

I've been thinking over what I told you. Last night I made myself sound like a moron, didn't I, wasn't that what I sounded like? I was one: but when I came to think about it some more this morning while I was taking the dog for a walk, I thought well why was I a moron, why was it? A dangerous one as well you know, I can't be arguing with that. What did I say to you, I'd done six months for rioting, then within six months of coming out I'd shot someone? That's a big jump isn't it, I mean in the nature of the thing? One minute a lad running around the streets throwing stones, the next a person with a gun trying to kill someone: a big difference between the two isn't there?

Well it was a girl you see, that's all I can say. I don't mean one put me up to it, nothing of the sort: no, it was because there was a girl I wanted to impress. Her name was Elaine, I'd known her at school, she was my first proper girlfriend.

You remember I told you I was in Crumlin Road for my six months? Well she came to see me and wrote to me: and me being in prison, it sort of kind of released something inside her, but don't ask me why. In those days as a lad I'd have told you the old story: you know, I didn't understand women. But when you get older you see things clearer: now I think I can see things clearer about her. Status I mentioned, right? Well that was it: in her eyes my stature had increased. I wasn't just one of a gang of lads, I was the leader of them. So she looked up to me, she admired me, I was a sort of a hero figure: or to put it another way, she was madly in love with me and made it plain she was. A very pretty girl: you know, long dark hair that she wore piled on top of her head like this, and beautiful big green eyes. And she was my girl and no one else's, and she told me she was. You remember yourself what it was like to be eighteen. To be told something like that by a beautiful girl, well everyone envies you don't they, it makes you feel like a king. To be sitting in the visiting-room in a stinking place like Crumlin Road, and a beautiful girl telling you she's waiting for you and when you come out she'll be yours: it makes you dizzy, completely dizzy in your head.

So that's how it was, just like that. She was clever, she was intelligent, she had a job with a finance company and a flat of her own she shared with another girl at work. It was all waiting: so inside I thought of nothing else but when we'd be together all the time. When it happened it was a dream, a fantastic dream, the biggest romance of all time. I don't want to put blame on her though for what happened afterwards, the shooting I mean: it was me who followed the path, I determined it and I did it for her but that doesn't mean she was to blame.

She was more of a fanatical Loyalist than I was, and a more thoughtful one: that ought to be said for definite. Family connections, her father big in the Unionists, two of her brothers active in the UDA which hadn't long been formed before that time. I remember their slogan: it was 'Law Before Violence', you saw it on their posters all over the place. And you can interpret it two ways: one way means it defines how they behave, but the other one was that the IRA ought to submit to the rules. That was how they intended it, the second way: and they were going to see it was enforced.

Not long after I'd come out, someone made an attempt on Elaine's brother's life. It was someone who was well-known, him and two of his associates in the IRA. More by luck than anything else it wasn't successful: but he was badly injured, he was shot six times in the chest altogether I think it was, and in hospital several months as a result of it. There was a lot of talk, and there was suspicion of who was responsible: it was fairly definite but nothing could be proved. The police questioned the man but they had to let him go.

I didn't see how this could be right: I couldn't accept it, not at all. Twice or three nights a week Elaine'd come back from seeing her brother in hospital and she was always very deeply upset: and there this man was walking around who'd caused it, and nothing had been done to him in the way of punishment at all. 'Law Before Violence', do you see the connection in my mind? I did, I became obsessed with the idea. When I'd been in Crumlin Road, I'd met one or two persons there: it's the best place you can go to, prison, for making contacts. I knew I could go to them and their friends for help in making a definite identification of the man who'd harmed her brother. Like anyone in those times, he'd two or three aliases and different places he lived: I went about it methodically and in a few weeks I'd found out all I wanted to know and finally I'd got him nailed. The only problem was a gun to kill him with: and for someone like me who'd been inside, that was the smallest problem of the lot.

Normally . . . that's a funny word to use in the circumstances isn't it but it'll do . . . normally if you set out to kill someone, you organise it carefully: you find others to help you, drive the car, keep lookout, one as a decoy if you're using one and so on. I didn't bother with any of that though: I went after the man by myself, entirely on my own. I knew where he was living, what nights and times he'd be there, and where he'd park his car when he was. I was waiting for him when he arrived one night about ten o'clock. He drove into the back alley off the road, stopped his car and locked the door: and all I said was his name. He turned round and I shot him five times from as close as this: it would have been six but the pistol jammed.

What went wrong was because of what I'd said, I hadn't bothered with the organisation side, I'd tried to do it all on my own, and that was where I came unstuck. I didn't know there was a police road block been set up three streets away: I jumped in my car to get away, took the first lefthand turn and drove straight into it. They'd heard the sound of shots, they saw a car coming fast, and when they stopped me there I was with the gun I'd just used still in the car. They didn't need to be brilliant detectives did they? I'd done it all for them.

Elaine came to see me three times when I was on remand: she asked me each time had I done it because the guy'd been the one suspected of doing for her brother. Each time I told her no. I didn't want her to think it was personal: I wanted her to think of me as a soldier obeying orders to shoot someone who'd been targeted. Don't ask me why I wanted it like that, because I really don't know. I'd done it out of love for her: but I didn't want to put it to her like that, that's as much as I can explain. Peculiar: no, more than that, crazy I was.

So that was how at the age of nineteen I got ten years. Inside I was a good prisoner, a model prisoner, at least it looked to them as though I was: so they let me out after I'd done half. But in that time, two things they didn't know about had happened, and they'd combined to completely change my life around. One was the obvious one: Elaine had found somebody else. She'd got pregnant, and so they married and before the child was born they went over the water to London. I never heard from her afterwards. She was a nice girl though, she was always straight was Elaine. She didn't write me the letter they call a Dear John, she came to prison to see me and told me to my face. I'd like to pretend I sat there and listened with my heart breaking but being noble about it and not telling her it was because of her I was there. It wasn't like that at all. I still liked her, but it was the thought of her getting pregnant by somebody else that I couldn't take: it turned me right off. I didn't say anything about her brother being the reason I was in prison. I just sat there and nodded, and said I understood and wished her all the very best.

Because like I said something else had happened to me too. It was the reputation thing I've talked about that I'd had in Crumlin Road: but this time it was much bigger than before. I'd taken on a leading IRA man entirely on my own, found him and gone after him and damn nearly killed him. All on my own: it was Lone Ranger stuff, very courageous and brave. So as a result I was getting approaches then all the time: I didn't have to go looking to meet the hard men in prison, they were the ones who were wanting to meet me. I was getting new lifelong mates by the score: I hadn't even known their existence till they came up and told me that's what they were. So by the time Elaine came and told me we were finished, what she said wasn't so important to me. I wasn't the same person at all. I hadn't actually murdered anybody yet, but that didn't alter what I was in my own mind. I was a professional killer. For the first shooting I'd had a reason, there was a kind of idealism in it: not letting the IRA get away with something, and retaliating against them because of my girl. But by the time she and I broke up, it was different. I was ready to do it just as a job.

– It's been good to talk: good for me anyway, I don't know how it's been for you. Jean said to do it. She's my sister's friend, we're getting married. She's divorced and she's got two grown-up boys. She's the brave one all right isn't she, taking on someone like me? We met in the prison two years ago: no it's three now. She was a part-time teacher. She's made all the difference to me. She's a Catholic, or she was, when she was younger.

In the last few years things have got a lot clearer in my mind, and it's because of being in prison. Ironic in a way. I've read books, I've attended education classes, I'm studying with the Open University to take a degree. You'll laugh when I tell you what the subjects are I've found most interest in: psychology, sociology, community relations. Repair work I sometimes think of it as: trying to repair myself's one part of it, and the other and more important one is trying to put something back into society, if that doesn't sound too grandiose.

What I want to do when I come out is some kind of community work or youth work, if I can get into that: I'd like to do something of that sort. Because I'm a Protestant by birth I want to work among young Protestants: I'd not be accepted anyway in Catholic parts of the community. I might be a marked man, I think I always will, I don't really know: some people have got very long memories. If you're inside for killing a Catholic no matter how long ago, they'll have your name on a list: they'll be waiting for you the day you step outside. The Loyalists too, they do the same: there's Republicans they're waiting for.

That's why I say it's young Protestants I want to work among. They're the ones who carry on this feuding for us on our side. A lad'll go after a released Republican prisoner who'd done life for murder, a man who'll very likely be old enough to be his own father, and who committed his offence when the lad had hardly long been born.

I think this is what I'd like to get at, if I could get a job with a chance of it. That mental state that says you kill someone not because of religious difference between you, but because you're told to, it's your duty as a soldier and it's your job: the sort of frame of mind I was in myself, yes. Those are the really dangerous paramilitaries, not the religious fanatics. I want to try and persuade them it's got to stop. I've no wish to remove people's religious prejudices, they can keep those: I couldn't do it anyway. To me Protestants can think the Pope's anti-Christ or whatever they like to call him, and be as hot and strong about it as they like. Argue, shout, debate, send their children to segregated schools, pray in their churches for Rangers to beat Celtic: all that. There's nothing as satisfying as a good one hundred per cent prejudice anyway: everyone should have one.

Bring it out and parade it around, why not? But not kill people: you don't do that. Be killed if you like, yes OK, go to the stake for what you believe. That's your prerogative, do that if you want, if that's how you feel. It's no crime. But to approach a bonfire where someone else is with a box of matches in your hand, strike them and throw them into the piled-up brushwood and start the conflagration that burns someone to ash: that's wrong, that's what's a crime. You mustn't do it: and if you see someone else about to, you should climb on the bonfire yourself and say to them if they do it, they'll have to burn you as well.

Protestants, Catholics: both of them must be helped to see it the same. I don't have it myself now, belief I mean: but I know how many people do, how much comfort it can be for them in sorrow. Religion as comfort, I'll go along with that. And religion as giving meaning to life, the hope of better things to come: those ideas if you hold them, yes they're fine. But religion as a reason for putting someone else to death: no, that's beyond the pale. To work to get that over, I think that'd be something worth doing: so that's what I want to do if someone'll have me when I get out, do a job where I can keep on saying that.

Peadar O'Donnell,

Republican

A few brief phone calls were made; terse and inaudible words behind almost-closed doors in other rooms. Waitings for calls to come back in reply, and queries about peoples' whereabouts.

Then a long and winding drive through a maze of dark streets in pouring rain round a series of housing-estates, until finally the car pulled up at the end of a narrow unlit path running between the back gardens of small semi-detached council houses.

The priest got out and stood on the pavement with the hood of his anorak pulled over his head and round his face to keep it dry. He pointed along the path.

– Go along down there to the seventh back door on the right. You'll be expected, it's seven o'clock, you're right on time. All you need do's just say your Christian name. He'll look after you. Good night.

Inside the bright warm kitchen the big man was standing in front of a three-bar electric radiator. A small dark plump middle-aged woman turned away from the pot of tea and fruit cake she'd set out on the table, smiled and nodded and went out. The big man pulled another chair out.

– Father Joe brought you himself did he, sure and that's typical of him, he's a good kind man. Did he give me a name? Well then I'll tell you what, put me as 'Peadar O'Donnell' will you in your book? Do you know who he was? Ah you should read some of his work so you should: one called *The Knife* he wrote, he called it 'A Novel of Strife and Love in Ireland's Troubled Times'. Beautiful it is, beautiful. 'Peadar O'Donnell', sure I'll be very proud I will to be given his name. Will you have some cherry cake now, she makes the best of anyone I know. We don't get it like this in prison we don't, and that's a fact it is for sure. Sit yourself down.

The one great ambition I had in my life, right from a boy you know, was to be a soldier and join the British Army. I fancied the Army life, because it meant security, good pay, special privileges and a bit of status. My father'd been a soldier himself, but in the Irish Army, and he told me to try and join the British Army because it was much better. He wasn't a Nationalist so he didn't see anything wrong with an Irishman joining the British Army, and when I was young nor did I. Politics didn't come into our lives. I remember once in Belfast one Saturday afternoon me and some friends got caught by a gang of boys near the Market and they gave us a kicking. They said we were Fenian bastards: I didn't know what it meant and when I went home I asked my father, I said 'What's a Fenian bastard?' He said 'The first part's to be proud about, and the second isn't.' I didn't know what he meant, but when I've thought about it since I reckon it was a good reply.

For a few months after school I was an apprentice joiner. But the wages were poor so I decided to take my life into my own hands and went along to one of the Army Recruiting Offices and took the Queen's Shilling. At first I was a junior soldier, then I joined the Royal Enniskillen Fusiliers. I was in the British Army for five years: I went to Germany, Kenya in Africa, back to Germany, then to Northern Ireland where I was in Ebrington Barracks in Derry. One of my duties there was as a sentry on the main gate. It all sounds farcical now: but I enjoyed my time. I'll always be grateful to the British: they taught me everything I know about weapons and explosives and how to be a fighting soldier.

In Derry I was told like the rest of us that certain clubs and pubs were off-limits because they were known haunts of Republicans. Tell any young man what he shouldn't do, and he'll thank you for giving him the information and go off straight away and do it. I did, with a lot of my mates. The difference was they were British and I was Irish, and I met people I felt at home with. Nobody tried to subvert me from my duty, but a lot of people asked me did I think the proper place for an Irishman was in the British Army? Before long I decided it wasn't. On my next posting, which was to our base depot in England, I went absent without leave. In a couple of months the military police found out where I was and what I was doing which was living in Middlesborough with a girl: so I was taken back to the depot, put on punishment, and then discharged.

I stayed in Middlesborough and got work as a long distance lorry-driver with a haulage firm. I married the girl, and not long after we had our first child. Then I moved on from that job to labouring on road construction where the money was very good. It was a happy period in my life but I had brothers and sisters here in Armagh, Belfast and Derry, and I kept hearing from them in their letters about what was going on here: the civil rights movement, the rioting, and the hard and unhappy time they were all having. I wrote regularly back to them, and they sent me all the information they had.

Before long I began feeling although life was pleasant enough for me in England, things for my own family and my own people back home were getting worse and worse. Imagine hearing about Bloody Sunday and the massacre of unarmed civilians from some of your own relatives who'd taken part in that march: imagine hearing another time your brother had been taken in to Castlereagh by the RUC and given a beating: imagine your sister writing how she'd been insulted on the street by British soldiers. When you heard about things like that and you were far away, you began to get angry. I talked to my wife about it and I said I couldn't explain it, I just felt there was no alternative, I should come home. And I said I could understand if she being English, and thinking of our two children which we had by then, if she wanted to stay out of it then of course she should. She didn't hesitate a minute: she said yes she thought I should come back to Northern Ireland, and she and the children would come with me.

We came to Belfast, and I took a job as a bus driver: then I moved south to a town near Newry where two friends had started up a motor repair business and offered me to join in with them. We did quite well to begin with: in those days there were clashes between the authorities and the Catholics, but there was a relationship between the RUC and ordinary people in country areas like the one where we were which wasn't too bad. Two particular RUC men used to come in to our workshop quite often when they were on duty, and we'd all sit and chat and drink a cup of tea. I don't think they were fishing for information: we were all on Christian name terms, and I think they'd

have got in trouble themselves if it'd been known they were
socialising on duty with us.

The other two in the business were IRA. The RUC didn't know
that, and neither did I. Having been a British soldier, I was regarded
with a good deal of caution: and if I'd displayed the slightest interest
in it, I'd almost certainly have been considered to be a plant. I've
often smiled when I've looked back at the situation: two RUC men,
probably not aware they were in the presence of two IRA men, but
hoping perhaps a remark would be made by mistake which would let
them find something out. And two IRA men hoping for the same
thing from the RUC in return, and me in the middle keeping my
thoughts to myself.

A lot of people have always said that it was Bloody Sunday in
Derry that was a watershed for the IRA. It hadn't many members
until then, it'd almost gone out of existence. It was what happened
on Bloody Sunday that brought them back into existence: after it
hundreds or even thousands of young Irishmen felt such a hatred
for the Parachute Regiment that'd been responsible, that they
determined to restart the armed struggle. I was one of those it had
that effect on: and the feeling stayed with me it did, and grew and
grew. More and more I knew I wanted to join, if I was given the
chance.

The way you joined was usually that if someone you knew had
been killed because he was an IRA man, what they call a 'cumann'
was formed in memory of him. It bore his name: and you could
apply to join it if you were a relative or a friend of his. In my case it
was because of the death of an uncle: he'd been killed by British
troops, and not long after his son told me a cumann was to be set up
in his name. Immediately I said could I join it. It seemed a good way
of commemorating someone, and it was a nice thing to be a member
of: a sort of family and friends group, in the name of someone you'd
liked and respected.

I was accepted because anybody who was connected with cars was
very useful. I didn't do much at first except take in vehicles for repair
that nobody wanted to be seen. My whole career was almost finished
right at the start because I was caught the very first operation I took
part in. We ambushed an RUC patrol but were captured and taken to
the local police station. I thought there was a chance I might even be

suspected of having set the whole thing up, but I was soon disabused about that: we'd hardly been in custody five minutes when the place was attacked by another group of our men. They don't do that unless someone important's been captured, but I don't know who it was in our group. The outcome was two got away, but I was still held by the police.

They treated people better in those days than they do now, and also they're not as bad in a country area: I didn't get anything like the knocking about I expected. I didn't tell them anything, and in due course I came up in Court and got four years. The biggest blow of it to me was after I went into prison, my wife said for the children's sake she was taking them back to England. She didn't want to be involved any more or have them involved, it was too dangerous: she wanted us divorced. I agreed. If she'd been an Irish woman and the children had been Irish, it would have been different, to her and to me. If you're married to an IRA man you have to be just as dedicated as he is. How could you ask that of an English woman? I was inside when the divorce came through, and I've never heard from her since. I don't know where my children are and I'm sad about it. But I made my choice to return to Northern Ireland and to go further and take part in the war: and so I have to respect her choice as well.

I did three out of the four years, and when I was released I remember it was a Wednesday. On the Friday I was back in my home town and volunteering again for action. But my release anyway coincided with a ceasefire which had been agreed: it didn't last long, and when active service was resumed I was involved again immediately. The motor repair business had gone broke, but if you're an Army member work will be found for you and I didn't suffer financially. You don't get paid as an IRA soldier: I did another job which they arranged, a legitimate one.

Before long they asked me to move to Belfast because I could be more useful there. I was something of an expert on arms and explosives, and what I did chiefly was training. That went on for a couple of years. Then there was an occasion when an informer said much more than could have been foreseen: the result was ten of us were arrested in a dawn swoop all over the city in different parts by the police. Being taken in for questioning was very different then. There was constant interrogation without stop, in my case it lasted for five days and I got no sleep in the whole of that time: I was questioned by different detectives, two at a time working two hour shifts. By the end of a period like that, when you've been continually questioned and punched and shouted at, denied food and denied sleep, you're in a bad state: you'll say almost anything. What I said myself wasn't of value in giving information about other people, but it left me personally very exposed. I was on remand for five months, then eventually I found myself in Court facing forty different charges. I got a number of fifteen year sentences, some twelve year sentences to run concurrently, and two life sentences. They ranged over pretty well every offence in the book including not having a dog licence and not paying a parking ticket. All told, without the life sentences, the fixed prison terms of imprisonment added up to two hundred and something years.

If I was still there doing it, I think it'd officially come to an end next year. I hope now you'll not be thinking I don't trust you: but would you mind if we moved on somewhere else, to another friend of mine's house? It's not a clever idea for me to stay too long in one particular place, you understand how I mean?

– Nothing that's ever happened to me has weakened my Republican convictions. The opposite: I wouldn't have been as firm in my ideas and beliefs as I am if the things done to me hadn't been done. You put a lot of people of similar ideas and ideals together in prison, and what they do is give each other strength. They exchange ideas, discuss them, learn things about the history of their country they didn't know before: and all of it helps them solidify their views. I've yet to hear of a single Irish Republican who didn't find his knowledge of what had gone on in the past in his country increased by what he learned from others in prison with him for the same reasons.

I was in the cages at Long Kesh, which're compounds of groups of huts surrounded by wire mesh: search lights are trained on them at night, and they've watch-towers at each corner with armed guards in. They're prisons within prisons: and you can't consider yourself a proper Republican if you've not been in them. The guards don't come in the compounds, they do the morning and evening head-counts from outside: and the food's brought by lorries which back up outside the fences. Well I say the guards never come in the compounds, but that's not strictly true: every once in a while they do, often on a Saturday night. A bunch of prison warders with dogs suddenly come in and give a beating to anyone they can lay hands on. It usually occurs after they've spent a couple of hours in their club tanking themselves up with drink. When that kind of thing happens it doesn't do anything to change any prisoner's principles: it just instils in him feelings of sheer hatred towards the authorities. They know even at the higher levels what goes on, but nothing's ever done to try and stop it. The result is everyone's increasingly de-humanised: the prison warders and officials and it has to be said yes the prisoners, the IRA men too.

People on each side you see, and outside as well, they've all stopped thinking. No one ever discusses anything properly any more, between themselves never mind with their opponents. They've long since forgotten there could be any other way to go about things: they've long since forgotten there were times when civilised people, if they couldn't agree they sat down and talked. Now everyone closes their eyes, puts their heads down and fights like drunken boxers in the ring. They're drunken because they've had so many punches to the head.

The Republicans are never going to surrender now any more than the Loyalists are. It's all being seen in terms of which side wins: and if one wins, then the other one loses and that's the tragedy of it, that it's developed into that. The Loyalists or the Unionists or whichever they call themselves, I almost feel sorry for them: they don't want to admit it but they're already seeing it's inevitable the British'll withdraw. They bluster and threaten but Irish Nationalism's a tide that'll never be stopped. However many IRA men are killed, there'll never be any shortage of recruits for the cause: but the Loyalists can't say the same. They don't have an endless stream of young people growing up and wanting to continue the repression of Catholics that their fathers and grandfathers carried on. Most young Protestant people I've met, they all want to live in a fair and just society, or seem to: or that's what they say.

I wish that what's gone on here and what's still going on could be got over to people on your side of the water. I don't think they know much really at all about the situation. One thing I do know is they know next to nothing about the motivation of the IRA. Your newspapers are full this week of this week's scandal, then that's replaced by next week's scandal, and that's all, trivial and unimportant things. Only the scandal of what's going on in Northern Ireland and has been for years and years, that really big and important scandal's almost completely ignored. It'll be seen one day in its true context as part of history: all the other ones won't even rate a footnote.

I'd like to say to British people 'Try not to judge me and others like me too harshly from over the sea, in your respectable middle-class liberal Guardian-reading homes. You've no proper knowledge of our history, and if you had you'd surely understand why we feel the only thing left for us is to fight you to the bitter end.'

Acknowledgments

I owe thanks to many people who gave me help at different stages during the preparation and writing of this book.

I first discussed the idea for it with my long-time friend and mentor Dr Anthony Storr, and then later with Professor Ken Pease of the University of Manchester. Both were encouraging and supportive, and gave me a great deal of assistance and perceptive advice. Breidge Gadd, Northern Ireland's Chief Probation Officer, prevented me from making too many mistaken assumptions, I hope: and her continuous warm friendliness and willingness to share her knowledge were always stimulating and refreshing. So too was the ready helpfulness at all times of Paul Casey, the director of Extern.

During my five months' stay in Belfast I talked with more than two hundred people. They were all always friendly and co-operative, without exception, but many of them asked me specifically not to reveal their names. Of those who didn't, I want to thank John Steel and Seamus McNeill of the Northern Ireland Prison Service, Duncan McLaughlan, Chris Thompson of the Department of Health and Social Security, Michael Ritchie and Martin O'Brien of CAJ, Terry Doherty of the Probation Service, Henry Bojdys and Major Tim Coles, and Mr McDowell of Flat Rentals who did me several favours. At the Linen Hall Library John Gray and his staff were most helpful and efficient, and my son John did a great deal of patient and careful research for me both there and elsewhere. I am glad he found Belfast and its people as endearing as I did.

I received a very generous grant of financial assistance from the Francis Head Bequest administered by the Society of Authors, where Mark Le Fanu gave me much enouragement and support. At my publishers Jonathan Cape, David Godwin was as sensitive and enthusiastic as he always is: and I owe thanks too to Marion Steel and Pascal Cariss there for their careful editing and patience.

Linda Ginn typed, re-typed, and typed again a flood of dictations and drafts and revisions and final versions of the constantly changing manuscript with impeccable precision and speed: yet again I am indebted to her for her willingness and cheerful acceptance of burdens as well as her skill. Her husband Richard helped me greatly too, and also has my thanks, as does Halesworth Adshop for its efficiency and exactness.

My assistant in Northern Ireland, Deborah Martin, not only had all the qualities I listed on page 3 as those I sought for, but also had an abundance of others: chief among them were the good humour with which she responded to all my challenging requests, and the enthusiastic determination with which she ensured they were satisfied. I hope my agent Gill Coleridge will take my dedication of this book to her as some indication of how much I depend on and am grateful to her, and have been now for such a long time.

Finally, the more often it is necessary, the less I seem to find myself able adequately to express how much I owe to my wife Margery. Her readiness to share household upheavals and changes of location once again was constant and unfailing, and additionally she uncomplainingly undertook hour upon hour of tedious transcribing of tapes and checking of drafts. For such things, but most of all for her companionship, I cannot thank her enough nor ever fittingly match her limitless love and support.

Tony Parker
Westleton, Suffolk

Bibliography

In the last quarter of a century alone there have been hundreds of books, articles and pamphlets written and published about Northern Ireland, and this doesn't attempt to be a comprehensive or even representative list of them. They're some of those I found in various bookshops in Belfast, Dublin and Cork while I was there, as well as many which were specifically recommended to me in answer to the question I asked almost everybody I talked to: 'What do you think I should read which would help me understand even better some of the things we've just been talking about?' Frequently I was astonished by the books which were suggested, because they put forward ideas and arguments almost directly contradictory to those the person I'd asked had been pressing on me with considerable fervour only a few minutes earlier.

Abrahams, M. & Sparham, L. *Still War*. Bellew Publishing, 1989.
Adams, Gerry. *A Pathway To Peace*. Mercier Press, 1988.
— *Cage Eleven*. Brandon Book Publishing, 1990.
Adamson, I. *The Identity of Ulster*. Pretani Press, 1982.
— *The Ulster People*. Pretani Press, 1991.
'An Phoblacht' (Republican News, weekly) Sinn Fein Bookshop, Belfast.
Arthur, P. & Jeffery, K. *Northern Ireland Since 1968*. Institute of Contemporary British History, Blackwell, 1988.
Beattie, G. *We Are The People: Journeys Through The Heart of Protestant Ulster*. Heinemann, 1992.
Belfast Evening Telegraph. Belfast, daily.

Bell, R., Johnstone, R. & Wilson, R. *Troubled Times: Fortnight Magazine & The Troubles*. Blackstaff, 1991.

Bishop, P. & Mallie, E. *The Provisional IRA*. Corgi, 1987.

Bowyer Bell, J. *IRA: Tactics & Targets*. Poolbeg Press, 1990.

Captive Voice. POW Department, Sinn Fein. SF Dublin, quarterly.

Care For Kids: Gingerbread Report. Gingerbread, Belfast, n.d.

Centre for Research & Documentation Annual Report. CRD Belfast, annually.

Committee On The Administration of Justice Annual Report. CAJ Belfast, annually.

Common Sense: Northern Ireland, An Agreed Process. Ulster Democratic Party, Belfast, n.d.

Conroy, J. *War As A Way of Life: A Belfast Diary*. Heinemann, 1988.

Co-Operation North Annual Report. Co-Op North, Belfast, annually.

Costello, M. *Titanic Town: Memoirs Of A Belfast Girlhood*. Methuen, 1992.

Curtis, L. *They Shoot Children: The Use of Plastic & Rubber Bullets*. Information on N Ireland, 1982.

— *Ireland: The Propaganda War*. Pluto Press, 1984.

Dickson, B. (ed.), *Civil Liberties In N. Ireland Handbook*. CAJ, 1993.

Dillon, M. *Killer In Clowntown*. Arrow Books, 1982.

— *The Shankill Butchers*. Arrow Books, 1990.

— *The Dirty War*. Arrow Books, 1990.

Divis Community Arts. *No Place For a Dog*. Divis Community, Belfast.

Downing, T. *The Troubles*. Thames Macdonald, 1980.

Doyle, R. *The Van*. Minerva, 1991.

Equality Working Group. *Directory of Discrimination*. Belfast, 1991.

Falls Community Council. *Falls In Focus*. Belfast, 1987.

Farrell, M. *Northern Ireland: The Orange State*. Pluto Press, 1976.

Faul, Fr D. & Murray, Fr R. *Plastic Bullets, Plastic Government*, Belfast, 1982.

Flackes, W. D. & Elliott, S. *Northern Ireland: A Political Directory*. Blackstaff, 1980.

Foster, R. F. *Modern Ireland 1600-1972*. Penguin, 1988.

Gay Star. PO Box 44, Belfast, quarterly.

Gearty, C. *Terror*. Faber & Faber, 1991.

Haldane Society. *Upholding The Rule of Law in N. Ireland*. 1992.

Hall, M. *Ulster: The Hidden History*. Pretani Press, 1986.

Helsinki Watch Report: Human Rights In N. Ireland. 1991.

The Humming Bird Drop-In Centre For Women. *Annual report*, Belfast, 1991.

Iris: The Republican Magazine. Dublin, monthly.

Irish Songs of Resistance. Vols 1 & 2. Sinn Fein, Dublin, n.d.

Jardine, Brother D. *Belfast's Bleak House*. Marshalls, 1985.

Justice For All. JFA Association, Shankill Road, Belfast, monthly.

Keane, J. *The Ram of God*. Mercier Press, 1991.

Keena, C. *Gerry Adams: A Biography*. Mercier Press, 1990.

Larkin, E. (ed.) *Alexis de Tocqueville's Journey In Ireland*. Woolfhound, 1990.

Leyton, Elliott. *Opposition & Integration in Ulster*. Memorial University of Newfoundland, n.d.

Life Sentence Prisoners: An Explanatory Memorandum. N. Ireland Prison Department, 1985.

Ligoniel Development Project: *Report*. Belfast, n.d.

Linen Hall Library Review. Linen Hall Library, Belfast, quarterly.

Maghaberry Prison: Fact File. POW Department, Sinn Fein. SF, Belfast.

McCann, E. *Bloody Sunday In Derry*. Brandon Publishers, 1992.

McKeown, M. *The Greening Of A Nationalist*. Murlough Press, 1986.

— *Two, Seven, Six, Three*. Murlough Press, 1989.

McKittrick, D. *Despatches From Belfast*. Blackstaff Press, 1989.

McLoone, J. *Being Protestant In Ireland*. Co-Operation North, 1985.

McMahon, S. *A Book of Irish Quotations*. O'Brien Press, 1984.

Moore, B. *Lies Of Silence*. Bloomsbury, 1991.

N I Civil Liberties Council. *Just News*. NICLC, Belfast, monthly.

N I Council for Voluntary Action. *The Political Vetting of Community Work In N Ireland*. Belfast, 1990.

North-South Newsletter. Co-Operation North, Belfast, quarterly.

O'Donnell, P. *The Knife*. Irish Humanities Centre, Dublin, 1984.

O'Malley, P. *N. Ireland: Questions Of Nuance*. Blackstaff, 1990.

O'Muilleoir, M. *Belfast City Council: Bastion Of Bigotry*. Sinn Fein, n.d.

Pilger, J. *Distant Voices*. Vintage, 1992.

Police Authority for Northern Ireland. *The Work of the Policing Authority. 1988-1991*, NI Police, 1922.

RUC. *The RUC: A Brief History*. RUC Belfast.
— *Chief Constable's Annual Report*. RUC Belfast, annually.
— *Police Beat: RUC Magazine*. Belfast, monthly.
— *Professional Policing Ethics*. RUC Belfast, n.d.
— *Statistical Information*. RUC Belfast, annually.
Ryder, C. *The RUC: A Force Under Fire*. Mandarin, 1989.
— *The UDR: An Instrument of Peace?* Mandarin, 1991.
Sands, B. *Skylark, Sing Your Lonely Song*. Mercier Press, 1982.
Shankill Activity Centre: *Annual Report*. Shankill Road, Belfast, 1992.
Sinn Fein. *The North of Ireland: A Resources Guide*. SF Belfast, 1985.
— *Republican Prisoners' Fact File*. SF Foreign Affairs Bureau, Belfast, n.d.
— *The Ulster Defence Regiment: The Loyalist Militia*. Sinn Fein, Dublin, n.d.
Stewart, A. T. Q. *The Narrow Ground: The Roots Of Conflict in N Ireland*. Faber & Faber, 1977.
Torbin, N. *The Irish Reciter*. Blackstaff, 1986.
Ulster Defence Association. *Beyond The Religious Divide*. UDA, 1979.
Ulster Newsletter. Daily.
Upstart. *Men's newsletter*, Upstart Publications, Belfast, occasionally.
Urban, M. *Big Boys' Rules: The Secret Struggle Against The IRA*. Faber & Faber, 1992.
Washington, G. *No Comment: Censorship, Secrecy & the Irish Troubles*. International Centre on Censorship, 1989.
Whyte, J. *Interpreting Northern Ireland*. Clarendon Press, Oxford, 1990.
Williams, M. *Murder On The Rock*. Larkin Publications, Dublin, 1989.
Wilson, D. *An End To Silence*. Mercier Press, 1985.
Wilson, G. *Marie: A Story From Enniskillen*. Marshall Pickering, 1990.
Wilson, R. (ed.). *Fortnight Magazine*. Belfast, monthly.
Women In Struggle. Sinn Fein Women's Department, Sinn Fein, Belfast, 1992.
Women's News. Falls/Shankill Women's Centre, Belfast, bi-monthly.